CAMBRIDGE LIBRARY COLLECTION

Books of enduring scholarly value

Music

The systematic academic study of music gave rise to works of description, analysis and criticism, by composers and performers, philosophers and anthropologists, historians and teachers, and by a new kind of scholar - the musicologist. This series makes available a range of significant works encompassing all aspects of the developing discipline.

Life of John Hullah

The composer and music teacher John Pyke Hullah (1812–84) enjoyed considerable success with *The Village Coquettes*, his 1836 opera with a libretto by Charles Dickens. He is best remembered, however, for his 'singing school for schoolmasters' which he directed at London's Exeter Hall in the 1840s and later at the specially built St Martin's Hall. Although his use of the French fixed sol-fa system was quickly superseded by Curwen's tonic sol-fa approach, his efforts - with the support of Sir James Kay-Shuttleworth - embedded music firmly in the school curriculum. An influence on the rapid growth of British amateur choral societies, he was also appointed the first government inspector of music in training colleges in 1872. First published in 1886, this biography was prepared from Hullah's notes by his second wife, Frances Rosser Hullah (1839–*c*.1921), a professional sculptor and writer on music for women's periodicals.

Cambridge University Press has long been a pioneer in the reissuing of out-of-print titles from its own backlist, producing digital reprints of books that are still sought after by scholars and students but could not be reprinted economically using traditional technology. The Cambridge Library Collection extends this activity to a wider range of books which are still of importance to researchers and professionals, either for the source material they contain, or as landmarks in the history of their academic discipline.

Drawing from the world-renowned collections in the Cambridge University Library and other partner libraries, and guided by the advice of experts in each subject area, Cambridge University Press is using state-of-the-art scanning machines in its own Printing House to capture the content of each book selected for inclusion. The files are processed to give a consistently clear, crisp image, and the books finished to the high quality standard for which the Press is recognised around the world. The latest print-on-demand technology ensures that the books will remain available indefinitely, and that orders for single or multiple copies can quickly be supplied.

The Cambridge Library Collection brings back to life books of enduring scholarly value (including out-of-copyright works originally issued by other publishers) across a wide range of disciplines in the humanities and social sciences and in science and technology.

Life of John Hullah

EDITED BY
FRANCES HULLAH

CAMBRIDGE UNIVERSITY PRESS

Cambridge, New York, Melbourne, Madrid, Cape Town,
Singapore, São Paolo, Delhi, Mexico City

Published in the United States of America by Cambridge University Press, New York

www.cambridge.org
Information on this title: www.cambridge.org/9781108062435

© in this compilation Cambridge University Press 2013

This edition first published 1886
This digitally printed version 2013

ISBN 978-1-108-06243-5 Paperback

This book reproduces the text of the original edition. The content and language reflect
the beliefs, practices and terminology of their time, and have not been updated.

Cambridge University Press wishes to make clear that the book, unless originally published
by Cambridge, is not being republished by, in association or collaboration with, or
with the endorsement or approval of, the original publisher or its successors in title.

JOHN HULLAH

PRINTED BY
SPOTTISWOODE AND CO., NEW-STREET SQUARE
LONDON

Yours truly
John Hullah

LIFE

OF

JOHN HULLAH, LL.D.

BY HIS WIFE

LONDON
LONGMANS, GREEN, AND CO.
1886

All rights reserved

TO

HIS PUPILS

DURING HALF A CENTURY

THIS MEMOIR OF ONE

WHOM THEY RESPECTED AS A TEACHER

AND LOVED AS A FRIEND

IS DEDICATED

PREFACE.

It is hoped that the story of a life spent in spreading a knowledge, among the youth of England, of a noble and refining art may prove sufficiently interesting to outweigh defects of plan or style in the telling of it.

The materials out of which the story has been woven are Mr. Hullah's own notes for an autobiography, put together at the often-reiterated suggestion of the late Sir James Kay-Shuttleworth; his letters to his mother, his brother, his first wife, and the present writer, together with one or two recovered from the friends (or their representatives) to whom they were addressed; from letters to Mr. Hullah, by habitual or occasional correspondents, and passages from different publications which illustrate and explain important crises in his life.

Thanks are due for permission to use the letters quoted. To those other friends who so kindly and so readily consented to the publication of letters submitted to them with that view, but which do not appear, it is necessary to explain that want of space has alone prevented the insertion of many interesting passages from them, for it has been deemed best to keep the book to its present limits that it may be within the easy reach of the many persons who, it is hoped, will care to know something of the private life of that 'Apostle of Music' who, nearly fifty years ago, first set them using their vocal gifts by the aid of his 'Manual'—the little volume which meant to them many hours of innocent recreation after toil.

FRANCES HULLAH.

GROSVENOR MANSIONS : *Dec.* 25, 1885.

LIFE

OF

JOHN HULLAH.

CHAPTER I.

AUTOBIOGRAPHICAL.

1812-26.

MOST autobiographies begin with the announcement that the subject thereof was born in such a place, in such a year, possibly on such a day—facts one and all that the writer can only have known by hearsay. When and where this event, so far as it concerned me, took place, I do not remember; but in Grove's "Dictionary of Music and Musicians" I find it stated that I first saw the light in the faithful city of Worcester on June 27, 1812. My earliest recollections would, I fear, prove vague and without interest. What took my parents to my birthplace I do not know. My only brother, who was four years older than I, had been born in London, and a few years later brought us back thither for life, as it proved. My first distinct recollection is of a journey with my mother in a coach, in the course of which I learned that I was not to be sent to school, whither, I presume, my fears had pointed, but that I was to continue for a time under her instruction. I must then have been about five years of age. This intention was not carried out, for my next recollections are of a school at Harlow, in Essex, where I remained some years. I suppose I showed some liking for music, for my schoolmaster, himself an amateur violinist who gathered together weekly a party of kindred tastes, occasionally allowed me to sit up on nights of practice to snuff the candles. From one or other of this orchestra I picked up enough to enable me on my return home for holidays to play the first strain of " God save the King "—an attempt which was received with much applause. I especially remember also being praised by my audience for not attempting the second strain of that popular tune.'

An aged friend of the Hullah family (still living in 1884), who knew John at this time, recalls a day when she received him in her house at Highbury, then 'thickly wooded,' and speaks of him as having been a 'beautiful boy' and 'a sweet child.'

'I may here mention that, though my father was without musical knowledge, he was not without musical taste, and my mother had received a good deal of musical culture. My maternal grandfather in early life had known intimately some of the most distinguished professors of his day. From John Danby, one of these, my mother had her first lessons in singing, and through him I have pleased myself with having, over a small number of steps, a connection with Palestrina; for Danby was a pupil of Domenico Corri, Corri of Alessandro Scarlatti, Scarlatti of Carissimi, and Carissimi of Palestrina. Some rumours concerning my mother's voice, then remarkable, reached the ear of Corri, and he visited her, and was so much struck by its quality and power that he offered to take her as a pupil.

' In those days—the latter part of the last century—a proposal of this kind was indignantly rejected by a prosperous, and I have heard at one time a wealthy, man of business. Some of my early recollections have reference to scraps of money which fell to my mother many years after—scraps left by the Court of Chancery out of many thousand pounds which had remained awaiting the decision or indecision of Lord Eldon. Another trace of my maternal grandfather's existence lingered in the person of Mrs. Alice Ingle, who received a small income bequeathed to her by him as the reward of many years' service—not so uncommon a transaction then as now. My visits to this good old woman I remember with much pleasure. Her room was decorated with drawings and models of carriages which had belonged to her husband, who had been a workman of my grandfather. These relics she treasured as she might have done those of her patron saint.

'Of my father's early days I know next to nothing. Rumours of the migration of his forefathers from France, consequent on the revocation of the Edict of Nantes, and of their settlement in Yorkshire—a common refuge of expatriated weavers—have come down to me, and from information more recently acquired from the "Essai Historique et Philosophique sur les noms d'Hommes" of Eusèbe Salverte (Paris, 1824), I gather that the word Hullah is identical with that of Wallack. Be that as it may, I have heard that the name still lingers in the neighbourhoods of Richmond and Hull.

'Why my father came back to London I do not know. It is far from unlikely that his strong political opinions, which would not be universally acceptable even now, but were received with horror seventy years ago, may have had something to do with his return. . . .'

From the sense of sundry broken phrases in Mr. Hullah's MS. it may be inferred that Mr. Hullah's father had imbibed the revolutionary principles which found their expression in the overturning of the French monarchical system. The faithful city became, probably, an uneasy abode for so advanced a spirit.

'Any musical taste that I may have been endowed with received little encouragement that I can call to mind during the first years of my childhood. I passed from my Harlow school to another at High Wycombe, in Buckinghamshire, and thence to another at Brixton, recently opened by a Mr. Hine, my parents' attention to which had been directed by a somewhat original course on their part. They advertised for a school, and received in response a letter and a prospectus from a gentleman unknown to them, whose sons had for some time been under Mr. Hine's care. Mr. Hine proved to be a person of somewhat original ideas on education, some of which have found and still find acceptance and favour. A few boys only learnt Latin, instruction in which Mr. Hine was, I fancy, only too glad to hand over to an assistant. But he was, I believe, a good mathematician, and from him I gathered with ease an acquaintance with the elements of Euclid. To this hour I have carefully preserved my school copy of Simpson, and have never looked at it since without pleasure. But the subject of all others favoured under Mr. Hine's *régime* was the English language, in which he expressed himself with a clearness and facility by no means uniformly secured by a classical education. My belief is that he knew no language but his own, but he knew this well. The, to this day occasional, French master presented himself to us twice a week, with results which time has not generally improved in the instance of the English boy. Of German I remained ignorant till some years after I left school. Among our *alumni* were three or four Spaniards, as many Greeks, and a single Frenchman. The business of these, one and all, as of ourselves, was to learn English—after the manner of young German governesses who visit Great Britain commonly with the same exclusive intent. Our means of communicating with these foreigners was through some execrable French, with which some of them were partially furnished. I might have picked up some Spanish, and even some modern Greek, had not all converse with those to whom these tongues were familiar been so strictly interdicted. But no power on earth will prevent a Frenchman using his own tongue, even with those who know not a syllable of it. The names of some of these gentlemen are not such as to be easily forgotten. Our Frenchman was a nephew of Volney, the oriental traveller, one of the "Idéologues" of Napoleon. He was a good deal our senior, and inherited, I fancy, some of the linguistic facility of his family. . . .

'Of the Greeks, one of whom I have never quite lost sight, was Mr. Ionides, long connected with the Crystal Palace. . . .

'My school-days ended at Mr. Hine's. His was the only school I ever heard of which the *curriculum* was almost made up of English literature. I suspect he was a self-taught man—one, therefore, of a class against whom much might be said. His acquaintance with his principal or one subject equalled that of any person with whom I have since been brought into contact. . . . Mr. Hine had a personal and intimate acquaintance with the poet Wordsworth, and was, I think, one of his earliest admirers, and communicated his admiration to his pupils and to all who came under his influence in very early days—days when "This will never do," and the like, was the language in which Wordsworth and Coleridge and Keats and Shelley were mentioned, if at all. I doubt whether an equal number of boys could have been elsewhere got together fifty years ago—I have doubts whether they could often be got together now—whose acquaintance with English poetry included the works of Shakespeare, Milton, Dryden, Pope, Percy, Goldsmith, Cowper, and many others with whose writings the majority of my schoolfellows were more or less intimately acquainted.

['As for modern literature, the very idea of its existence had never dawned upon these youths, none of whom knew any language but English,' testifies the late Mark Pattison of his fellow-undergraduates.]

'I must not bid farewell to one to whom I owe so much without recording one at least of his many peculiarities. In common with many men who lived through the French Revolution, he caught many of the opinions which preceded and led to that prodigious event; among others, those of one of the later French "philosophers," Helvétius. This writer held that the views of equality on which "the rights of man" were based should be extended to the head and even the heart of all mankind; and that, could the latter be freed from the accidents by which they are insensibly affected, they would be found to be all but identical; that, placed under the same or like circumstances from infancy, the powers of a Milton and a Tupper might be found equal. That such a statement as this, boldly put before mankind, should be scouted indignantly is not surprising; and that a thoughtful man, accustomed to all the instances to the contrary presented every hour to the eye of a schoolmaster, should, after many years' experience, maintain it and laugh at any views about "gifts" for this, that, or the other, does seem indeed extraordinary. The theory propounded by Helvétius, it is needless to say, was held strongly

by most of Mr. Hine's pupils—by myself among the number.
I am not sure that some of it does not hang about me still.
Encouraged by the unshaken belief of Mr. Hine that anybody
could do anything he put his mind to, I at least learned to
speak, and my elocution was, apart from my acting, I remember, much applauded by audiences far above those of an
average theatre, when, on my return to school after the holidays, I played the parts of Shylock and Sir Giles Overreach, in
which I had seen the elder Kean, of whose acting of these
characters and of the part of Richard the Third I still retain a
vivid recollection.

'The science of education may or may not have advanced
during the last fifty years, but it certainly has not been brought
to bear on the art of speaking clearly the English tongue in
everyday life.'

CHAPTER II.

AUTOBIOGRAPHICAL (*continued*).

1826-33.

' OF the gradual and insensible progress by which I became acquainted with music I can give no account. Of my mother's voice, and somewhat slender musical acquirements, I have already spoken. Of my own, in these earlier days, I should say nothing had not experience as a teacher shown me how the smallest musical power picked up in childhood (even such as the first strains of " God save the King," already alluded to) may prove worth something in after life. Had I been asked, when I left school, in 1826 or 1827, what my vocation in life was likely to be, I am certain that the musical art in any shape would have been the last that would have occurred to me. A very early experience of its effects was, I had been told, anything but promising. Taken for the first time to a theatre, I was said to have manifested such terror at the sound of the double basses that I had to be taken home and put to bed forthwith. To be sure, something of the kind *à propos* to the trumpet is recorded by Mozart. My violin playing subsequently has been shortlived ; but during my holidays I got some pianoforte lessons from an elderly maiden lady, a Miss Brown, which, good or bad, stuck by me till I finally left school. I cannot call to mind that among our acquaintances at that time there were any that were " musical," or any that could have directed me in the cultivation of my voice, finger, or musical skill of any kind. All sorts of careers were suggested for me. I was to be made a civil engineer (the day for civil engineers was approaching), a doctor, a lawyer, an architect, &c. &c. I have often dwelt on what I might have made of any of these callings. This at least is certain—nobody suggested the calling of a musician.'

In a letter addressed to the writer in 1884, Mr. William Chappell says: 'It was the friendship with the Smart family that induced Mrs. Hullah to bring up your husband to music as a profession, and to give him the best assistance in first-rate tuition.'

'Meanwhile two or three precious years rolled on, I can hardly say how. I made acquaintance with a few people, more or less musical, and in the year 1829 became a pupil of William Horsley, Mus.Bac., Oxon, who, though but little past his prime, looked even then a "grave and reverend senior." There are always in the world old-fashioned men, and he must have adopted that character early in life. When I first knew him he had already a considerable reputation as a theorist, which he had evidenced by the production of a number of compositions of a class in which he may be said to have attained the highest perfection—the glee. The child of a still greater ancestor—the madrigal—the glee revived in a somewhat different shape about the middle of the last century; and through the compositions of Webbe, Stevens, Callcott, and a few others, continued to uphold the character of English music till the time when I first made its acquaintance. As a pianoforte teacher Horsley had a considerable and deserved reputation, and possibly I might have profited more than I did by his instructions had not my late musical beginnings rendered success in that department of the musical art impossible. I followed the course I was directed to follow with the results that might have been expected from their observance, and then after a time made some attempts at composition. These were of course chiefly vocal, for naturally my tastes came out again, and what I had already read came back to me in unison with the new art I was striving to acquire. My struggles with the keyboard were still, however, unrelaxed; though, for the most part, carried on through the agency of music I never liked when I first knew it, and do not like to this hour. With the preludes and fugues of J. S. Bach I made acquaintance, and the acquaintance ripened into love, before I could play them. But along with those I was set to work upon certain sonatas—shall I be forgiven if

I call them "old fashioned?"—with a disinclination or disgust that extended itself to a vast number of pieces of like facture and dulness. Numberless compositions now easily accessible were in those days unattainable or frightfully costly in this country. The four parts, or books, of those preludes and fugues of Bach cost me, I recollect, three pounds sterling, and a full score of one of Handel's oratorios about as much. The more recent sonatas of Beethoven were costly, and slow in finding popularity. I remember attempting the performance of—now one of the most popular—the "Sonata Pathétique" in the presence of some half-dozen musical friends of my master, not one of whom, save the latter, had ever before heard it or heard of its existence.

'Not long after this (to pass from greater to smaller things) a glee of my own composition was performed at the same house by five eminent performers. Among these was Mr. Sale, a bass singer, then of some reputation, and known as the composer of a duet for tenor and bass—"The Butterfly"—who was good enough to say some encouraging words about it. Among the other auditors was the Chevalier Sigismund Neukomm, then in the height of his transient reputation, who kindly loaded it with commendation. Gradually I became better acquainted with these and other professors, and I was admitted from time to time by Mr. Horsley to the meetings of the Concentores Sodales Society [founded in 1798 upon the suggestion of Mr. Horsley, dissolved in 1847], a social band of men of "a certain age," for the most part good musicians, and each a centre of his own circle, greater or less. The lives of such, obscured by those of better known artists, are in their effects prodigious. Through them, musical skill, knowledge and taste are handed on from generation to generation, and on the whole increased and improved. The majority of these I can remember, from whose words and notes I gathered much from which I, and eventually others, profited more than they or I can ever know—composers, singers and organists, who have now passed away. The very names of some of them are, or at least will be ere long, forgotten; and these I willingly revive. My acquaintance with some of them sprang up and blossomed

after the period of which I am speaking, and must be spoken
of later; but I call to mind with pleasure the names of Giles,
Spencer, Terrail (an amateur), E. Taylor and Bellamy. I remained under the instruction of Mr. Horsley till some time in
the year 1833, when I stepped into a new world of art and
became a pupil of the Royal Academy of Music. My introduction to this establishment I owe to two friends, pupils there,
who gave me such accounts of the teaching of Crivelli as inspired me with curiosity concerning his method of voice cultivation. One of these had profited largely by his instruction,
and I was desirous to know whether anything of the kind could
be done for me.

'The Royal Academy of Music, then in its tenth year, though
as yet unpopular among English musicians, had attained in
1833-34 a reputation which it has not at any time exceeded.
Every school has its periods of irregularity, and that of 1832
had just been marked by the production of the first concerto
of Sterndale Bennett, then in his seventeenth year, and who
followed up its composition by a rapid succession of similar
works, soon to be brought to an end by the curse of English
music—pianoforte teaching. But of this elegant genius it will
be time to speak later.

'So with respect to G. A. Macfarren, now Principal of the
Academy and Professor of the University of Cambridge, in
both of which offices he succeeded Sterndale Bennett. In
this year (1834) were held the rehearsals and performances for
the festival in Westminster Abbey. These were the first performances on so great a scale that I, or any one not greatly
my senior, had ever taken part in. My recollections of them
are certainly not favourable. The choruses of which I formed
an increment were placed right and left of the orchestra, and
behind the columns of the aisles. Save by the eye, there
seemed to be no means of keeping time, either with the band
or with the opposite choir. That this, however, was done
may be considered as certain; for the approval of the result
on the part of the audience was universal, and the satisfaction
on that of the majority of the performers was certainly also
considerable. Of these the soloists were Madame Grisi, the
Misses Stevens and Masson, Signor Rubini, Messrs. Braham,

Sapio, H. Phillips, Sale, Seguin, and Signor Tamburini—one and all now dead.

'Of these the last assuredly produced the greatest *effect*. His voice, then in its prime, seemed to possess a penetrating power that found its way to every part of the auditory. I record this after an interval of more than forty-eight years. I heard Tamburini again and again subsequently, in his prime and after it, when he seemed to have exhibited every conceivable imperfection, but always, I think, retaining this extraordinary peculiarity.

'I remained in the Academy about two years, during which I profited greatly by the instruction of Crivelli—in his art, I believe, *ultimus Romanorum*—one of two or three persons with whom I have been brought into contact who taught, or who seemed to know what is meant by teaching, singing. He was but slightly accomplished as a musician, but in all that concerns the *formation and delivery of the voice* transcendent. Singing, however, is one of those arts in which a teacher must not be judged altogether by his pupils : their health, strength, habits, general culture, and a thousand other causes are only in a slight degree under his control and observation. The paucity of singers in any given age may best be characterised by the expression of Imlac to Rasselas in respect to poets : "Enough, thou hast convinced me that no human being can ever be one of them."

'The years of which I have just spoken were marked by a number of incidents which contributed to my musical progress and the formation or increase of such taste as I was "gifted" with. I heard for the first time, in 1829, a great singer and a greater violinist—Davide and Paganini.'

Mr. Hullah evidently purposed to give a somewhat lengthened account of his knowledge and opinion of the leading musicians of his early days, but failing health and limited leisure stood in the way, and he has left but the few preparatory notes which follow. From these it will be easy to gather how very high a value he placed at all times on flexibility, clearness, penetrativeness and power of expression in the human voice rather than on mere technical skill.

CHAPTER III.

AUTOBIOGRAPHICAL (*continued*).

1833-36.

' DAVIDE was the second of a great race, for years one of the most renowned artists of his time, and one who maintained his power till long after the age of seventy. Davide *fils*, when I heard him, somewhere about 1829, possessed a voice of enormous compass, but with a style and flexibility to that time unheard and inconceivable by me. He was followed by a succession of singers who in other respects perhaps surpassed him, for he was said then to be failing ; but he dwells on my mind as the last of a kind of which I cannot call to mind having heard another specimen.

'Of his successors, whether in point of voice, style, or sustained power, such as never before or since occupied the Italian stage, Lablache, Tamburini, Rubini, Grisi were beyond comparison the most remarkable. Signor Lablache stood apart from all singers of whom we have records in every conceivable particular. He was exceptional in birth, face, figure, voice, variety and musical talent. Years ago I remember being told with a positiveness that there was no possibility of questioning that the Italians could *sing* and the French could *dance*. Lablache, though actually born in Naples, was of French extraction. His face (though it is hard to speak of the face of so multiform an actor) was more like that of the Phidian Jupiter than that of any living human being I ever saw ; his figure, though enormous, was never clumsy, while his tread was like that of Taglioni ; with a voice the volume of which seemed inexhaustible and the sweetness and purity of which were at moments unequalled ; a man who would seem to have been equally fitted for every part he touched, and who touched every part with equal ease and success; a face and a voice and an action as capable of drawing forth tears as inextinguishable laughter. Of Lablache's physical strength I remember witnessing two uncommon exhibitions. During a rehearsal, in which he was not taking part, his attention was called to a contrabasso (an instrument he played), the head of which leaned over the orchestra on to the stage. He stooped, lifted it with one hand, examined it, and, having satisfied his curiosity, deposited it again gently in its proper place. On another occasion Lablache was playing the part of Leporello in "Don Giovanni," and had to remove Masetto from the stage. This latter part was taken by Giubilei, a man of nearly equal height with Lablache. When the moment arrived for dealing summarily with Masetto, Lablache picked him up, tucked him under one arm, and carried him across the stage and out at the wing as easily as he would have carried an umbrella.

'Rubini was wanting in all the personal graces of Lablache. His face was deformed by small-pox. He acted only at moments to save himself trouble. He had attained his apogee, if not passed it, when he came to England. Yet he stepped into a reputation, and did a number of things no tenor had ever done before. . . . At moments his force was enormous, and his alternations of loud and soft effected apparently without exertion, . . . every note, whether of the *voce di testa* or *di petto*, being most completely under control and at his command. In a most eminent degree Rubini's voice possessed the quality of tenderness.

'During my connection with the Royal Academy I became acquainted with Miss Fanny Dickens, then a student there. She had formerly made some reputation as a pianist, and had recently returned thither to study singing under Crivelli. She was an excellent musician, *one who knew the sound of what she saw*, and could reproduce it by voice or hand readily and correctly. Some time in 1835 I first met her brother Charles, then just of my own age, who was connected with the "Morning Chronicle," and over and above reporting had written sundry articles under the well-known title, "Sketches by Boz." I had, a year or two earlier, set to music some portion of an opera called "The Gondolier," which had appeared in a periodical rejoicing in the promising title of "The Rejected Drama." I had been captivated by the title, "The Gondolier," and though I believed Mr. Dickens was then unpractised in dramatic literature, it occurred to me that we might combine our forces—he of words and I of music. He entered into the scheme at once, and, after a few days' thought, addressed to me the following letter, which, as initiatory to many others, may be of interest:

'The moment I am quite certain of an hour or two I will beseech you to take part in a very grave discussion. What I am anxious to suggest to you is the expediency of dropping the Venetian idea altogether and making the drama an English one. I really cannot please myself with any of the sketches I have made for an opera to which the title of "The Gondolier" would be applicable; and remembering the popularity and beauty of many of the old English operas, I am strongly prejudiced in favour of a simple rural story. I am the more induced to offer this notion when I consider with how little expense such a piece might be produced, and how very effective its situations might be made, while "The Gondolier," on the other hand, would require a great many supernumeraries and some rather costly scenery. Add to these considerations the increased ease and effect with which we could both work on an English drama, where the characters would act and talk likepeople we see and hear of every day, and I think you will be of my opinion.

'I have a little story by me which I have not yet published, which I think would dramatise well. If you approve of my idea, it is done in a twinkling; if not, I will work out your original notion; but I will frankly confess that, while I am at home in England, I am in Venice abroad indeed.

'Yours very sincerely,

'CHARLES DICKENS.'

'At this time Mr. George Hogarth, whose daughter Catherine Mr. Dickens subsequently married, had not long left Edinburgh, of which he was a native. He had become musical critic to the "Morning Chronicle." . . . Some compositions of mine were at this time shown to him, and he, fortunately for me, thought well of them, and volunteered, when any progress had been made in the contemplated work, to introduce it to the notice of Mr. Braham, who was about completing and opening the St. James's Theatre. During the latter part of this year (1836) the opera was completed. The title of "The Gondolier" was abandoned, and an original subject having presented itself to Mr. Dickens, it was, after many consultations, put forward as "The Village Coquettes," of which certain songs, duets, and concerted pieces soon formed constituent parts. These, accompanied by Mr. Hogarth, I took one morning to Mr. Braham, then living at a house no longer existing, The Grange, at Brompton. This interview was, of course, to me an important and a trying one. At no time was I ever a skilful pianist; to sing at any time in the presence of Mr. Braham was a serious matter, and what would be the end of the presentation I knew not. A very few moments swept away the nervousness with which I began. It is needless to say that Mr. Braham was an admirable musician. His once unparalleled gifts of voice were then, though a little failing, still considerable. He almost immediately took his position near the pianoforte, and in spite of the unfamiliar handwriting of the MS., read bar after bar as though he had known it all his life, accompanying the performance with kind words, never to be forgotten. Some half dozen friends strayed in, and the audience was completed by Mrs. Braham, Miss Braham, and others of the family. A long morning, during which I heard nothing but praise, brought this session to a close, and I left The Grange with a sort of understanding that my opera was accepted, and would be put in rehearsal at the earliest possible moment.

'Not for many months, however, did this moment arrive; not till December 6, 1836, was "The Village Coquettes" played for the first time. The performers were Miss Rainforth, then a *débutante*, Miss Julia Smith, Messrs. John Parry, Morris Barrett, James Bennett, Strickland, Gardner, Sidney Harley, and Mr. Braham.

'In the course of rehearsal many changes ensued, as well among the performers as in the piece they had to perform. One part intended for a singer was performed (without a note of music) by a comedian, Mr. Strickland, and the first solo was executed by another young comedian, who has since risen to high eminence—Mr. Alfred Wigan. Miss Rainforth had not then long made her appearance. She exhibited much

talent as an actress, and possessed a fresh and beautiful voice.
Mr. John Parry, an excellent musician, with a pleasant organ
and pleasanter style, afterwards became known in an entirely
different walk of art. Mr. James Bennett was a refined artist
who had not very long before appeared with much success;
the voice and style of Mr. Braham are hardly yet forgotten.
In respect to his voice there had hardly ever been two opinions, on his style opinions were divided. As a matter of fact
he had two styles—one to which he was kept by enthusiastic
admirers in the gallery, another which he reserved for audiences
of a very different class. He was endowed with one talent
cherished by both classes of hearers—an articulation of a kind
which I do not remember to have heard touched by a single
English singer before or since. You could have taken down
from his lips a song delivered for the first time; as was said
of him more than once, "even the dots of his *i*'s and the cross-
ing of his *t*'s were attended to." All these performers, young
and old, great and small, have now (1882) passed from the
scene. . . . To each and all I owe much, and though such
reputation as I have may have been earned in another sphere,
I have never forgotten what I owe to them all for such success as they helped me to in this. For "The Village Coquettes,"
notwithstanding the various opinions expressed as well on the
book as on the music, was a success, and that of a very decided
kind. It was played in London about sixty successive nights,
and afterwards in Edinburgh, under the management of Mr.
Ramsay, an actor and manager still remembered in that city
as the friend of Scott.

'Its migration northwards was attended by a sad accident.
Not many days after its first performance the theatre was
destroyed by fire, and the score and separate parts with it. A
few copies of these were all that ever came back to me, and,
save some songs, I never saw the work again. The concerted
music perished utterly, and, my head filled with designs for
other work, I never gave myself the trouble to write it out
again. I hardly know how to speak of the feeling of my col-
laborator respecting his share in the matter. I have a considerable number of cuttings from the various papers of the
time. English musical criticism, save in a few instances, was

at the lowest ebb, and a tone of contempt, as well of the words as of the music, pervaded the greater part of them. With Mr. Dickens I remained, till nearly the close of his life, on excellent terms. He had, like the majority of " literary " Englishmen of that day, no critical knowledge of music; but I fear he never quite forgave me for being mixed up with him in this matter.'

The philosophical resignation with which Mr. Hullah bore the loss of his MS. is very characteristic. He always accepted the inevitable with at least outward composure, and put away a sorrow or an annoyance with a silent decision that is, to say the least of it, extremely rare. To this faculty, however, may certainly be attributed his long and well-sustained career of work, so trying to mind and body, carried through till nearly the end of his life with but few and short pauses for real rest. But then he took his rest as he did his work—with all his mind and with all his strength. No one ever more thoroughly followed out the Miltonic admonition that—

—— disapproves the care, though wise in show
That with superfluous burden loads the day,
And when God sends a cheerful hour, refrains.

Hence the gladsome tone of all his holiday letters, and the power of enjoyment he communicated to his fellow-travellers. As Mr. Hullah speaks with so little respect of the critical ability shown in his earlier days by the musical staff of the leading newspapers, it is perhaps not paying him a high compliment to quote any of the contemporary criticisms. Still, it seems but fair to point out that he underrates the opinions expressed in the various journals of the day on the music of ' The Village Coquettes.' The critic of the ' Morning Post' announced that that opera burletta was a ' triumph.' ' And we are happy to congratulate him on his triumph—a triumph which we hope will not render him careless of his future efforts, and indifferent to the further development of the powers with which he is unquestionably gifted.' Having administered this lofty piece of advice, the tone of which may be found echoed in other journalistic utterances on the same subject, the writer proceeded : ' The great beauties of his music consist in its great freedom from servile imitation and its ingenious and appropriate instrumentation. Mr. Hullah has been particularly happy in the latter quality. There is no vulgar noise.' The 'Morning Herald' told its public that 'Mr. Hullah's music is, for the most part, quite genuine to its subject—simple, lively, and melodious;' an opinion endorsed by the 'Morning Chronicle': 'The music is admirably in accordance with the subject—simple, unaffected, and full of beautiful, expressive, *English* melody.' The 'Spectator' devoted two columns of close and most laudatory criticism on the opera as a whole. The 'Athenæum' was distant, cold, not to say scornful, merely glancing sideways at the work; but even the 'Athenæum' took time to observe that 'there are some sweet things in it.' 'Have the English a style of their own?' the 'Satirist' asked; and thinking it best to settle the question, at once dogmatically asserted, 'Unquestionably; and we point, without going any further out of the way, to the music of "The Village Coquettes" as being essentially of the English school.' The 'Sunday Times,' though hard on the words of the operetta, had to speak condescendingly favourable opinions on the music.

CHAPTER IV.

AUTOBIOGRAPHICAL (*continued*).

1838.

' DURING these years—for the most part occupied with " The Village Coquettes "—numerous social as well as musical incidents fell to my lot. I became organist of Croydon Church, a post of some importance. The church, which dates from the fourteenth century, is a noble and interesting one, and contained in 1835 an organ by Avery, a builder of considerable repute, and, though old-fashioned in its keyboard, of great sweetness and beauty. The office of organist brought me into communication with a family of high culture, with the remaining members of which I still retain a close intimacy. At the time I made their acquaintance the head of the house was Mr. Thomas Miller, already well advanced in years. He had taken a very high degree at Cambridge, and was a man of great accomplishments, a scholar whose recollections of men of the latter part of the last century were clear to him as things of yesterday, and a Tory of the strongest and most unchangeable order, who had made up his mind on all subjects—and they were many—*and never altered it.* . . . His detestation of Napoleon Bonaparte was without measure or stint. . . . He had never crossed the Channel, for, as he once said to a lady who affected to believe in his personal knowledge of the Continent : " I thank God, madam, my own country is good enough for me." With all this he kept his mind open to conviction on one subject—music—and saw merit in men as recent as Spohr and Mendelssohn.

' My musical occupations during this [1837] and the following year were various. I wrote a madrigal, " Wake now, my love " [printed in ' Vocal Scores '], which was honoured by performance by the Madrigal Society; also two songs, " I arise from dreams of thee," and " Rarely, rarely comest thou, Spirit of Delight," both for Miss Masson. The second she sang at the concerts of the Vocal Society, then existent. This great artist, whose appearances headed the subsequent rage for the German language, was chiefly educated in Italy. . . . Her general accomplishment in English, as in the Italian and French languages, all of which she used with freedom, was consummate, and her familiarity with the literature of the countries was unusual. No one could have spent an hour in her society without profit from her talents, of which music was but one, and that not the greatest. I do not remember her as a distinctly *popular* artist. Her comparatively rare appearances, chiefly among persons of taste and refinement, were never made without lasting effect. I may speak of her performance of the above-named songs as having obtained especial encomiums from two great composers—Atwood and his pupil Goss.

'At the close of this year I formed an alliance with Mr. Madison Morton, with whom I made an excursion to Malvern for the purpose of completing a second opera, " The Barbers of Bassora," neither so well performed nor so successful as the first. And in the following year I made my third and last essay in dramatic music in the production of a short one-act drama, " The Outpost," to which the fates were apparently no more propitious than to its predecessor. To speak frankly thereupon, I believe this little piece ought to have succeeded, and might have maintained its hold on the public. The book was by Mr. Serle, many of whose works had attained real success, and the principal characters were well sustained by Miss Shirreff, a favourite at that time, and Mr. Wilson, whose tenor voice was singularly beautiful. . . .

'In the latter part of this year Mr. John Foster, subsequently my father-in-law, whose affairs frequently took him to Paris, invited me to accompany him thither.'

In the August preceding this important visit, Mr. Hullah wrote from Martins, in Dorsetshire, to his mother, beginning the letter with a description of a railway journey in those days.

I went (he says) in a steam-carriage, a position in which I trust, except in cases of great hurry, I shall never again find myself; the shaking, bumping, and jarring gives you pains in the head; the smoke blinds you, and if you would let it, suffocates you and covers you with dirt, and the noise puts all conversation out of the question; you never pass within sight of a town, and frequently travel for miles between walls of mud—*i.e.* embankments and *cuttings*. Altogether it is a fatiguing, noisy, inodorous method of conveyance which people may resort to when they are in a hurry or cannot get a stage-coach, but which I would no more use from choice than I would have a sound tooth drawn out of my head or drink salt and senna to the health of my friends after dinner.

The closing paragraph of the letter reveals that among the *eight* girls around him there was one who was already of great importance to him. The oldest tale in the world was being told again to willing ears. Her name is mentioned as one of four venturesome souls who confided themselves to his charioteering on an expedition to Lord Shaftesbury's seat. Thanks to the family Dobbin, no disaster ensued, however, and very soon after this sojourn in the country he went to Paris, and wrote home letters giving his freshest impressions.

To his brother, September 20, 1838, he says:

On Tuesday, Mr. Foster, having given me a few general directions about the streets, launched me into the Boulevards and left me to find my way as I could by the aid of a 'Plan de Paris' and my tongue. I started off, passing through the Place Vendôme and walked about to get a general notion of the place. I went to the Tuileries Gardens, the Luxembourg, the Hôtel des Invalides, to Notre Dame, and through numberless streets, *places*, bridges, quays, &c. &c. Mr. Foster and I then met and dined, after which I went to the Théâtre des Variétés, where I saw a piece of Paul de Kock, called 'Moustache,' the 'Bayadères,' and a vaudeville, 'Le Père de la Débutante,' in which Vernet played. . . . The 'Bayadères' won't do in London. . . . Vernet deserves *all* his reputation. I have been to the Louvre. . . . The whole quadrangle is just opened in which are the new Spanish pictures. . . . I was knocked up merely walking through the rooms without seeing anything in detail, and I have not yet entered the sculpture rooms. Last night I went to the Académie Royale and saw 'Guillaume Tell'—Arnold by Duprez. . . . Paris is one of the most beautiful sights in the world. . . . At night the whole effect is like enchantment, and a thing not of reality, but . . . the Arabian Nights!

In a second letter he says:

I have been several times to the Louvre, where I have encountered several acquaintances—a Mr. Dickinson [Lowes Dickinson], who is studying here, as likewise Miss Combe, who is in a state of anxiety about the Lawrences [Mr. Samuel Lawrence], with whom she is going to Florence. . . . I have visited all the lions of Paris— Père la Chaise, the Chamber of Deputies, the Gobelins, the Arc de Triomphe . . . St. Cloud, Versailles ; the sights that everybody must see and be heartily sick of . . . a splendid bore ! It is, however, necessary to say to the French that all is ' *superbe, magnifique!* ' They are content. . . . I have been three times to the Académie Royale, twice to the Opéra Comique, once to the Variétés, once to the Gymnase. At the first I have seen ' Guillaume Tell,' ' Les Huguenots,' and ' Masaniello.' At the Comique I have seen ' Zampa ' and ' Le Perruquier de la Régence. . . . Cinti is ill, so they don't play the ' Domino Noir ' or ' L'Ambassadrice,' or I would have seen them also. . . . At the Gymnase I saw Bouffé, a most splendid comic actor, if possible more comic and more natural than Vernet. . . . I hear he can be exquisitely pathetic. . . . I find he is the *real* Monsieur Jacques, and that Barnett, Vizentini, &c., are all Bouffé and water. . . . The papers here are full of an absurd story of Mr. Green taking a tiger with him in his balloon. . . . I shall bring you a lot of little *Journaux*, in one of which you will find a capital letter from the tiger to his friends in Bengal. . . . I have bought, or rather Mr. Foster has bought me, several scores ; and I have picked up a beautiful copy of Molière and another of Beaumarchais. . . . Love to mother.

CHAPTER V.

AUTOBIOGRAPHICAL (*continued*).

1838–40.

Doughty Street, December, 1838.

Monday evening, 11 o'clock.

MY DEAR HULLAH,—I am very sorry indeed that an engagement of pure business prevented my being in the way to see you to-night and shake hands with you as a bachelor for the last time. Believe me that my warmest and heartiest wishes are with you and your amiable wife, and that among the many sincere wishers for your welfare whom you will both—happily—be enabled to number, neither of you will count one more true or stedfast than myself. I say God bless you with the gravity of an old man and the warmth of a young one, and am always,

Faithfully yours,
CHARLES DICKENS.

Mr. Dickens's congratulatory letter marks the date of Mr. Hullah's marriage with Miss Foster. She was somewhat his senior in age, something more than pretty in person, and possessed, in addition to sprightly manners and not a little wit, of great musical talents, cultivated, as had been his own, in the Royal Academy of Music, and bearing already such good fruit that at the time of her marriage she was earning a very fair income as a teacher and pianoforte-player.

Like most women she found, as years went on, that domestic cares, the bringing up of a rather numerous family, keeping close accounts of expenditure, and the management of social life generally, filled up her time, leaving none for money earning; so gradually all trace is lost of independent work of a remunerative kind on her part. The records of her husband's earnings and of their joint expenditure are minute, and date from the earliest days of married life. One is filled with respect for the patient industry these methodical records display, and with sympathy for what must have been her anxieties as each closing year, with sadly few exceptions, showed the balance to be on the wrong side.

As having some bearing on Mr. Hullah's life, and throwing light on some of its incidents, it may be mentioned that deficits in the exchequer of the young *ménage* would seem, as a rule, to have been made good by her generous and presumably rich father, the young husband being rarely, if ever, disturbed by any revelations concerning them. Indeed, from the beginning of her married life, Mrs. Hullah seems to have made the kindly and generous, but, as after years proved, the grave mistake of suppressing all unpleasantnesses, whether financial or personal, from the husband's and father's eyes. A too complete immunity from the small trials and disagreeables unavoidable in family existence left him in later life inexperienced in the conduct of domestic rule, and unable decisively and efficiently to assume at need that attitude of authority which can only be taken and maintained unquestioned and uncriticised after years of gradual preparation. But prophetic reflections of this nature found no place in the meditations of the young couple, who did not, for many a day after December 20, 1838, dwell on matters of greater importance than the enjoyment of existence—the preparation for Mr. Hullah's future career being, however, by no means the least enjoyable part of it.

In delightful simple language *he* tells his mother—*she* often adding a word—of their honeymoon sayings and doings as they progressed towards Tunbridge Wells, and thence homeward by Hastings, where they were made much of by an old army officer who had known Mr. Hullah's mother, and over whose severe and quaint mode of existence they made merry.

Mr. Hullah's own notes begin again with the year 1839, when he and his wife were established in their first home.

'My first work on my return home this year was the completion of six vocal duets, in co-operation with Mr. H. F. Chorley, with whom I had contracted an acquaintance which ripened into friendship which was maintained for many years.

He had recently been made musical critic of the "Athenæum," one of the few journals in which, at that time, anything readable about music was to be found.

'About this time the idea of forming a school for popular instruction in vocal music first dawned upon my mind. Something similar had before this occurred to two or three persons —to a Mr. Hickson, an amateur, and possibly to others, for it will be found that such schemes are never quite solitary. Rumours of the work of a German musician, Maintzer, in Paris had early reached my ear; but a second visit to that capital had proved that they had come to nothing, and that neither classes nor any fruits of Maintzer's teaching had maintained an existence. It was during this second visit that I first heard of Wilhem, whose books, classes, &c., were already beginning to excite notice. This second visit was made in company with my wife and Chorley.'

Having reached Paris, he writes to his mother:

> I have completely gained what I wanted in Paris without using the introductory letter [through] Madame Carson, a pupil of the singing school conducted by M. Hubert on the Wilhem Method. M. Wilhem, being an old man and having a good pension from Government for the invention of his system, only exercises a general superintendence of the singing classes in Paris. The working man is M. Hubert, whom I have found most obliging and willing to tell me all I wanted to know. . . .

'Through the interest of Mr. Henry Reeve I was brought into contact with Sir James Kay-Shuttleworth (then Dr. Kay), whose interest in the subject, although he was not a musician, was greatly excited. Shortly before this the Normal School for schoolmasters had been opened at Battersea—the only school for schoolmasters then existing in England. It consisted at first of some ten or twelve youths, two or three of whom only had any knowledge of music, and as many any voice or apparent knowledge of the subject. Any beginning less encouraging could hardly be conceived. I remember, after walking some time before the gates of the establishment, at length summoning up courage to make my appearance, and finding two ladies, the mother and sister of Sir James, and two other strange ladies, who had made their way into the place and asked permission to see it—there being as yet nothing to see. This party was soon joined by Sir James, and I found myself, for the first time in my life, called upon to give a lesson in music. In this, I believe, I was considered to have been fairly successful. At any rate, others were attracted to my lessons. A few days later came Lord Carlisle (then Lord Morpeth), subsequently one of my kindest friends, Mons. Guiyot, then French ambassador, Lord Lovelace, Mrs. Austen, &c. . . .

'In August, 1840, Sir James Shuttleworth went with me to Paris. We visited the Normal School at Versailles, the public classes at the Halle aux Draps, and those of the Frères Chrétiens, whose relations to their pupils greatly captivated Sir James. He followed their teaching with close attention, and at the termination of one of the classes burst into a passion of tears, exclaiming, " Would to God we had anything like these *men* (he would have said *papists* an hour before) in our schools!" A strange exclamation from a man habitually very reticent on the subject of religious belief, and certainly, at the period of this visit to Paris, holding in horror everything bordering on Roman Catholicism. . . . Our return to London was marked by a visit to Battersea by the then Bishop of London (Blomfield), a man who added to his general culture a knowledge of music and skill in its application. The first person of his class with whom I had as yet been brought in contact, he remained till the end of his days one of my most kindly enthusiastic friends.

' At the close of this year (December 26, 1840) a conference of schoolmasters was got together at Sir James's house, whereat I remember among others the presence of Dr. Hawtrey, of Eton. On this occasion I made, for the first time in my life, something like a sustained speech on the principal subject which had brought us together.'

At this point the effort to write his own recollections—made, alas! too late—fails. For many pages back the writing betrays how the hand became less and less firm, the body weak, and the sight weary. Very sad it was to see him sit down to his table each forenoon, according to long custom, determined to profit by his morning strength, and then, ere an hour was passed, to witness the fading energy and gathering lassitude, and the mournful expression in his eyes, as slowly he would remove his glasses, lean back, and say he 'must rest awhile.' The last page in his own handwriting was written at Pesio in June 1883.

From the time of the visit to Paris of which he last speaks, Mr. Hullah was launched on the musical career, and pledged to work out to the utmost of his power the diffusion of music among the people of England. A firm believer in the softening and civilising influences of his art, he worked with the single-minded faith of a genuine reformer and the zeal of an enthusiast. Encouraged and seconded by his wife, he henceforth gave himself up, without stint of his physical or mental resources, to the task to which he had put his hand. His first public lecture to which he alludes was often present in his mind on subsequent occasions, when he would speak of his extreme nervousness on having to face an audience that famous day. To those who knew Mr. Hullah only in after years, when constant practice in addressing large numbers had given him confidence and nerve, this condition of mind will excite an amused and half-incredulous smile.

Two or three of his old friends of that early period have been heard to affectionately rally him on his appearance and manner at that first lecture, recalling the thin, spare, active figure, which appeared shorter by some inches than it really was by reason of the large head made to look still larger by an unusually thick growth of dark hair, kept then by no means as trimly short as it came to be of late years, when, as he would say, he had passed under military rule. The large keen eyes, with their boundless power of expressing (or concealing) any and every passing phase of thought or emotion, and the quick emphatic action of the right hand; the clear, resonant voice that penetrated to the farthest corners of any room—the whole man giving promise, even at that 'prentice hour of his life, of the qualities and *physique* which enabled him afterwards to attract, retain, and drill into a musical army the incongruous materials with which he had mostly to deal.

CHAPTER VI.

BIOGRAPHICAL.

1841-43.

SUPPORTED by the recently accorded approval of the Council Office, a meeting was held in Exeter Hall on February 4, 1841, to which Mr. Hullah explained his system with the aid of musical illustrations by the Battersea boys.

Among the audience might have been observed Mr. Charles Greville, taking mental notes of all he heard and saw for the benefit of that 'Journal,' so interesting to the present generation. The editor has enriched Mr. Greville's remarks with the following note, one sentence of which will be read with surprised edification. (See p. 25.)

I had myself put Hullah in relation with the Government and Mr. Eden, who tried his system of musical instruction (based on Mr. Wilhem's plan) at the schools at Battersea. *Indeed I persuaded Hullah to go to France to study Wilhem's system,* which was in operation there. Lord Lansdowne saw that musical education was a neutral ground on which all parties (those most divided) might agree; and he took up this idea with success. Sydney Smith went to this lecture, to Hullah's great delight, and it was successful. . . .

People in every position, from Prince Albert downwards, were showing curiosity about the new musical movement— going to the new classes, listening to Mr. Hullah's lectures, and writing to each other about them and the lecturer as quite one of the important topics of the day. Already, from distant colonies, came demands for, and inquiries about, the Hullah-Wilhem Method. The booksellers had for a while to reply that the Method 'was out of print.'

The teaching work would seem to have gone on ceaselessly throughout the year, for, when Mr. Hullah was absent from London, Mrs. Hullah was arranging fresh work and helping to keep together what was going on. One of his journeys took him to Cambridge, where, under the auspices of Mr. Eben Kay, he was made acquainted with Trinity College, and welcomed by Dr. Whewell. Mr. Hullah reported himself as having a 'pleasant sojourn' and 'getting rapidly better, thanks to two glasses per diem of Trinity ale among other good things!' He 'had not a moment's breathing time,' not even to record some remarks of Macaulay's on Keble's 'Psalter' (just published), though these were 'noteworthy.' All the time when he was not 'rushing about' or 'talking' was spent in answering letters from all sorts of people about the new method; as, for instance, a clergyman's wife wrote in haste to ask if he could *immediately* send her a teacher for her charity school, for a Miss ——, whom she had just engaged, demanded on the spot a set of musical-glasses, 'costing 4*l*., wherewith to *pitch* the voices of her scholars. She would like instead one of Mr. Hullah's instruments—that '*diapason of Wilhem!*'

A short summer trip taken with the late Rev. M. Mitchel, in the course of which he did much walking in Wales, 'as much as thirty miles in one day,' refreshed him for his autumn campaign, which opened with a great meeting (with Lord Wharncliffe, President of the Council, as chairman) of elementary classes for the purpose of forming a singing society. Then, as the year drew towards its close, he started for Manchester with Sir James Kay-Shuttleworth, Mr. Carleton Tufnell, and six Battersea boys. The account of this journey—a very illustrative one—of the work on which he was constantly engaged and the way he did it, is best given in his own words, taken from a letter addressed to his wife, to whom the minutest personal details were interesting:

On Monday morning we all met at the railway station in good time; and in consideration of Castles and Pope [two of the Battersea boys] being *small*, I got the clerk to put us (the six boys and me) into *one* carriage, in order that we might practise a little on the road. Dr. Kay and Mr. Tufnell went into another. We had a pleasant ride to Derby, singing occasionally, though we could hardly hear one another for the noise. On our arrival we found Mr. (the late Lord

Belper) and Mrs. Strutt with a carriage waiting to take us to their house. The boys were packed into a fly, and we followed, first stopping at the Athenæum, that I might see the room where I was to lecture. Here I found Mr. Elliot, and after a little talk we walked on to Mr. Strutt's. A glorious grand old house—the perfection of a comfortable and even elegant English home—built, I should think, at twenty different periods, with rooms in the oddest places imaginable, and six or seven staircases. . . .

There were no end of people to meet us and to go to the lecture. Among others Archdeacon Shirley, a most cheery person, whom I had met before. After a very magnificent dinner we adjourned with the boys to the room, a most elegant place, supported by pillars and beautifully fitted up. It was, to everybody's surprise, crammed to excess. In fact I could hardly get in. I have never been so nervous. Hitherto I have always addressed either people I know something of, or at least people who have had a leaning favourable to me. Here was a room full of strangers perhaps expecting a *concert*. And, to make things worse, there was a feeling in the audience which, when understood, was very well, but which made it dull at first, that we were not to be applauded, and that it would be even disrespectful to me, as Mr. Strutt's guest, to betray any enthusiasm. However, all went very well, the good folks were most attentive and soon got interested and warm in the matter, and the boys sang very nicely. After the lecture the Archdeacon made a speech—very complimentary—speaking of the spread of music as a *great subject*.

. . . .

The next morning after breakfast the boys and I started for Manchester before nine o'clock, Dr. Kay and Mr. Tufnell going with the Strutts direct to Mrs. Davenport's at Capesthorne. Our journey lay through a most beautiful country, Matlock and the Peak, but the cold was intense. A light snow had fallen and frozen, and the road being hilly we reached Manchester, not at five o'clock, as was expected, but at a quarter-past six! I had now to seek out Mr. Langton (Dr. Kay's friend), to find out when and where I was to lecture, to dine, and to dress. Luckily Mr. Langton lives close to an hotel, was at home and expecting me. After five minutes' talk we came back to the hotel, ordered · a tea-dinner, and, after dressing pretty smartly, ate it. . . . Mr. Langton came to take me to the Athenæum, where I was to lecture at half-past seven o'clock. Here I was presented to loads of people, and found Seymour and all the Manchester professors and Barnett. I peeped into the room, hung up the great sheets, and then waited for the awful moment of addressing the Manchester audience. At length we marched in and were received with great cheering. In five minutes I shut up my book, and was talking away to the people just as I do at Exeter Hall.

. . . .

Every point was well taken and understood by the audience, and the success was perfect. I touched the most formidable intervals, and made the boys tell what notes composed some passages I sung, all of which pleased the good folks vastly.

November 19.—To-day I have been over an embroidery factory, a cotton factory, and Museum of Natural History. Now we are off to the Mechanics' Institute for the second lecture. When I come back I will fill up the page and tell you how we got on.

Eleven o'clock.—Glorious success! The Manchester people are certainly excellent judges of lecturing! We have just come from a very full audience (in the Mechanics' Institute) whose enthusiasm was past all bounds . . . . Their attention was extraordinary, as if they would not lose a word. If anybody moved or coughed or made the smallest noise he was instantly put down by acclamation.

The indignation of the assembled multitude at an unfortunate boy who attempted to leave the room while I was speaking was almost ludicrous. There were a dozen people at least with books (manuals) in their hands. The touching of the fingers was rapturously received, and I sang some passages and made the boys tell me the notes beautifully. To-morrow morning we shall go and see more factories, and in the evening lecture at the same place as to-night.

From Manchester he went on to Macclesfield and Congleton, lecturing at both places. He then returned to London to take command of the 'Upper Singing School,' which met for the first time in Exeter Hall on December 1, and began the courses of choral practice which went on for so many subsequent years.

Taking plenty of 'notes' for lectures to be prepared for the ensuing year, Mr. Hullah spent his Christmas holidays at Capesthorne, the house of Mr. and Mrs. Davenport—that same Mrs. Davenport who, the author of 'Philip von Artevelde' tells us, all unconsciously sat to him for the portrait of 'Rosalba,' the heroine of his 'Sicilian Summer.'

The Capesthorne of those days (it was subsequently destroyed by fire) presented many attractions to the young musician. The house was roomy, luxurious, and made socially agreeable by the hostess; while his craving for knowledge, guided by that ' true literary *instinct,*' already much developed —which, years afterwards, the late Rector of Lincoln College found so marked a characteristic of Mr. Hullah's intellect— was fed and encouraged by Mr. Davenport, who, over and above his classic culture, was a student of modern linguistic accomplishments generally, with a decided partiality for Italian. Many a time in later years Mr. Hullah has spoken of the hours passed in the library at Capesthorne, and of the benefit and delight he derived, especially in respect to Italian literature, from the wide knowledge and delicate literary tastes of Mr. Davenport.

The following extracts will give an excellent picture of the kind and amount of work done under Mr. Hullah's influence. He was clearly working onwards, carrying conviction to the minds of his countrymen and women as to the civilising influences of music on the habits of the working and leisured classes of the land, arousing sincere enthusiasm, and lifting high the hopes of dreamers and philanthropists of England's future condition, when, throughout the realm, music should have lulled to rest all savage passions and made love and joy the rule of the peasant's life. His own dreams were so vivid on this aspect of the subject, and his own belief in the humanising power of song so profound, that it is no wonder if he carried all hearts with him. A friend writes to Mr. Hullah:

I wish you could have been with me yesterday at a little village nine miles from Derby. I think you would have been gratified. The Archdeacon, whose parish it is (Shirley), has been enlarging his church, and at its reopening there was a service in which the singing was performed by some of your pupils, not indeed *your* pupils, nor Mr. Elliott's [a direct learner from Mr. Hullah], but by the pupils of Mr. Elliott's pupils. The fact is that in Longford and Shirley, two neighbouring parishes, the Rector of Longford and the wife of the Rector of Shirley have respectively, week after week, repeated the singing lessons which they received in Derby to a class of some twenty or thirty labourers' and farmers' children and artisans, and it was the result of this that I could have wished you had witnessed. There were twenty-five from Longford parish and fifteen from Shirley. The former have received thirty lessons, the latter thirty-three. One of Mr. Garnier's best performers is a young carpenter, who up to last spring had been pronounced utterly devoid of what is popularly termed an ear for music.

In the afternoon Mr. Garnier gave a little lecture on your plan of teaching. . . . The account which he gave of these carpenters, bricklayers, and labourers being seen at their dinner hours and after the day's work was done constantly busying themselves going over the *do, re, mi* on their fingers, and practising themselves in beating time, was very amusing, or rather I should say very gratifying when one calls to mind how great an advantage it must be to such a class to interest them in anything save the most obvious wants of the passing hour.

The irregularity of attendance was a constant obstacle in the way of improvement. But what interested me most was the account which Mr. Garnier gave of the perceptible moral influences resulting from the opening of his class. Several of his pupils had in previous winters been unsteady in their behaviour from having no object of rational interest to occupy their attention during the dark evenings, but these lectures had not only kept them to habits of regularity but also had drawn them invariably to the church whenever it was open for service.

Farther north the 'method' was being actively brought into operation by one of Mr. Hullah's fellow-labourers, Mr. Constantine. The following account of a week's work in 1842 is taken from 'All the Year Round.' Though not published till January 5, 1861, it may best find a place here:

A striking illustration of the diffused influence of Mr. Hullah's enthusiasm is to be found in the results of the labours of Mr. Constantine among the mountains of Cumberland and amidst the whirr of the machinery of Northern England, among a people famous in these days [1861] for their good choral singing. When, in 'forty-two, Mr. Constantine began working Mr. Hullah's system, under the direction of Mr. Crowe, at Liverpool, he taught first a mixed class of ladies and gentlemen in the national schoolroom at Birkenhead, and gradually undertook the following round as his week's work. We begin it in the middle. Wednesday, the first business was to get to Ulverston, twenty-two miles distant; the way being across the sands of Morecambe Bay. This journey in winter time had to be made often in the dark, because the low tide and the morning sun would not always keep in harmony together. The winter fogs, too, are, at Morecambe Bay, not very welcome to a lonely rider travelling on horseback, and obliged to rely on his horse's knowledge of the track. Class-day in quiet Ulverston was always a gala-day. The singing-master's horse was sure to be well looked after, for Ulverston, the town farthest north in Lancashire, stands on a tongue of land where there was nothing to enliven its work but the market-day, till the musicians came. The four thousand inhabitants yielded three singing classes: one contained about fifty ladies and gentlemen, another forty children, and the other was a general class of a hundred. The excellent organist kept up the work, and has conducted an Ulverston musical society from that time, we believe, to this. People came from miles away to be taught in these classes. A cartload of poor children used to be sent by a kind lady from Bardsea. A hale old clergyman walked, in all weathers, nine miles into Ulverston and nine miles out again, to qualify himself for teaching, upon Mr. Hullah's system, his schoolchildren and parishioners, that so he might elevate not only the music in his church, but also the happiness, and even the morals, of his district. He was rewarded with a success beyond his expectations. On Thursdays the lecturer went on to Ambleside, a ride of twenty-one miles, to a place that is, in winter, very quiet, with its five or six hundred inhabitants sorely in need of wholesome entertainment. Here, where there used to be the most horribly nasal and inharmonious imitation of church music, there is now sung by the people a plain musical service, irreproachable in taste. On Friday the round was from Ambleside, fourteen miles on, to Kendal, where there were four pretty good classes, but these did not live to a second course. Sixteen miles on next day, Saturday, brought the teacher to Casterton Schools. Having taught, then a ride of seventeen miles to Preston was followed by a railway journey to Lancaster and back, to meet classes there. Sunday was spent at Preston. A ten-mile ride on Monday to Blackburn carried the music-master to three classes, the last a very large one, chiefly composed of factory hands. On Tuesday the Lancaster classes were visited by way of Preston, and so the week's round ran for one of Mr. Hullah's propagandists in the winter of the year one thousand eight hundred and forty-three.

CHAPTER VII.

BIOGRAPHICAL.

1842-45.

DURING these years Mr. Hullah's work awakened the attention of several men and women of note who showed intelligent interest in the educational and political aspects of his teaching. Among these were the Prince Consort again, the Duke of Wellington (whose entrance into Exeter Hall one evening was recognised by a pause in the proceedings, the audience rising at the same moment), the Marquis of Lansdowne, the Queen Dowager, the Chevalier Neukomm, Moscheles, Keble, and Lord Wharncliffe, whose presence at Mr. Hullah's choral classes was not the result of mere curiosity. Lord Wharncliffe's observation bore fruit when, in July, speaking in the House of Lords in favour of granting financial aid to the musical movement as a recognised branch of national education, he said:

> The first classes that were established were singing classes, and their original idea was confined to the instruction of schoolmasters and mistresses—of persons who attended for the purpose of afterwards instructing others—and so it went on for some time; but by degrees the direct sphere of utility became enlarged, and class after class was formed of persons who attended for the purpose of learning singing on their own account. The undertaking was originated in the latter end of 1841, and at the present moment (July 13, 1842) there were no fewer than 50,000 persons attending the singing classes of Mr. Hullah and his pupils.
>
> . . . . . .
>
> In the beginning of this year it was found that the instruction in singing had induced the persons who attended these classes to form a strong wish for instruction in other elementary branches of education; and on this desire being made known, the persons who originated the instruction determined to accede to it; and accordingly classes were formed, one for writing, another for arithmetic,

and a third for linear drawing. These had also answered the purpose well.

Should these institutions be enabled to continue their useful labours, there could be no doubt that in a very short time a large portion of the lower classes in the metropolis would be withdrawn from the public-houses. During the first year this institution was supported by the payments from the persons instructed and by private contributions. The schoolmasters and mistresses paid 15*s*. for sixty lessons; mechanics and persons in a still more humble sphere paid 8*s*. or 10*s*. for the same number of lessons; while those who could afford it paid 30*s*., or 6*d*. a lesson.

It was soon found, however, that there was so large an increase of attendance, that the former payments were quite inadequate; and, accordingly, towards the end of last session, a petition was presented from these institutions to the Committee of Privy Council, praying for support out of the Education Fund; but the reply of the committee necessarily was that, however cordially they might support the views of these institutions, they were precluded by the form of the grant for education from applying any portion of it to this purpose. He (Lord Wharncliffe) then recommended to the gentlemen who managed these institutions that choral meetings should be publicly held for the purpose of at once making the value of the institution known, and of adding immediately to its funds. The choral meetings had accordingly been given, and with success to a certain extent, for 900*l*. had been realised by them, and a most interesting and valuable spectacle had been afforded to the public of 1,600 pupils of this institution singing together in the most correct and excellent manner, and giving proofs of how much had been done in a very short time.

The question, then, was—these classes having been established with the most beneficial results hitherto, and with the certain prospect of conferring upon the people of this country a great national and individual boon—whether it was not most desirable that Parliament should lend them its support.

With reference to Mr. Hullah himself, who had been spoken of as having made so good a thing of these classes, the fact most honourable to himself was that, up to the present moment, he had given his valuable time and services for nothing. All that he had ever asked for himself was 30*s*. per night, but not one shilling of this had been received, for he had invariably declined pressing for one moment this very moderate claim, in order not to embarrass the very limited funds of the institution.

The Christmas of 1843 Mr. Hullah again spent at Capesthorne, the visit being even more than usually pleasant by the presence of some Italian gentlemen. Signor Prandi among the number, who made the atmosphere of the house so very Italian as to exercise a quite magic effect on Mr. Hullah's vocal organs. He writes at midnight on New Year's Eve to his wife:

> You won't know my voice! What with the air and exercise [of speaking as well as singing Italian] I think it is better than ever it was in my life, and this morning I found, to my great satisfaction that I could sing all manner of passages of execution, make shakes to Crivelli's exercises, and sing the chromatic scale in a style worthy of a Tamburini.

Among the guests are also mentioned three English gentlemen named Crawford, who, during a life spent in Italy, had learnt to play the guitar, and were 'not ashamed to let us hear them,' comments Mr. Hullah, bearing in mind the idea still very prevalent forty years ago that music, in its executive form at any rate, is fit only for women, and men who are also professionals.

Before the end of the London season not only were numerous classes going on in Exeter Hall, but King's College, the Charterhouse, Merchant Taylors', and Eton and Winchester now took up fixed hours of his time. At Winchester College, as elsewhere, Mr. Hullah's relations with the head and staff of masters was of the pleasantest; and if any among them perpetrated a good *jeu d'esprit* at his expense, no one laughed more readily than he. It is easy to imagine how amused he must have been as he copied, and assuredly in so doing learned by heart, the following verses by the Rev. Charles Wordsworth, Master of Winchester College, and sent off to 'Punch,' whose own talent was several times exercised in poking fun at the new musical movement:

Teaching against time.

'Take time by the forelock,' said one to another,
'Take time by the key,' said his musical brother.
'Take time by the lock, and take time by the key,'
'And *keep* time, and beat time!—nice tidings for me.'
Quoth Time, 'I had better be off on the wing,
Or those urchins will catch me as sure as they sing.
Up, down, right, and left! 'tis but poor fun, I tell ye,
For me all the while to be beat to jelly,
So I'll leave Mr. Hullah in Wykeham's old hall,
To teach the boys music in no time at all'—

in which process he was zealously aided by Mr. Edward
May.

Every other week or so he made a *sortie* to some provincial town to see local notabilities about teaching matters, and at Easter paid a flying visit to Paris, where, among other incidents, was the melancholy pleasure of assisting at a mass for the soul of the man on the lines of whose method of teaching he had modelled his own—Wilhem. A day or two afterwards he met Spohr, who, he remarks, ' did not play very well.'

In August he paid his first visit to Sellinge, which, during the life of the then rector, Mr. Bellamy, was as another home to him. While the ' Apostle of Music ' was thus busy in setting, or keeping others at work, friends now and then took thought for his worldly affairs, and proffered advice. Sir James Kay-Shuttleworth, reviewing Mr. Hullah's financial position, says :

> I think that your expenses are now so slight, that you may derive a considerable income (500*l.* per annum at least) from the singing classes at the Apollonicon, if you think it worth while to give your personal attention to the classes.
>
> The day classes for tradesmen and their wives and daughters, and members of the middle classes, ought to pay much better, and if properly managed should give a clear income of 800*l.* or 1,000*l.* per annum.

Had he followed, or perhaps, writing at this distance of time, it ought to be said, had he been *able* to follow out this good advice, he might have secured for himself that ' learned leisure ' he was so well qualified to enjoy. It was not to be, however. Work, unintermittent and severe, was his destined portion in life. Nor was he always permitted to work with the sunshine of friendship's affection to cheer and encourage him. Now and then some caviller, unable to realise a higher moral level than his own, would accuse Mr. Hullah of this, that, or the other departure from the path of rectitude. These attacks he passed by in complete silence, or, if made by letter, with a mere acknowledgment of that letter. One instance of Mr. Hullah's mode of dealing with calumnious attacks will suffice.

Being in Lancaster in the autumn of 1843 on musical business, a clergyman present at an evening meeting put into his hands a letter written by a Mr. H. Crow, which letter, he says, 'had appeared nearly a week since addressed to me in some local newspaper. It contains the usual matter of such letters and a long extract from a pamphlet called "Hullahish," about granting certificates by the thousand to people I never saw, at I can't say how many guineas per head, and ending by calling on me publicly to declare whether it is true! Poor dear man! I wrote the following in answer:

'SIR,—I beg leave to acknowledge the receipt of a letter bearing your signature and dated September 8, and which has only this evening reached me. Yours &c.
'Every man, they say, should have his letter answered.'

Rarely, indeed, did Mr. Hullah even allude to disagreeables of this sort. It is necessary to seek elsewhere than in his letters to learn that malice and envy often strove to blacken his name. It is an open question whether he would not have been wiser in his generation had he now and then, at any rate, disproved the falsehoods uttered against him. Reticent and silently contemptuous of libels he seems to have consistently been in his earlier years, and reticent and silently contemptuous he remained to the end of his life. While admitting the dignity, it is not possible to admit the expediency of this habit of his mind. When urged, as sometimes he was, to meet a lie by a simple denial, '*Qui s'excuse s'accuse*,' he would say, and that settled the matter.

The year 1844 was again begun at Capesthorne, whence he visited Alderley and other adjacent great houses. In February, having been elected to its chair of music, Mr. Hullah delivered his introductory lecture at King's College, London, and arranged an opening class at Trinity College, Cambridge. In May the name of Mendelssohn occurs for the first time in his diary at a party at his own house, when the 'Walpurgis Nacht' was performed; also that in this year he came across Sir Arthur Helps (then Mr. Helps), with whom his acquaintance must have ripened very quickly into friendship, judging by the free and frequent correspondence which went on henceforth through many years. So rapidly indeed did Sir Arthur's interest range itself on Mr. Hullah's side, that early in 1845 he offered aid of every kind towards the scheme, which had already for some time been floating in the air, of a definite and fixed home for the great singing classes which Mr. Hullah had for three or four years been carrying on in Exeter Hall, the Apollonicon Rooms, and other places. Once seized with the idea himself, Sir Arthur urged others to join in the scheme. It is interesting to learn how many generous hands were ready to give assistance to a venture the failure of which was not unlikely, and the success of which the most sanguine could not hope would ever be very brilliant, looked at from a business point of view. But it was not from a business point of view that any of the gentlemen and ladies who came forward at this early stage of the undertaking did look at it. They thought of nothing, in the first instance, but making their young friend Mr. Hullah happy, and enabling him to do that which, when they came to question their philanthropic impulses, they felt to be a great and civilising work. Rome was not built in a day, however, nor was St. Martin's Hall!

The usual records of a busy season drew to a close in July. His 'play time' began in August, by a visit to Tunbridge Wells, with a party from the Charterhouse, headed by the late Dean of Peterborough, Dr. Sanders. Then, in September he joyously packed up his 'toothbrush and sketch-book' and departed for Dover *en route* for Florence. It was his first visit to Italy, and was destined to be made under exceptionally felicitous circumstances, for at Cologne he made a highly promising discovery concerning one of the two travelling companions with whom he had already established some sort of acquaintance. He says:

> One of my fellow-travellers had puzzled me all day; in fact I never remember to have met a person about whose calling I was so puzzled. His criticisms on art and exquisite feeling for the beauties of atmospheric and linear effects in the scenery would at once have made me set him down as an artist, but his acquaintance with literature and his most polished and gentlemanly manner were so *un*artistlike and *un*professional, that it seemed impossible. He and his friend inscribed their names before me and vanished. I approached the book and saw—George Richmond, painter. When Mr. Richmond came down in the morning, I introduced myself and we became friends in an instant! and also travelling companions.

The light-hearted pair of newly made friends travelled by

vettura, 'doing but fifteen miles a day,' and having endless time for loitering at every tempting spot—and there were many—lunching on green figs, black bread, soft goat's-milk cheese, and grapes purchased in the bunch, which bunch was sometimes of such magnitude that, held between them by the stalk as each was seated on a stone, the last grape trailed on the ground! The *vetturino* meanwhile dividing his patriarchal attention between his '*bestie* and his jubilant charges.

At Lugano Mr. Hullah noticed the gravity with which the church services were performed, but the half-operatic style of the musical accompaniments displeased him much.

Still (he says) it is impossible to be in an Italian town an hour without feeling that music is in the hearts and lives of the Italians as is the case with no other people. I cannot but feel now how forced a thing it is in comparison with the French, the English, and even the Germans.

When Milan was reached the travelling party was increased by the presence of Sir William, then Mr., Boxall, and enjoyment ran, if possible, higher. Following his usual habit of talking to everybody, Mr. Hullah had made acquaintance with the clergy of the cathedral, and was accordingly requested by the *Canonici* to play on their great organ, a feat he performed with infinite pleasure during one of the services. Of the success of his operations on so gigantic an instrument he, perhaps discreetly, says nothing. Onward to Florence, stopping at many a beautiful old town rich in the things they loved, went Mr. Hullah and his genial friend, running against acquaintances here and there, and then, having for a brief space revelled in *Firenze la bella*, Mr. Hullah turned back, his heart yearning for home as 'after all more beautiful than even beautiful Florence.'

CHAPTER VIII.

BIOGRAPHICAL.

1846.

AFTER only one night's rest from his journey, Mr. Hullah plunged into full work, which lasted without intermission till Christmas. Even New Year's Day of 1846 did not pass without the daily portion of work—an arrangement of Palestrina's Gloria,' as it happened.

Towards Easter he began to flag over a lecture on the 'Duty and Advantage of Learning Music.' But a visit to a country house *en route* to Leeds and the exhilarating society of an Irishman given, in and out of season, to letting off ridiculous anecdotes, partially rested and cheered him. 'As I arrived, he says, ' Sir William —— had the circle around him in a roar, and was at the moment telling a story of his Irish servant, who, having dropped a trayful of delicate porcelain, shook his head disapprovingly at the ruins, with the remark, "By Jasus! how brittle ye are this mornin." '

At Leeds he was the guest of Dr. Hook, who, to their great amusement, laid out a scheme for the migration of the entire Hullah family from London to Leeds, and was at great pains to point out how advantageous an arrangement it would be. Dr. Hook threw himself completely into the object of his guest's visit, becoming so interested in the working out of it that he insisted on printing the explanatory lecture Mr. Hullah had delivered on his arrival, and grew quite excited over a sudden controversy that burst forth between his guest and some ' Gregorians ' who were at the preliminary lecture.

One of these gentlemen, with great energy, set out his arguments on four folio pages, which Mr. Hullah proceeded to deal with. All cognisant of the dispute were on the *qui vive* to know the result of the paper war, and there was immense exultation when 'universal opinion pointed to the demolition of the Gregorians.' Dr. Hook kept him pretty hard at work. There were lectures every evening, one or two unexpected speeches to be made, all manner of people to be seen and introduced to, and Sunday schools to be inspected. 'But,' he says, 'at last work is over, and successfully, and now I shall have a day or two's *play*.' He then proceeds to give a vivid picture of the *ménage*:

Dr. Hook's power of doing work is tremendous, and it had need be, for he is never let alone a moment after nine o'clock. People come to him about everything: cases of conscience, arbitrations, advice—every difficult knot in the county seems to be submitted to his fingers for untying. It is an open house. Dinner is at any hour—people coming and going.

The conduct of church matters under Dr. Hook greatly attracted his notice, and he embodied his impression in a closing paragraph of his last letter:

On the whole, I owe *this* impression to my visit—that, whereas I have hitherto had to use a little imagination to think the Church a living thing, here I *see* that it is so.

For some time there had been a good deal of expectancy among musical people concerning a forthcoming performance in June of Mendelssohn's 'Lauda, Sion,' at Liège, and a Mendelssohn festival, superintended by the great man himself at Cologne, during which a chorus of 2,500 tenors and basses were to perform on the top of the Sieben Gebirge. To hear these Mr. Hullah departed with Mr. Chorley. He involuntarily 'enjoyed' (!) a whole night on the deck of a steamer, saw the sun rise and admired it as much as a sleepy and extremely bad sailor could be expected to do; but required a bath, a supper, a night in a 'delicious bed,' and a successful journey to Liège before he felt a man again. He tells how,

Following a crowd (going, as they imagined, to hear the Mendelssohn music), we found ourselves 'involved' with a group of ringers in blue blouses, who, with the assistance of a good-natured man with an ophicleide under his arm, came by, and somehow cajoled the doorkeeper of the Town Hall to let us through. We mounted a sort of ladder, and found ourselves at the back of an orchestra preparing to play a mass of Cherubini, and discovered on inquiry that the Mendelssohn music was not till the evening at six. Of course we had no objection to two good things instead of one, and heard the mass with great satisfaction. That over, we went to seek Mendelssohn, who is staying with a Liège grandee. He was at home, and in an ecstasy of delight at the sight of us, so he kindly said; full of inquiries and self-congratulations at our arrival. Of course we now get reliable information about everything. The new work is the Latin hymn Lauda, Sion,' the whole of which Mendelssohn (for the first time) has set to music.

. . . . . .

Mendelssohn's host is to get us in, a matter seemingly of some difficulty. He (the host) has moreover invited us to spend the evening. It will be something to assist at a Belgian *soirée*. Probably, too, Mendelssohn will be serenaded, which happened last night. It appears that it is to be one of the grandest festivals there has ever been in Germany, going on Sunday, Monday, and Tuesday

Having heard the 'Lauda, Sion,' he says of it :

Mendelssohn's hymn is really a very fine work, and, in spite of a very indifferent performance, produced a great effect. The ceremony, of which it formed a part, was very imposing, not excepting a sermon preached to a great body of ecclesiastics, among whom were fourteen bishops! The chanting of the Psalms, too, in the vespers was the best I have ever heard; this, of course, was the business of the priests. The *choir*, on the other hand, was most inefficient, the bishop having refused to allow the soprano and alto chorus parts to be sung by women, though he permitted one female solo singer. I should have liked to preach to *him* !

. . . . . .

This morning we went to the cathedral and heard Beethoven's mass in C ! ! ! After service we were taken all over the works (which are going on with great spirit) by the architect.

Fired with a spirit of emulation, Mr. Hullah organised a monster choral concert on his return home and carried it through, with a body of 2,500 singers, on June 18.

In the autumn Mr. Hullah, accompanied by Mr. Headlam and a younger friend, again went abroad, intending to get as far as Venice. The journey began unpropitiously, and his first letters are most mournful. His rooms were always fusty, and with peculiar frequency looked into unsavoury 'stable-yards;' the skies were leaden, 'like London on a Sunday;' the interchange of letters 'took such a frightful time;' the rain came down 'every day and all day long;' he waxed vengeful against an inopportune baby, the cause of all his trouble and loneliness; he would give up Venice and go back at once, only that 'Headlam did so urge his going at least as far as

Nuremberg.' So to Nuremberg he allowed himself to be taken; and once there, the great beauty and picturesqueness of that enchanting place dispersed the dark clouds of discontent; and, the sun having shone for an hour or so, the trio immediately bought the largest white hats procurable, and started—two of them gaily—for Aschaffenburg, picking up Mr. John Gurney on the road.

Mr. Hullah's letter about Nuremberg is as good a traveller's letter as can be imagined; but, now that all the world has been to Nuremberg, it is too long, like its many interesting companions, to be given *in extenso*. He kept his eyes open to everything, from the design of the weather-vane on the highest steeple or tower down to ridiculously worded advertisements. One of these *vis-à-vis* of his hotel windows— which ran to the effect that the advertiser ' recommends himself as a teacher of English and a Kentish man, *la prononciation de Kent, dont la capitale est Cantorbéry, étant réputée la meilleure* '—gave rise to so much wit and laughter that Mr. Hullah's natural *gaieté de cœur* returned in full force. He forgave the baby, and went blithely on with his journey, his letters, his German studies, and his *sketch-book*, the contents of which were to ' give perfect satisfaction when he got home.' The German church services bored him greatly, and the music was far from being a source of delight to him. The fact that the sound of the German language then, as always, was, when spoken by the class of persons usually in communication with travellers, a perpetual irritation to him, accounts for the disproportionate prominence given to an Italian hotel-keeper at Nuremberg, whose vowel utterances smote the more sweetly on his ear by contrast, and enhanced the comfortable amenities of an Italian *cuisine* after a long course of German simplicity:

A wonderful man! (writes Mr. Hullah) about six feet high, and immensely bulky, with a most Pickwickian countenance. His power of eating exceeds everything I ever witnessed; his gastronomic judgment is shown in his table. He seems to have grafted German gluttony on Italian discrimination, to have subposed a Teutonic digestion under a Latin palate. His habits were curious. He passed the morning in a sort of den not much bigger than himself—the shell to the snail. From one o'clock he devoted himself to society. He took the head of the table at that hour. When we left it we left him; when we came down again from our rooms to go out he was still at his post; when we returned he was taking his coffee and a cigar. If we walked out again soon he was perceived to have begun supper (*i.e.* another dinner); when we returned he had never finished it.

At Ratisbon a curious fancy to spend some time in the torture-chamber seized Mr. Hullah. He made a book full of sketches of the dreadful instruments he found there, dwelling (surely for the first and last time) on things capable of giving physical pain. After describing the place, well known now, he says, as he took up his position, sketch-book in hand, 'there is a possible fascination about the subject, partly due to its being the relic of another age, which I, who am not given to horrors, could not resist. . . . It was a strange sensation to sit in a corner of this precious remnant of what the Gregorians have the impudence to call "the days of faith," and call up in one's mind the horrors that have been acted in it.'

Linz was the next halting-place, and here a truly astonishing 'development of German' helped the party to see thoroughly the Monastery of St. Florian and its library. Mr. Hullah writes:

It is a perfect palace in size and splendour, but realising rather a fairy tale than presenting a reality. Conceive a suite of about twenty rooms in a row, commanding one of the most beautiful prospects conceivable, furnished in a style of regal splendour, literally for the Emperor, which nobody has occupied in the present century; chairs in which nobody has sat; beds in which nobody has slept; looking-glasses that have never seen more than one or two human faces; drawers which have never held clothes, and writing-tables with never an *inkstand*; all these things of the last century, and having never been used. Then there are rooms full of preserved birds and insects and cabinets of minerals. The shutters were opened to let us see what the rooms contained: a collection of indifferent pictures, also kept in the dark. . . . There is a gorgeous church, with a nave almost as big as that of St. Paul's, in which vespers were chanted by eleven individuals, the only persons we saw to occupy a building which I should say would easily contain a thousand people. It appears there are no monks now in the establishment, but that it consists solely of sundry ecclesiastics, some of whom are professors in various colleges about, and some of whom manage the *farms*, which are very celebrated, and in appearance quite equal to our best English farms.

We finished our inspection of this extraordinary place by a

development of German, for which you will hardly give us credit. There is a very large library. This we asked to see, and were conducted by the guide to a door, on the other side of which we were told we should find the librarian. I entered, and found myself face to face with a person in an ecclesiastical costume—a real *bonâ fide* German professor. In my best German (!) I requested to see the library. In answer he poured out a flood of words, evidently civil and apparently with a question, not one of which Headlam or I understood. 'Did the Herr Professor speak French?' 'No.' 'Italian?' 'No.' 'English?' 'Not a syllable.' There was no help for it but to plunge into the German, which I did vigorously, and maintained a conversation for an hour and a half on books, England, Mr. Newman, Dr. Pusey, pictures, taste, Shakespeare, and the musical-glasses, in the course of which I received many compliments on my *pronunciation* ! and many regrets that we had not come in the morning, when the Herr Professor might have had our company to dinner. . . . I hope you will now have more respect for my German. . . . P.S. I now speak French, German, and Italian— indifferently.

At Linz Mr. Hullah parted from his friends for a while, and made the final start towards Venice. 'At 4 A.M.,' he says, 'I stepped into a little covered carriage, and dashed out by myself into the rain and darkness. But, oh! the delight of thinking that in a few hours I should be in Italy again; and, oh! the blessed sound of the first " *buon viaggio*," and my elation when my charioteer asked me what countryman I might be, for I could not be an Englishman, said he; *they* were all so *concentrati*, and never laughed!' Presently he ran short of the current money, and his *vetturino* had to pay his bills till, Treviso being reached, the collective financial resources of the town enabled him to change a few sovereigns and push on to Mestre, where he gleefully took his seat in a gondola, and was borne swiftly away to the beautiful city Who that knows Venice will not follow with sympathy and interest the eager, expectant traveller wending by tortuous water lanes the way to the Piazzetta di San Marco on that lovely moonlit night? A week passed by before he found a moment to write home his impressions—a week of

Long, blue, solemn hours serenely flowing,
Whence earth, we feel, gets steady help and good.

Every evening I have been out so late looking at the moon, and I have come home so knocked up in body—not to speak of my poor brain'—that I have been fain to go to bed in the smallest

number of moments possible. This evening and its moon I have
given up to tell you how I have enjoyed other evenings and their
moons, and other days and their suns. How to begin I know not.
How am I to convey to another any notion of a city which has
been for centuries the theme of wonder and admiration of every
traveller who has had to tell of it, and which yet far surpasses the
most glowing description and the most sanguine expectation?—
which is in every respect in which a city can be beautiful—in
climate, architecture, and living interest, excels almost every other,
and is in one respect quite unique. . . . Oh, that you could have
seen the moons of the last two or three nights! The Persian
ambassador smiled when he was told that a round muggy-looking
thing which he saw in London was the sun which he had worshipped
in the East—' his informant was pleased to be facetious.' I confess
it is hard to believe that *we* have ever been lit by this Venice moon,
whose shadows are so intensely hard and black, and by whose light
the smallest type may be read with ease, and by which I think
even colours could be distinguished.

And so he runs on through page after page, rhapsodising
over each building, each point of view, troubled that he cannot convey yet more distinctly an idea of what delights him.

CHAPTER IX.

BIOGRAPHICAL.

1847.

To turn from Mr. Hullah's letters—warmly tinted pictures as they are—to the daily routine of work in London is depressing, until, following him, interest is revived in the humanity of the busy existence. Scarcely could he have shaken off the dust of travel when he was at his classes, lectures, and writing again, despite the autumnal chills and the grey gloom of the London atmosphere. Frequent social gatherings are briefly recorded at home and abroad, at which were present Chorley and Helps, the Brookfields, the Richmonds, Miss Masson (the singer), the Procters, Lord Monteagle, Sir A. Codrington, and many another genial or interesting or influential personage. At a final gathering of the year—on New Year's Eve—the Hullahs being hosts on this occasion, were present Charles Dickens and his wife, her father (Mr. Hogarth), old Mrs. Hullah, and two or three more, who all found each other so delightful that the party only broke up when 1847 was two hours old.

No notes exist of the conversation that took place on that or any other evening, but it may reasonably be surmised that the scheme for the building of St. Martin's Hall, daily approaching maturity, formed a prominent topic. Certain it is that most of the ladies and gentlemen named took an active part in advancing it. For this purpose also a concert—the first of a series—was given in Exeter Hall on January 18. Naturally the attention of the general public was becoming aroused by these means to the subject uppermost in the mind of Mr. Hullah and his more immediately interested friends

E

and pupils. Still the undertaking was a large and most costly
one, calling for great sums of money not easily collected for
any purpose, and decidedly difficult to collect in furtherance
of a project in which, after all, the greater number of persons
actively concerned were of the more needy sort. Private
friends came forward with help handsomely, but still a good
while elapsed before a contract for building a new music-hall
was signed. However, in May the contract did get signed,
and on June 21 the foundation-stone was laid, before a vast
concourse of spectators, by Viscount Morpeth, M.P., in due
masonic form. Several notabilities spoke, each according to
his light, and the proceedings terminated by the presentation
to Mr. Hullah of a cheque for 500*l*. ' in furtherance of an
undertaking launched that day ! ' accompanied by good wishes
enough to have floated it triumphantly there and then. But,
reviewing the subsequent history of the speculation just taken
in hand, one is constrained to think that his guardian angel
must have been engaged elsewhere that day, for had he been
by he could never have consented to a man of Mr. Hullah's
disposition hampering himself with financial operations of
so difficult and intricate a nature. While perfectly able to
grapple with, and lay out statements of accounts in a ' style
worthy of a chancellor of the exchequer,' as a correspondent
took occasion to tell him, Mr. Hullah so disliked business
details, was so little inclined to exercise the degree of caution
indispensable in dealing with all sorts of men, that it is hard
to comprehend how he ever took courage to launch into any
undertaking involving almost daily monetary transactions.
It can but be supposed that the advantages likely to ensue
from his getting entire control of a building suitable for his
great educational classes were brought with undue prominence before him, and that he realised these more vividly than
he ever did the equivalent drawbacks, and that it was only
when the latter forced themselves on his daily, hourly existence that he understood how dearly he would have to pay in
pocket and in peace for the realisation of his pet scheme. It
would be instructive to know whether, in the year 1847,
building operations were carried on for a fifth or sixth of
their cost now. It surely must have been so, since a body

of gentlemen conceived it possible to undertake a great brick structure like St. Martin's Hall with only a few thousand pounds to begin upon, or the measure of their trust in the generosity of the public must have been sadly miscalculated.

To the work carried out in St. Martin's Hall is undoubtedly traceable the present all but universal study of music by every class in England; but it may certainly be said that for the chief director of that early movement, splendidly as he was supported and encouraged by his immediate friends, the results were ruinous in every way. Nothing but the marvellous elasticity of Mr. Hullah's temperament, thanks to which he was at any moment able to cast care behind him and plunge with the most complete power of concentration into whatever he had on hand, could have enabled him to bear up against the wear and tear of his life from June 21, 1847, till the day when, fourteen years later, he stood free from the crushing burden of St. Martin's Hall. It must be remembered that all through these years of anxiety Mr. Hullah was so happy and so fortunate as to have by his side a companion who shared his every labour, his every care, possessed of capacity and energy little, if at all, inferior to his own.

In this same important month of June took shape a scheme for the foundation of Queen's College in Harley Street, the first collegiate chartered school for girls. The initiatory meeting was held at the house of the late Rev. F. D. Maurice, with whom Mr. Hullah had the good luck to be associated in this project, the growth of which was a source of active interest to him during the remainder of his life. He was a man quite peculiarly fitted to be connected with any educational institution for young women or girls.

Respect for womanhood, merely as such, was so deep seated in his nature that it coloured spontaneously his relations with women, producing in them at every age an enthusiasm that called forth all that was purest and truest in their nature. As his pupils, girls, with few exceptions, felt that Mr. Hullah expected of them, as a matter of course, nothing short of their best efforts, and they—involuntarily, so to speak—responded loyally, and showed the best of themselves in every way when working for him. For several years before the present writer met Mr. Hullah, it was chiefly from young Queen's collegians she heard his name—never mentioned but with a loving respect really remarkable.

A little incident which Mr. Hullah was fond of recalling is shown by the 'Daily Remembrancer' to have occurred one evening just before the break-up of the London season, and the consequent flight to holiday lands. There had been a small dinner-party at the Hullahs' house. The guests were just about to depart when in walked two poets, Samuel Rogers and Thomas Moore. A little chit-chat followed, the dinner guests postponed their exodus, and Tom Moore asked his host to sing some of the Irish melodies. Placing himself at the piano Mr. Hullah began, and Mr. Moore listened attentively and without comment to the end, when he said, 'Ah, I see you've found out it doesn't do to sing them as they are written.' This was fortunate, since Mr. Hullah, whose rendering of the melodies was most beautiful, never sang them twice *exactly* in the same way!

Mr. Hullah's companion on his autumn holiday was Mr. Richmond—than whom a more genial could scarcely have fallen to his lot. The two were always 'in luck,' getting just the rooms and the dinners they liked at Petracchi's in Paris, that matchless host never forgetting to provide them with a daily surprise in some new preparation of their favourite food —macaroni—the effects of which he watched with the anxiety of an artist and inventor. Very rarely did they get permission to dine *en ville*. Indeed, the excellent Petracchi would give no sort of consent till he received good assurance that the dinner they were going to eat was not likely to be inferior to the one they left behind; as on the occasion of dining with a certain Mons. P——, famous for his cellar of ancient date and his delicate appreciation of its contents. Having many kindred tastes, the two friends visited with nearly equal interest schools, galleries, and studios together.

Of the schools Mr. Hullah writes :

This visit has been very valuable for Richmond and for me, as showing how enormously *we* have advanced on the French in the last few years. Defective as is the School of Design in London, it appears to be incomparably in advance of that of Paris. And in respect of the singing schools, though I must give them the credit of precision and a sort of exactness of intonation which yet never appears quite in tune, our people are enormously ahead in time, in feeling, and I suspect in reading. In the children's schools there is no comparison to be made for a moment. As to the music they sing—it is everlastingly rubbish; no great works, nothing grand; nothing with any *outline*—no passages overlapping one another as in the music we sing; but little chopped-up successions of four-bar phrases, with chords of accompaniment by way of under parts. I mentioned to M. Foulon that we were going to have a concert of Mendelssohn's music, upon which he remarked: ' *Ah ! voilà une musique très ennuyeuse.*'

. . . .

At another school I have just heard a lesson given by a M. Chevé, who has invented '*un horrible chiffre*,' as one of my companions called it, from which some boys sang. The *chiffre* may or may not be ingenious enough, but the inventor is a most conceited little fellow.

Indeed, so angry did M. Chevé and his *chiffres* make him, that Mr. Richmond had to take him for a turn round the studios that afternoon, by way of clearing up the atmosphere.

With a good deal of the modern French School of Painting Mr. Hullah would seem to have had but scant sympathy.

Ary Scheffer's work, which he saw for the first time, he speaks of with dislike; though the large style, imaginative force and solemnity of Paul Delaroche's work, also new to him apparently, impressed him much. It was only in the Italian galleries of the Louvre, however, that his full pleasure in pictures revived. The holiday performances were wound up by a long hunt among the old bookstalls and shops, in search of Spanish literature likely to be useful to Sir Arthur Helps, who was about this time bringing his ' History of the Spanish Conquest ' to a conclusion. To receive the ' treasure trove ' was, doubtless, the special object of Sir Arthur's arrival to dinner the very day after Mr. Hullah's return home.

CHAPTER X.

BIOGRAPHICAL.

1848-54.

THROUGHOUT the year 1848 few weeks passed without a meeting between the two houses of Helps and Hullah. Frequent intercourse, based on sympathy of tastes and a joyousness of temperament remarkable in both men, became a pleasant habit. During long after-dinner discussions, all manner of subjects, grave and gay, were disposed of. Probably, during one of these sessions, the duty of citizens in times of national disquietude was expounded by Sir Arthur in his best manner, and led to so strong a conviction as to his own duty on the part of the musician that, in the spring of the year, he became a special constable during the Chartist riots. His Conservative tendencies were much braced by the chilly perambulations of those April evenings, after which he always maintained that ' popular outbreaks result in a considerable increase in the noise and dirt of the world.' Certainly the birth of his aversion to Radicalism was always referred back to that period of his life when the beat of his *bâton* would have produced quite other sounds than those which usually followed its timely flourishes. He gives an insight into his political bias in a letter to his mother, written from Paris, in which he tells her of a visit to the National Assembly, whence he had returned at 6.30 P.M., after a sitting of six hours.

There was a full attendance — 750 members — and a very animated debate on the Education question. Among those who spoke was Odillon Barrot, one of the most distinguished of the French parliamentary orators. De Falloux and St. Hilaire also spoke at some length. The debate ended with a ' division,' during which the *noise* exceeded anything I ever heard—except, *perhaps*, that in a room in a cotton mill at Manchester, which contains 900 looms. Paris is suffering in reality very much from the follies of last year. There is still, however, an outside of life and gaiety—very noisy gaiety —but what a great change is apparent even on the surface! Of *gentlemen* we saw few, of *ladies* none. The best places in the theatres, are filled by people who certainly would be more in their element nearer the ceiling : a charming *égalité* in dirty hands manifests the spread of Republican sentiments. The influence of an uncultivated audience manifests itself in a coarseness and want of finish in the performance which would not have been tolerated a year ago.

But active participation in passing political events was but an interlude in his life, which was becoming daily more absorbed in educational work.

Queen's College had opened in 1847, when he had given an introductory lecture, and had commenced his classes there with twelve pupils, his own daughter being one of them. Ere long the success of Queen's created a desire for a second college for girls, to which end, in the following year, a committee was formed, and the preliminary details arranged for an institution subsequently known as Bedford College, with which Mr. Hullah was also associated, the number, efficiency, and zeal of his musical assistants enabling him to relegate to their hands from time to time the conduct of many of the classes which met at the Apollonicon Rooms, awaiting the completion of the new hall in Long Acre. Financial complications in connection with this ill-starred building began to draw indeed to a climax in 1849; but friends discovered his perplexities and voluntarily invited his confidence. Having learnt the state of affairs, several, among whom Sir John Coleridge and the present Lord Chief Justice (then Mr. John Duke Coleridge) took a most prominent place, were unremitting in their efforts to get subscriptions for the purpose of finishing St. Martin's Hall. A statement was drawn up and largely circulated, in which the history of the Hall was briefly narrated. It was assumed, as generally admitted, that Mr. Hullah 'had laboured hard and to good purpose' ; but [that] it was not commonly known that he had reaped but slender fruits personally from exertions almost beyond his strength and injurious to his health ; nor 'that to several hundred of schoolmasters and mistresses his instructions had been from the first given gratuitously, . . . nothing in the way of general public help having as yet been extended to him.'

The public responded to the appeal to some extent, and on October 10, 1849, a portion of the building having been finished, the Upper Singing School met there for the first time.

'I am right glad to hear that the Hall has got its hat on,' writes Sir Arthur, always to the fore in cheerful congratulations. 'Great will be the day when it puts on its nether garments and appears in proper trim with well-tied neckcloth and pumps.' And he did not fail to be present when, in February of the following year, the Hall was brought to such a point of completion that, amid a flourish of trumpets, it was placed under the protection of St. Martin and opened for public use.

All parts of the building shared Mr. Hullah's care and exercised his ingenuity, the library perhaps more than any other, for it was then the only musical library in the country. During the following years he made it a singularly complete library of reference, the MS. catalogue of which has survived the fire, and testifies to the patient, indefatigable hand of the founder. Being now 'at home,' Mr. Hullah's ardour for musical instruction redoubled. Ceaselessly the classes went on, gathering force as time progressed, but financially none of the prophesied benefits accrued to him, the enormous working expenses absorbing all available funds.

Curious difficulties, adding not a little to the daily harass of life, sometimes arose in the composition of the choral classes. For instance, now and then soldiers (who cannot lay aside the regulation uniform at will) desired to join the classes, to which proposal sundry civilian members, unaccustomed to such close proximity of the military garb, made objection, though, when called upon to give their reasons in plain language, they were naturally embarrassed and much exercised how to avoid saying in so many words that, though the soldier might be good enough to fight for them, suffer for them, die for them, he was not worthy to stand in the civilian ranks of a choral class—for to this the whole objec-

tion was reducible. To such prejudices, alike cruel and
irrational, the director never yielded. Those who objected to
the uniform—he was careful to point out that it was the
uniform which made all the appreciable difference—might
go, but that if the soldiers wished to stay they were welcome
to do so. In many other, though less marked, instances
English exclusiveness exhibited itself from time to time in
offensive or ridiculous ways, and had to be tided over with
tact and good temper, qualities brought into daily requisition
in business relations with composers and their patrons, quite
as much as with vocalists, solo or choral. A difficulty of this
kind arose at this time between himself and Mr. Chorley,
who, having found ' a new composer, Gounod by name,'
wished to secure him a hearing rather on trust, Mr. Hullah
preferring to wait till he could call on Gounod in Paris, where
he meant to pass his next Easter vacation. Fortunately he
was able to agree with Mr. Chorley in his estimation of
Gounod, though he wrote somewhat cautiously : ' I carried off
four compositions from Madame Viardot's house . . . Of these
things it is difficult to speak confidently. A great original
musical genius is such a creation that one is slow to come to
any conclusion. That the pieces I have seen and heard, in a
way, are thoroughly workmanlike is their least praise ; perhaps
their most extraordinary quality is their simplicity.'

To return to the summer of 1848. As August drew near
its close the great question, ' Where shall we take our holiday ? '
was debated in joint family conclave on some breezy slope of
Vernon Hill. It was agreed—with acclamation we may be
sure—that Sir Arthur Helps and Mr. Hullah should escort
Lady Helps to the Rhine country, Mr. Hullah to act as
cicerone-in-chief. Full reports, to which all three contributed,
were sent daily to Mrs. Hullah, detained at home by ' urgent
private affairs,' but requiring to be kept posted up in everything, jokes included, of which the following is a specimen.

Having written at great length concerning the restorations of the Dom-Kirche at Cologne, the cicerone-in-chief
adds, ' And now you will be looking for personalities—accounts of other restorations—and reports on the edification

of (k)naves other than that of Cologne.' He has to tell of
endless merriment extracted from 'unconjugated verbs and
undeclined nouns' in the 'for-years-much-studied-but-there-
fore-not-the-even-yet-perfectly-acquired' German tongue, dis-
charged at the heads of all persons who had information to
give, and he has to confess that these grammatical missiles
not infrequently failed to hit their mark. But this 'summer
nonsense' soon came to an end, for Mr. Hullah was recalled to his post, leaving his fellow-travellers to finish their
holidays. It was decided that he should be kept faithfully
au courant of all the incidents thereof, and as soon as he
was gone they sat down and sent off a final report to Mrs.
Hullah.

'Johannisberg has in this journey outdone himself in kindness,
good-nature, considerateness, and skill, in managing men and things,
writes Sir Arthur; and Lady Helps adds: 'We have got so fond of
him that we are quite miserable at his going away. When we are
alone we do nothing but talk of him. He is well and as full of life
and energy as you could wish.'

The next amusing letter from Sir Arthur was from Coblentz, dated September 27 :

Johannisberg-Zimmer.

Have we not done great things, considering that on Sunday last
[when Mr. Hullah had started for England] we lost our right hand,
our best leg, the only eye we saw clearly with, and the front part of
our head? Well, but *what* thing? Why, man, we have been to
Ems, to Schwalbach, to Schlangenbad, to Biebrich, and we have
composed a very difficult letter in German, for which no model was
to be found in the book, to the postmaster at Coblentz.

I get on pretty well with my German, but I do not fash myself
with it, but let it quietly soak into me. A German master has been
routed out of an old garret over the water there, and he gives
lessons at 10 groschen. He is very severe. and I have notions
about pronouncing *ich* and *mich* and *auch* which had not before been
conceived of my mouth. I tell you what I have got also—a translation into German of Montalembert's speech, which will form an
excellent study.

When the travellers returned they found their friend more
entangled than ever in his ceaseless circle of work, in which
he continued to whirl round and round till, fairly worn out, he
was compelled to seek rest for his body and relaxation for his
mind in the as yet never-failing remedy of a Continental trip.

So soon, therefore, as his working season was over, Mr.

Hullah descended on his Sellinge Rectory friends *en route* for the Continent. It seemed likely when he left home that he would have to take his holiday alone, but while at Sellinge he drew such attractive pictures of a run through Belgium and the Rhine country as fired the President (then a Fellow) of St. John's, Oxford, who was staying at his father's house, with a desire to accompany him. They departed, leaving the rector and rectoress in a state of much anxious disapprobation, for they, never having crossed the Channel, could not dissociate foreign travel from the idea of great danger, and were also a little by way of 'thanking God their own country was good enough for them.' However, they recovered their usual serenity of mind so soon as letters containing brilliant reports and no record of mishaps began to arrive. Having travelled for some days, Mr. Hullah writes to his wife :

> Cock has just gone, having set off at some unchristian hour to *walk* (with a guide to carry his toothbrush) through the Black Forest.

[The late Rev. T. A. Cock was one of the oldest and most beloved Professors of Queen's College. For many years he made a practice of taking a walking tour in Switzerland, and became a great authority on all matters relating to pedestrianism, the last but by no means least important point— the portability of luggage—having occupied his attention, until, according to his friends, he had acquired the art of compressing in the compass of a pocket-book every luxury and convenience that heart of traveller can desire.]

> We are come to Freiburg, where I have made a very agreeable addition to a small circle of acquaintance in Professor Hüber, of Berlin, the author of a book about the English Universities which Frank Newman has translated—a great German Conservative and High Churchman, who knows A—— and H——, and the Coleridges, and writes occasionally for the 'Guardian.' We were fellow-travellers both on Wednesday and yesterday. On Wednesday we spoke only a few words (of German), when my 'beautiful pronunciation' took him in, for he thought I knew the language perfectly. Yesterday I found he spoke English, and at the *table d'hôte* he told me who he was, a compliment I returned without expecting to produce the sensation that it did. He knew all about our doings, about the Hall and everything else, and was full of curiosity and inquiry.

He continues his letter from Basle :

... He wishes to write some articles about us in the German reviews. So far as I can gather, we are as much ahead of the Germans in musical (popular) culture as in some other things. The accounts of the teaching in German schools, which have been published formerly by Hickson and latterly by Joseph Kay, are somewhat exaggerated, according to Mr. Hüber.

Further communications concerning Mr. Hüber were broken off by the arrival at the door of the omnibus (the progress of which across the bridge at Basle had been watched by the letter-writer), out of which emerged Sir Arthur Helps. Later on arrived Mr. Butterfield, and immediately the party started for Venice, taking Verona and many other neighbouring cities on their way out and home, and getting all the enjoyment and refreshment to be expected from a party so constituted. With the return to London recommenced anxieties. Such comfort as may be drawn from much sympathy and some help he had. A friend of long standing writes :

I cannot, my dear Hullah, let this opportunity go by without expressing to you my pleasure at having been in any way connected with your good work, and telling you that I have a feeling of gratitude to you, at having been as it were permitted to act with you at all in this matter. You will not perhaps see at first what I mean, or you will fancy that it is merely a well-turned phrase (part of my craft), but it is not so. When you think how often money is ill used and how rarely a man can look back with thorough satisfaction at what he has done with any portion of his possessions, you will agree with me that one may well be thankful to anybody who puts one in the way of using any money to the complete relish of one's own conscience. Allow me heartily to congratulate you on the success already attained at the Hall, and to say how pleased I should be if circumstances should allow of my being of further use. Kindest regards to Mrs. Hullah, who has throughout been such a helpmate in the enterprise, and who has always kept up our spirits in the worst of times.

One other entry in the Diary for May of this year must be briefly noticed. Mr. Hullah notes having heard Dr. Newman lecture at the Oratory. It was the first time, and marks the moment when Newman's influence was brought to bear on the life of one whose existence was as nearly as possible perpetual movement ; excluding, it might not unreasonably be assumed, the leisure needful for theological reading or purely speculative thought. Merely controversial writings or discourses would at no time have much attracted Mr. Hullah, but the earnest, spiritual, eloquent utterances of Dr. Newman moved him profoundly, and raised an echo in his own pure moral nature. Throughout his life there was an undercurrent of sympathy, partly spiritual, partly poetic, with the Romish Church. He felt its far-searching power over the mind, and was not altogether unwilling to bow beneath that power when exercised by an intellect great as Newman's. When, in the last two years of his life, Mr. Hullah had hours, instead of moments of leisure, he would constantly begin the day by taking down a volume from the 'Newman shelf,' furnished mainly by various friends, aware of the interest he took in all that Newman put forth, and whose letters show them to have been fully alive to the value of such meditative reading to one whose pursuits tended to over-excite and weary the brain. The pressure and anxiety under which, it has been seen, Mr. Hullah lived increased appreciably with the years at this period of his life. Fortunately for him, body and mind were in perfect working condition, enabling him to carry out from early morning till midnight, day after day, the crowded programme of his existence during the winter and spring months of 1851 to 1854.

The musical work was stretching out in all directions under his general guidance, he as often as possible bringing his personal influence to bear on the classes as well in the country as in London. Thus he is found one week spending many hours daily in the 'Hall,' conducting choral classes at forenoon rehearsals and evening performances, lecturing on various points of practical or theoretical music at divers institutions in and about London, composing or arranging music, and giving lessons with unfailing punctuality at the Training Colleges of St. Mark's, Battersea, and Whitelands; at King's, Queen's, or Bedford Colleges, and at the Charterhouse. Another week, and he is seen going in post-haste to the assistance of some county magnate wholly bent on converting the local peasant into a musician, and placing implicit trust in the power of the 'Apostle of Music' to help him to that end. In the occasional leisure moments gained while passing from place to place, he contrived to get through an amazing number of books on general subjects in the four languages with which he was more or less familiar.

If, happily, there occurred an evening unfilled by professional or social engagements, his Diary records that it was spent pen in hand—some article or pamphlet being the result; while in the comparative leisure of the autumn months he prepared lectures on musical topics for delivery on special occasions arranged for long beforehand, the matter of which was pronounced by experts to be 'most excellent,' and the manner and style of which drew cordial commendation from judges as competent as Mr. G. L. Craik. Such a lecture was the one given by Mr. Hullah at the inaugural meeting of the Musical Institute. A second, written soon afterwadrs, and published in pamphlet form, entitled ' Music as an Element of Education,' excited Mr. Craik's admiration. ' I have read your lecture with interest, delight, and admiration,' he writes. ' It will make many of us wish we had fallen into such hands as yours before we were too old to learn; you ought to give us a dozen such; you might come out with one every year.'

And another correspondent, in allusion to the same pamphlet, says:

I wish you could ram your lecture into the heads of our educational rulers of the present day. It is a reproach to their judgment, and it makes their professions questionable, that you, the author of a great national movement, in which they assume an interest, should not speak in Downing-street as well as at St. Martin's Hall. Is there no Lord Ashburton to discover that music is a 'common thing'?

Yours truly,
Cambridge.   D. J. S.

The Press also marked Mr. Hullah's efforts with generous appreciation, pointing out the civilising effects of his teaching, as evidenced by the brightening expression and gentler bearing of the members of the poorer singing classes. ' They are a sight most attractive to any one who loves his kind,' wrote the ' Guardian,' ' and full of instruction for a political philosopher. Honour to the " great unconscious demagogue," as he has been called, to whom we owe it, in the first instance, that there is such a spectacle to look upon.'

A few days' respite from his various occupations enabled

him to cross the Channel and refresh himself with a whiff of the 'fine continental smells' he always declared to be preferable to the perfumes of Araby.

Among other agreeable incidents of his brief stay in Paris, Mr. Hullah mentions a dinner with Meyerbeer.

Rested and invigorated, he returned to carry out a lecturing tour in the South of England, meeting at every turn with a welcome; but his journey was overclouded by anxiety on account of his mother's health; and when he returned home in October, it was to see her gently pass away at a ripe age, regretted by all who knew the clever old lady.

As the winter drew near, arrangements had to be made for a move into the dwelling-house attached to St. Martin s Hall. Returning from one of his numerous journeys out of London, he slept in the new home for the first time on January 11, 1854.

Henceforth the conduct of the great classes and important concerts given in the Hall were less fatiguing, and wasted less time, but did not prevent Mr. Hullah from feeling urgent need for a real holiday in the autumn of 1854. He was much disconcerted that his wife could not see her way to accompanying him on his projected journey, but as the exigencies of family life again detained her at home, he packed up his valise, put in a new sketch-book and some work to do at odd moments, and betook himself to Sellinge. There he devoted a day to hearing and criticising the village classes taught on his own system, and enjoyed a few post-prandial chats in the rectory study, and finally he succeeded in securing as his travelling companions Dr. and Miss Bellamy. The party went by Ghent, Malines, Liège, and Cologne, listening now to musical services, now climbing belfry or church tower, or wandering about in quest of the 'sketchable' bits in back streets or on quays, or—witness his own confession!—getting into quiet boyish mischief. He reports to his wife with glee how, at Liège, he made close acquaintance with a '*carillonneur*,' whose professional enthusiasm he brought up to the point of setting the bells going at an hour when bells were not usually heard—to the consternation of the surrounding inhabitants.' On descending from this exploit and passing 'with an air of innocent meekness' through surprised groups of the afore-mentioned inhabitants, he adds that he joined his friends in listening reverently to a service in the Church of the Redemptionist Fathers, where we heard noble chanting and a capital sermon all about St. Liguori, their founder.'

From Cologne he sends home an effective picture of an unusual scene. 'We stood among a crowd,' he says, 'of two or three thousand people collected in the Grande Place, all with uncovered heads, and at the windows of the houses around the inmates stood, also taking part, like us below, in the open-air service going on. It was a service in honour of St. Martin—*our* saint.'

When the Bellamys turned off in another direction, Mr. Hullah, who hated partings, 'felt the waters close over him' as he went onwards alone to Basle; but his cheery soul quickly came to the surface again on meeting Sir Arthur Helps and Mr. Butterfield. With them he went into Italy, visiting many places they already knew and a few as yet unfamiliar to them. Among these was Ravenna. Coming back from his first glimpse of the Pineta he writes:

I have been to the top of the old round tower of the church, whence I could see the Adriatic covered with shipping and *hear* the murmur of the wind through the forest which Dante, five centuries ago, described so exquisitely. A strange, weird, fascinating thing is this forest of immensely tall pines, growing sufficiently apart to allow of their full development and of the sky shining through them, and such a sky! 'Dolce color d' oriental zaffiro [1]—a blue

[1] The passage from which these words are taken is thus blocked out in the prose translation of the 'Purgatorio,' to which Mr. Hullah makes frequent allusion:

'Dolce color d' oriental zaffiro,
 Che s' accoglieva nel sereno aspetto
 Dell' aer puro infino al primo giro,
 Agli occhi miei ricominciò diletto,
 Tosto ch' io uscì fuor dell' aura morta,
 Che m' avea contristati gli occhi e 'l petto.

Tender hue of {oriental / eastern} sapphire, that gathered in the {clear / serene} expanse / aspect} of the pure air, even to the {edge of the horizon, [as far] as the} first circle to my eyes again brought delight so soon as I issued from the {stagnant / dead} air that had so {saddened / oppressed} mine eyes and {heart. / breast.}

with green in it and, when seen in little bits, having the concentrated lustre of a jewel. Such stillness, too, broken only by a gentle wind, the cries of grasshoppers, and the occasional rustle of a bright-eyed lizard or slowly moving snake.

As he turned away he was like one who had gazed into the mournful shadowland of the Purgatorio, and, as was the way with him when under the influence of strong emotion, he poured out his feelings to the person dearest to him before seeking rest. With the morning light his spirit passed into a gayer mood, and, taking up his letter again, he ends it thus :

Life is very delightful, very full of incident, but, with Rasselas, nothing external to my Happy Valley of the moment excites my admiration so greatly as the *post* when it brings me budgets from home ; and to the post I am going when I have told you that Butterfield is just down, and as lively as a bird and eager for breakfast and churches.

From Ravenna he was homeward bound. Once more re-established in his home quarters, *bâton* and pen vied in activity throughout the winter. A large number of musical works of interest and importance were performed in St. Martin's Hall during these years which were well appreciated by audiences daily growing in intelligence. In the midst of many tasks an odd fancy to learn the violin seized him. Truth compels the admission that the reputation of Paganini was not at any time imperilled by the execution of the new practitioner.

CHAPTER XI.

BIOGRAPHICAL.

1855-56.

MR. HULLAH would seem to have contributed to the 'Saturday Review' for the first time in 1855. His connection with it threatened to be of but short duration, for he would not brook Mr. Cooke's free use of the editorial prerogative to take or to leave as much of an article as he pleased. After a sharp passage of arms, however, a better understanding was arrived at, and Mr. Hullah wrote several articles for the 'Saturday in the course of the following years. To the 'Guardian' and to 'Fraser's Magazine he also contributed from time to time, and early in the year prepared a series of lectures on musical history for his students at Queen's College. But the most important lecture of the year was given at Newcastle, at a meeting of the Durham and Northumberland Association for the Promotion of Church Music. The entire lecture, from which the following passages are selected as having especially provoked criticism and controversy, is well worthy of study, as much for general information as for guidance on a subject he had clearly thought out in all its aspects and made in a particular sense his own :

Music in the Parish Church.

Is there any tradition which dictates, or any principle involved in the closing of the choir gates against the many persons who, even now, at a few hours' notice, would be ready and willing to devote their musical powers to the praise and glory of God, by reinforcing the regular staff in those passages which can only be fitly rendered by large numbers of voices—by a real chorus ? Such gatherings are of frequent occurrence in other countries—in France, in Italy, and especially in Germany. This I know from personal

observation and experience. The finest musical service in Europe
—I am speaking now simply of the music—a service far more
ornate than anything one would strive after, or even desire, among
ourselves, is produced almost entirely by non-professional musicians
—*volunteers*—persons who, with us, would be mute listeners, not
from want of *will*, but from want of any arrangements or facilities
for turning their talent to account. I say that even now the
number of persons ready to contribute, by the exercise of their
musical skill, to the Church's expression of praise and thanksgiving
on special occasions, would be found very large. It will be one of
the results of the popularisation of vocal music to make it still
larger, and by a gradual action to develop a few individual vocalists
into a multitudinous chorus—a choir into a congregation.

. . . .

As our cathedral choirs are at present constituted, the finest
church music cannot be performed in our cathedrals, be the individual members of the choir ever so skilful. No compensation, no
substitute, can be found for the element of *number*. The two or
three most accomplished tenors or basses in the world cannot form
a chorus; nor will any number of *diapasons, mixtures,* or *posauns*
from the workshop of any human organ-builder make amends for
the absence of those pipes, one of which—' the best member that
he has '—it has pleased God to give to each of His creatures wherewith to sing His praises.

. . . .

On what principle is the introduction of music as an element of
divine worship to be justified at all? In what does it differ from
other arts or accomplishments, that whereas one or other or all
of *them* have, in their time, been debarred entrance into the sanc-
tuary, music we find to have been an instrument in the religious
ceremonials of every people, from the earliest ages to the present
time? The Jews allow of no representations, pictorial or plastic,
of natural objects in their synagogues; so also the Mahometans in
their mosques. The Greek Christians, freely admitting painting,
studiously exclude sculpture from their churches. Some sectaries
have rejected the help even of architecture, and, from choice, have
worshipped in the forest or even in open day. But music appears
to have formed some part (with one insignificant exception) of every
religious ceremonial. And rightly. Not merely because it is a
beautiful thing in itself, influential with, and delightful to the mass
of mankind, but because it has been felt to be an instrument through
whose agency man can give utterance to thoughts and emotions at
once too deep and too vague to find vent in mere words.

I have often thought that the one limited sect of Christians
which rejects music *altogether* from its religious meetings is far
more consistent in doing so than many of those among ourselves
who could and do introduce it into *their* services very freely—not
as a means of expression, not, properly speaking, as a part of the
service at all, but as a *relief* to it—to afford a few moments' rest to

the officiating minister, or to fill up some pause or hitch which silence might render awkward.

. . . .

In the course of a controversy . . . which grew out of the recent mutilation of a choral service in the neighbourhood of London, an expression was used by one of the parties concerned which considerably puzzled some of the lookers-on. Having protested against the fitness of any service which could be called choral for the particular institution in which it had been carried on for fourteen years, he recommended that, in future, only the Te Deum, Jubilate, &c., should be sung 'in addition to the *customary psalmody.*' More than one of those interested in the discussion, not unreasonably anxious for greater precision of language, asked, I believe, for an explanation of this expression—What was the 'customary psalmody'? In what did it consist? Where was it practised? . . . I believe I am safe in saying that the 'customary psalmody' is still undefined, and that its nature, properties, and abiding-place have not yet been pointed out by the writer who used it, or anybody else. Were a musician called upon to describe it (as it has come under my own notice, either by means of personal observation, or the hundreds of communications I have, within the last ten years, received on the subject) he would perhaps say that the 'customary psalmody' was a noise produced, for the most part, by the youngest and least instructed members of an average congregation, accompanied by a sort of cacophonous humming, the result of an impotent sense of duty on the part of their elders.

The speaker then enters into a discussion concerning the difficulty of forming a choir:

Our last and greatest difficulty still remains. A choir implies not only tenors and basses, but sopranos and contraltos. Of whom are the latter to be composed? In cathedrals, as everybody knows, the sopranos are all boys, from the ages of seven or eight to those of fourteen to fifteen. The cathedral system ignores the existence of half the creation, and that the most musical half. As I have said, however, our business now is not with the exceptional cathedral, but with the average parish church. We are not now called upon to reform that which is old, but to form something new; and we are only concerned with the old in so far as it may serve as a model or as a warning.

Of the cost and time necessary to keep up the number of singing boys in a cathedral choir any cathedral organist or precentor could tell. He might also have something to say about the evils sometimes resulting to the boys themselves from the exclusive direction of their attention to one pursuit; of the (apparently inevitable) sacrifice of their general education; of the nourishment of small vanity consequent on the possession of a somewhat rare and fascinating accomplishment, expiated after a year or two by neglect and indifference as little deserved as the adulation they had formerly received, and of being thrown on the world with one single talent —that of playing on an instrument they have lost for ever. It is possible that these evils may be inseparable from the cathedral system. But if I thought they were necessary attendants on that which I am now proposing, I would recommend any system, even the maintenance of the 'customary psalmody' itself, in preference. But why, I would ask, are *we* bound to follow the cathedral system in the parish church? Why must *we* also ignore the existence of half the creation, and that the most musical half? Why are those who possess a talent of which the Church stands in such pressing need to be debarred the privilege of devoting it to the honour of Him who has given them the wish and the opportunity to cultivate it? It is possible that a proposition to admit, or, more properly, to invite the co-operation of, women in our choirs will come with a sort of shock on many who now hear me; the same kind of shock with which others a year ago first heard that a party composed for the most part of young and highly bred women were going to bind up the wounds of, and speak words of comfort to, our soldiers in the Crimea; the same kind of shock, in fact, which is caused by the first mention of every attempt to bring feminine tact and energy to bear on any of the thousand good works which still ask their help, and which will never be done completely without them.

The fact is, that the objections to women singing in church *avowedly* (for nobody objects to their singing unavowedly) belong to, and apply to, a state of things entirely different from any that I am now proposing—a state of things involving music of a character that ought never to find its way into the Lord's temple, and persons to perform it of habits of life and tone of mind the furthest possible removed from those which should be the first qualification for admission into a real choir—meretricious music and self-contemplative performers. Arrangements can always be made with regard to placing those who compose a choir as are at once conformable to ecclesiastical propriety and common sense; such arrangements, in fact, as will make it possible for *any* members of a congregation, female as well as male, that possess the requisite skill to belong to it, and to feel it a delight and a privilege to do so.

The lecture and its subsequent publication brought down a shower of letters, for the most part narrow-minded or inconsequent. The following, however, are among the exceptions. The first is from Mr. G. L. Craik; the second from the Rev. J. M. Jephson, of the 'Guardian':

The lecture is first-rate. But, although there is no answering you on artistic principles, I need not tell you that to nine-tenths of the more religious feeling of the country your notions will seem quite atrocious. The fact is, that the worse we sing in church, the more piously we think we acquit ourselves. Whether we sing in tune or out of tune can make no difference to God Almighty; and as for anything else, the more deplorable our performance the more do we exhibit of the spectacle upon which heaven has always been held to look down with especial delight, that of all good struggling with adverse circumstances. If our more musically constituted neighbours were in a more proper frame of mind they too would find nothing in our efforts, however unsuccessful, to excite other feelings than those of respect and sympathy.

I went to Parker's (succeeded by Messrs. Longman) (writes Mr. Jephson), to buy your treatise on 'The Stave,' for Mrs. Jephson's benefit, and on the counter I saw your lecture given at Newcastle, which I immediately added to my other purchases. I fear you will think me very presumptuous, but I cannot resist the temptation of telling you how admirable I think them both. When I read your preface to 'The Stave' I jumped up and cried 'Bravo!' not that there was anything in it like 'fine writing,' but because it seemed to me a perfect model of terse and nervous English. There is something very mediæval in your witty device on the title-page, something like one of Sir Thomas More's quaint concerts, that delighted me. But I soon was startled by your proposal in the lecture to *legalise,* as it were, the employment of women's voices in choirs. The female voice is so full of passion, and is so powerful to awaken feelings of personal admiration in the other sex, that one can understand why the old ecclesiastical tradition excluded it from public worship. This objection is, however, perhaps less applicable to England than to more southern climates, and female singers may be said to be already a *fait accompli.* I must take an early opportunity of visiting the chapel in Long Acre when you are carrying out your theory. The piece of irony about the customary psalmody is delicious. You have been doing a great deal lately in the literary way.

But, though ready and willing at all times to give a patient hearing to those who held views more or less opposed to his own, he did not therefore abandon an opinion once formed. The less likely was he to do so in regard to matters involving principles of justice as well as of expediency. To bring that opinion, when matured to conviction, to the light of public judgment was part of his creed as reformer. It is therefore not surprising to find him seizing other opportunities of unfolding his views. Such an opportunity seems to have occurred at an archæological meeting or Church Congress. The passages which follow are extracted from the undated proof-sheets of Mr. Hullah's contribution to some such gathering. Having rapidly sketched an amusing picture of the ordinary condition of a village choir and country parson, ambitious to get something done with the musical part of the service, he says:

Regarded strictly on its own merits, I will venture to express a conviction which has long been growing upon me, that the limitation of choirs, of whatever kind, to men and boys, as it is attended with great musical disadvantages, so it is attended with social disadvantages of a much more serious kind—I mean disadvantages to the performers themselves, the boys especially. . . . As members of a choir, boys are no more a complement to, no more a match for men than they are as members of any other society or association whatever. It is all but impossible—certainly it is not to be desired—that a boy should be able to *sing*. He may read music and utter musical sounds sweetly enough, but sing he cannot; he wants alike the sentiment which only experience and knowledge of life can give, and the physical powers by which, after proper training, this sentiment could be made manifest. A boy is, and ought to be, an unformed, incomplete being, who, save at the utter sacrifice of everything that is most engaging and most lovable about him, cannot do anything perfectly; he is, of necessity, a beginner in art and science as in life itself. By the limitation of church choirs to men and boys, one, and that perhaps the most beautiful, variety of the human voice is entirely excluded from them—the contralto, for which is substituted the male counter-tenor, which in most cases must be regarded rather as an anomalous, artificial mode of utterance than as a voice in the proper sense of the word. It is singular that the use of this mode of utterance or production, the very name of which, *falsetto*, is a reproach, and the result of which is a quality of sound which, if not exactly effeminate, is certainly epicene, should be confined to a people so justly priding itself on manliness of character and simplicity as the English. The *falsetto*, or third register, is of course not unknown in Italy, France, and Germany, but it has been regarded always as an adjunct to, and an occasional resource from the first or second registers, even by singers—the late Rubini, for instance, who had it in the highest perfection and under the most perfect control. The very existence of the male counter-tenor is ignored by continental musicians, and, with the single exception of Handel, I cannot call to mind one who has made use of it, even in writing to English words and expressly for English performers. The second part in the choral works of Haydn, Mozart, Beethoven, Spohr, and even Mendelssohn, so familiar with our musical resources, are, in every instance with which I am acquainted, written for the contralto, or lower female voice.

But to return to the boys. I am not unaware, of course, that the argument I advanced this moment in respect to them may be turned against my own position. It may be said that, as a musician, I picture to myself and crave a kind of service and a state of things in our cathedrals which a large number of pious and cultivated persons do not at all desire to see introduced and brought about in them; that the very imperfection which I have described as essential to the voice and execution of a boy has of itself a charm—nay, is its principal recommendation; and that the absence of sentiment manifested in the very want of expression of which I complain is the thing of all others to be denied in a place from which everything like human passion should be banished, and on occasions when its manifestations would be altogether impertinent and unbecoming. I hope I appreciate what there is of truth in all this. I never hear—I hope I never shall hear—the clear treble ring 'through the long-drawn aisle and fretted vault' without experiencing something more than mere musical gratification. But when it has died away upon my ear I cannot forbear asking myself whether my emotion has not been raised at too great a cost; I cannot forbear asking myself what is likely to be—what is in many cases—the effect of all this on the clear treble himself.

. . . .

A very strong feeling in this matter has led me to say more than I had intended, and to treat as a principal topic what is, after all, only an incidental one, so far as my present object is concerned; for what I want to show is, not that boys should *not* be employed in choirs, but that women *should*. Moreover, the choirs of the formation of which I wish now to speak are not cathedral choirs—any change in the constitution of which would be attended with difficulties that I should be the last to underrate—but parish choirs, which, more often than not, require formation rather than reformation.

Does there exist any decree or even strong expression of opinion which a member of the Church of England is bound to obey or called upon to respect forbidding women to sing in churches? That their introduction as choristers has, in former times, been often impossible, or might have been sometimes attended with much inconvenience, need hardly affect us, for even in former times expediency has met with its usual indulgence. Plenty of examples existed even before the Reformation, as such exist still, of choirs composed exclusively of women—those in convents and conventual schools, for instance; and nearer to our own times—in our own Church and country—boys have been dispensed with altogether, music having been composed expressly for men, the treble parts having been performed by instruments. This was the case for some time after the Restoration of Charles II., when boys skilled in singing were not to be had. It is to this accident that we owe our large repository of equal-voice anthems (by P. Humphreys. Blow, Wise, Purcell, and others), and possibly our culture and employment of the male counter-tenor voice. Our ancestors, to whom we so often look for precedents, were sometimes very indifferent to precedents themselves; they often took very common-sense practical views of the cases before them, and dealt with them accordingly. In matters of art—in architecture, for instance—they often showed themselves singularly contemptuous of the works of their predecessors, pulling them down, re-making them, or covering them over with new work, without the slightest compunction, and sometimes it would seem without the slightest necessity.

With their example before him, one about to organise a new choir is surely not called upon to prove why women *should* sing in it, but has rather a right to ask why they should *not*.

He closed his remarks by giving technical reasons why congregational singing carried out in the customary manner could not produce satisfactory musical results. In his character of a missionary of music, he hoped and believed in a future when training in musical science would make congregations as intolerant of cacophony as they would be of the misuse of the letter 'h' in the pulpit. Musical culture brought to this point would, he thought, eventually become indispensable to the calm serenity of mind in which alone concentration of devotional feeling is possible.

In addition to his purely professional writings, Mr. Hullah's literary efforts showed about this period an inclination to branch out in other directions, for he alludes in his letters home, during a short trip up the Rhine, to his 'Dante studies,' and some slight beginning of a prose translation of the 'Divina Commedia,' 'much interfered with,' he complains, 'by the usual necessity for recovering, with the aid of grammars and dictionary, the separable prefixes of the German tongue.' He might have added that the constant excursions from his head-quarters at Godesberg in search of musical dissipation must have also stood in the way of serious study of Dantesque Italian.

After hearing at Cologne a good deal of Glück and an oratorio by a composer then living—Herr Rheinthaler—which greatly pleased him, he says:

I went into the music gallery of the cathedral, where I was most courteously received by the Herr Capellmeister (a nice old gentleman) and Herr Weber, the director of the *Männer-Gesang-Verein*, who is organist of the cathedral. It was a high festival, the Bei-Bischof (Suffragan Bishop) celebrating mass with a perfect crowd of clergy, and perhaps 5,000 people within the areas.

. . . .

After mass I went to Rheinthaler's, who played me the first part of his oratorio, some of which I like greatly. It is very little Mendelssohnian, but deeply impregnated with the old Italian spirit, for Rheinthaler has lived two years in Italy, and is an enthusiastic admirer of the *seicentisti*. . . . I find there is to be a grand service, the music chiefly performed by the children of all the neighbouring schools at Brühl. They are going to do some of the Missa Papæ Marcelli at Bonn on Wednesday!

CHAPTER XII.

BIOGRAPHICAL.

1857-58.

SOME time in the summer of 1858, Dr. Horsley, the organist of the Charterhouse, died, and Mr. Hullah was elected to the vacant post, which he still held at the time of his death. The appointment had its pleasant side, for it brought him into closer relations with the officers of the institution, and enabled him to enjoy their society more frequently, since it entitled him to a place at those weekly dinners in Brook Hall which are now among the memories of Carthusian hospitality. In the autumn, being on his way to Staunton-on-Wye, whither one of his most intimate friends among the *ci-devant* masters of the Charterhouse school had migrated, Mr. Hullah bethought himself that he had not seen his native city, Worcester, for many a year—not indeed since that long-ago period when he had unfolded to his mother with youthful confidence his scheme of succession to the organistship of the cathedral; so at Worcester he halted.

I descended (he says) at the Star Hotel, just opposite the house in which I was born. Its smart red brick face is—*stuccoed*! It is lucky it wasn't stuccoed once—some—well—some *twenty*-five years ago, or I should certainly have made a point of being born somewhere else! . . .

Working his way round by the Malvern Hills, Mr. Hullah arrived at Hereford, where for some hours he and Mr. Butterfield—also bound for Staunton—played unintentionally at a game of hide and seek, to the embarrassment of Mr. Phillott, who had come to meet them. Finally, however, both guests were recovered and carried off, and duly reported results of the pleasantest sort; Mr. Hullah adding that, in spite of delightful society and scenery, he secured his 'four hours' morning work,' not only while at Staunton-on-Wye, but throughout a round of visits paid before his return home. A visit to the Continent, however, he could not manage, hard as he tried to do so. His disappointment was, of course, great —all the greater that his companion would have been Sir Arthur Helps, who, buoyed up by the hope that Continental temptation would prove too strong for his travel-loving friend, had gone off alone 'in advance merely,' and, sad to say, had gone by the long sea-route to Ostend with woeful consequences to himself, concerning which he felt constrained to give an account:

> Wisdom is justified of all her children (he begins), and therefore amongst them of John Hullah and Cato, both of whom have expressed a strong opinion against going by sea the least more than is absolutely needful. I, in my folly, neglected the advice of the aforesaid Cato and John Hullah, and I have suffered. . . . I am now . . . .
>> Remote, unfriended, melancholy, slow,
>> And therefore have not in myself the go
>> Ahead which I last year was wont to know,
>> When friend and wife conspired to drive me so.
>
> I am going to Bonn, where I expect to find you studying German.

But Sir Arthur's expectations could not be gratified, for the poor friend was working day and night, his spirits flagging sadly. But in sadness or in gladness his active brain worked, it would seem, equally well, and having, as a friend said of him, 'what Bacon denies Aristotle, a teaching patience, and being a learned thinker and a master of his own knowledge,' he succeeded in producing in a very short time, among other smaller essays, a 'Grammar of Music,' much lauded by his correspondents, and a certain article in the 'Guardian' which much pleased Mr. Butterfield, who writes:

> Your review of the Handel Festival scheme . . . . is very capital indeed (he says); I shall frame and glaze the supplement and keep it among the things I like best. It is full of force and liveliness, and shows how much such a subject gains by being treated by a man who cares for and knows about other arts as well as the one he is writing on. Just as people are, in their 'used-up' state, asking

for immoderate noise in music, so they are too much viewing hugeness as a grand thing in architecture. My whole soul rebels against such vulgarity. The age is like an old drunkard, with no true or refined taste left for anything, alas! . . .

For months back it had been observed that Mr. Hullah was suffering in health and spirits. It has not been possible, however, to trace this condition, so abnormal to him, to any definite cause other than the non-success of the Hall, yet his depression must have been altogether remarkable to suggest to anyone the advisability of friendly intervention offered from time to time. How far he broke through his habit of reserve and responded to these invitations to unburthen himself cannot now be known, but if he responded it must have been to a very slight extent. Meanwhile, the cloud that darkened his life did not obscure his mental activity. On the contrary, the inventive faculty never seemed stronger with him than now, when he wrote the melody to Kingsley's 'Three Fishers.' Taking a retrospective view of Mr. Hullah's inner life, his compositions are seen to have been expressions of, and outlets for, his sadder moods. Hence, doubtless, the peculiar vein of melancholy which is so marked in his happiest efforts, each of which, it will be found, was put forth during some period of powerful though restrained emotion or protracted disquietude.

From Mr. Kingsley, with whom Mr. Hullah had become acquainted some five years previously, came the following letter:[1]

My dear Hullah,—I am much pleased to hear of the success of the song. I have heard of it from other quarters beside you, so that the public voice seems quite unanimous. But I take no share of the credit—words are naught without music and singing; and it is to you and Miss Dolby that the praise is due. Pray present my compliments to her and thank her for the honour to which she has brought me (so I hear) by her marvellous voice and science. I hope some day to hear her myself. As it is, I have not been at a concert this ten years; seldom in London, and then always over-busy and getting no 'amusement' there.

A little later Mr. Kingsley writes:

I only heard the 'Fishers' sung a few weeks ago for the first time, and was much delighted. It was the only setting which I

[1] See *Life and Letters of Charles Kingsley*, by his Wife.

have heard which at all rendered what I meant to say and entered into the real feeling of the words, and there seemed to me in it much true music, simple, noble, and original. Your approbation of my powers gives me great pleasure. I feel more and more inclined to suspect that they are what I can do best, and that I am like Camille Desmoulins, *une pauvre créature née pour faire des vers*, and only likely to get myself into wars by meddling with politics and lofty matters only to be handled by Disraelis and Clanricardes. The public has been very kind as yet about the poems, and Heaven knows I have been humble enough about them; for it was in exceeding fear, and only after long solicitations, that I put them forth, and I am more dissatisfied with them than any critic can be. Farewell and prosper.

Brief notes were not unfrequently exchanged between poet and composer, and acquaintance ripened to intimacy of sympathy and mutual comprehension rather than of personal intercourse. Each understood and was ready to give honour to what was best in the other. Now and then they met, Mr. Hullah often in after years recalling with delight a few summer afternoons passed by him and his wife with Mr. and Mrs. Kingsley at Eversley. It would have pleased him to know that the surviving head of that bright household also remembers those occasions with pleasure.

It was not long before Mr. Kingsley's verse was again a source of inspiration. 'The Sands of Dee,' and a duet, 'The Starlings,' sung by Miss Dolby and Miss Kemble, had a great success. Shelley next inspired him, and 'I arise from dreams of thee' was the fruit. Sung by Mr. Santley at one of the Orchestral Concerts, it produced in 1858, as it cannot fail to produce when efficiently sung, a deep impression. In common with an earlier effort, 'Rarely, rarely comest thou, Spirit of Delight,' this song requires, in addition to great compass and flexibility of voice and much technical skill, a delicate and cultured intelligence; not often, therefore, can it be adequately rendered.

His life seemed very eventful, very full, each day appearing to have rather more than a fair share allotted to it, and yet bundles of letters, expressing—in awkward phrase enough at times—deep gratitude for this, that, or the other kindly act, reveal how he spent some of his leisure hours in giving lessons or advice to young people requiring but quite unable to pay for such help. It is pleasant to get another peep into how he got through some other of those rare leisure hours, such as is afforded by a note from Mr. George Richmond, addressing him as an *amatore stupendo*, and enclosing a students' ticket for the National Gallery to enable him to 'work' there at the same time with Miss Hullah, who was understood to be pursuing a course of study with the definite purpose of turning her talent to account.

CHAPTER XIII.

BIOGRAPHICAL.

1860-61.

THE death of Mrs. Hullah's father cast a gloom over the usually gay Christmas season. To afford her a change of scene, Mr. Hullah took her to Dover, and no sooner were they settled in lodgings than he brought out his Spanish grammar and dictionary and beguiled the time by doing exercises and looking out words, the result of which was that in a short time he was able to make out the sense of books on common subjects. Here, also, he completed the music to Kingsley's 'Last Buccaneer;' and it seems probable enough that, while watching the sea some tempestuous day, he conceived the music of 'The Storm,' that beautiful music that interprets so perfectly, and has helped to make so famous, Adelaide Procter's dramatic poem. Later on, when back in his study at St. Martin's Hall, may he not be pictured working out the original idea on Ash-Wednesday night—he has recorded that he composed 'The Storm' on that day—when even in prosaic Long Acre the March winds were howling and raging so weirdly as to call up the spirit of the storm and breathe to him the closing phrase? Who is there that has heard that song well sung without an abiding sense of its expressive force and grandeur?

The year 1860 would seem to have been fruitful to him in musical ideas, for he published several small efforts in the 'Singers' Library, and in 'chill October' he wrote 'O, doubting heart' (to Adelaide Procter's words), a sweet mournful strain expressive of his discouraged mental condition.

If a musician's compositions may be regarded as revealing

passing thoughts and emotion, may not the choice of his next song, 'Turn, Fortune, turn thy wheel,' be accepted as telling of a heart moved to impatience by unkind Fortune's persistent frown? For years he had worked unceasingly, cheerfully, and yet success did not come to him. But other complaint or note of anger than that which is traceable in his music there was none. On he went, producing important musical works at short intervals at the concerts at St. Martin's Hall—that 'bequest' which was, to quote from a clever article which appeared in the 'Times' subsequently to the fire which destroyed St. Martin's Hall, as the Peau de Chagrin to Raphael in Balzac's novel. . . . 'The more he made use of it the more was he a loser;' . . . . 'succumbing,' indeed, 'under the weight of reiterated successes.' In the intervals between these ruinous successes he wielded his pen as efficiently in his sanctum above as he did his *bâton* in the Hall below, holding, among other matters, long discussions by correspondence with Dr. William Pole and the late Mr. Griesbach on the vexed question of musical pitch, and contributing his influence to the adoption in 1860, by the Society of Arts, of Pitch 528. In the brief pauses which could now be given to relaxation he paid two or three visits to Gadshill, where the late Mr. and Mrs. Dickens were in the habit of making life joyous to their guests, and with great delight secured a few days in his beloved France with his wife, eldest daughter, and Mr. Butterfield. Rheims was the central point of interest, and it was enjoyed under exceptionally favourable circumstances as regarded the beautiful cathedral, thanks to the courtesy of the learned Abbé Cerf, whose acquaintance, thus begun, was kept up many years by letters, accompanied on his side, as occasion offered, by the latest literary efforts of M. l'Abbé. It may safely be assumed that Mr. Butterfield's presence was an additional pleasure, affording as it did opportunity for innumerable discussions on the work going on at All Saints', Margaret Street, under his direction. Now, it not infrequently happened that Mr. Hullah's admiration for his friend's work was so great, that by sheer force of sympathy he was apt to imagine that he had done more than half of it himself—a conviction that in no wise diminished his pleasure in watching the progress of whatever was going on. Many a time, at his own table, with Mr. Butterfield and other friends around him, he would preface learned little dissertations on architecture by ' You remember, Butterfield, when *we* built that church?' or ' when *we* were planning that house?' And Mr. Butterfield, with an indulgent smile, would look up quizzically, but accept this view without protest—to the amusement of initiated auditors.

With August the holiday time was drawing to a close, and dates for the resumption of work were fixed on, when Mr. Hullah decided to spend the intervening days at Stanford. How little he dreamt, as he left home that Saturday morning, that he had slept for the last time in the home of many hopes and disappointments!

Sunday passed in peaceful rest. The evening services were over, and he was sitting with Mr. and Mrs. Tylden in quiet talk, when a messenger belonging to the Hall, Patrick by name, arrived, bearing a letter from Mrs. Hullah, in which she told him in a few words that the Hall was destroyed by fire. In her never-failing thoughtfulness in all that concerned him she ' had rapidly decided that the unavoidable shock would be less severe if all known details were told by an eye-witness.'

Mr. Hullah's own memoranda are of the scantiest:—
' *Monday*, Aug. 27. Left Stanford for London. Found W—— and C—— at station [a brother-in-law and Mrs. Hullah]. To the Hall—a ruin.'

What that brief entry meant to him and his but few can realise, for, happily, there are but few on whom such a calamity has fallen.

For five days he went regularly to the scene of the fire; on the sixth Mr. Dickens carried him off to Gadshill.

On September 4 he was at his work at Battersea, and fell into the regular round of college classes again, aided at every point by his firm and tried friend Mr. Edward May, and his other many and not less kind assistants.

On the 5th the Upper School, burnt out of the usual haunt, assembled in St. James's Hall, and continued to meet there for a time.

On September 20 the Hullah household was reunited under one roof at a house in Langham Place.

And Mr. Hullah's friends—where were they? Those among them who were near gathered around him and his wife as quickly as they could, opening their houses, purses, and hearts without stint.

From all parts of the country, from people in the highest position of social and political life, and from people of humbler degree, came letters thick and fast, numerous enough to fill a large volume, expressing deepest sympathy and sorrow. All end with bright words of encouragement, kind words of consolation.

Nor, in the majority of cases, did the writers rest content with mere expressions of sorrow, hope and counsel; they were up and doing all that in them lay to try and rebuild his broken fortunes and enable him once more to go on with his mission in life. Some of the schemes are royal in their largeness and generosity. Had nothing tangible ever resulted from any of them, it would still have been an honour for any man to have been the object of regard, respect, and confidence as unlimited as was felt by thousands of men and women for John Hullah. A very substantial something did however result from these schemes, though falling short of the noble intentions of the originators; and, but for the sympathy and support extended to him, he would certainly have succumbed beneath the weight of the necessary but humiliating investigations and legal proceedings which followed the catastrophe of the fire.

The general feeling and the active assistance to which it gave rise would be best described in the language of those who came to the front, did space admit. While all alike, whether professional or not, were equally eloquent in expressions of condolence, there were some among his literary friends, who at once assumed the initiative in helping him materially by their personal exertions on his behalf. Foremost among these were Charles Dickens, Mr. Henry Chorley, and Mr. Harry Chester. Among his non-professional friends none took a more important place than Sir James Kay-Shuttleworth, or, as before, a more prominent than the Lord Chief Justice, then Mr. J. D. Coleridge.

Who knows (says Mr. Chorley, concluding a letter brimful of kindly plans for the future)—who knows, as I come to think over the whole affair, but it may have an issue more wholesome than damaging so far as your future life is concerned.

. . . .

On all sides I have but one assurance, that something hearty and honest and kindly may, and should, and will be done by the musicians to show that neither your past services to music, nor your late calamity, can pass without an earnest wish among many to offer you something more than *word* sympathy. . . . Will you leave the chances of my scheme in the hands of your friends ? I think you *would*, if you knew with how much delicacy and high respect you are spoken of on every side. But rest assured that if *I* be concerned in the matter, nothing shall be done which can or shall place you in any false position. . . .

On the same day Mr. Chorley despatched a long letter to a mutual friend, setting forth how aid could best be given. His views took in an extensive programme of musical entertainments, likely to be organised by various societies or individuals for the purpose of helping Mr. Hullah through the difficulties resulting from the fire. In course of time these ideas were realised, almost every leading musician giving personal assistance with a cordiality that went to Mr. Hullah's heart. But while there was but one opinion among Mr. Hullah's friends as to the need for rendering aid, there was a direct divergence of opinion as to the way in which he ought to use the money proceeds.

While one party, headed by Mr. Chorley, and counting friends of such undoubted influence with Mr. Hullah as the Millers of Croydon, Sir Arthur Helps, and Sir Henry Dryden, begged him earnestly not to dream of resuming life at St. Martin's Hall or elsewhere quite as before; another group of his friends held a different view of the case, and among these was one at least who had a right to a hearing—Sir James Kay-Shuttleworth. Of three letters Sir James wrote on this matter, the last, addressed to Mr. J. D. Coleridge (now Lord Chief Justice), is the most comprehensive.

I was more cognisant than anyone else of Mr. Hullah's earliest efforts to introduce instruction in vocal music among the classes supported by wages. I accompanied him to Paris to examine the schools taught on Wilhem's method. I was for three years responsible for the rent of Exeter Hall, in which his first classes were taught. This relation to his earliest efforts enables me to say that they

were characterised by an *entire absence of any self-seeking whatever.*
Mr. Hullah has always been most disinterested in his pecuniary
transactions. He gave up the profits derived from his classes at
Exeter Hall, above what was required to meet the *enormous rent,
to pay the teachers of other classes of the Method*—reserving
nothing for himself for three years' most laborious exertion.

The whole annual charge and income of the enterprise in what
was called the *School of Method* amounted to 3,000*l. yearly.*

I have had the pleasure of being cognisant with Mr. Hullah's
relations with the training colleges, great elementary and other
schools, and public establishments. They have all been characterised by a fastidious delicacy of spirit in everything that related
to his own or his assistants' remuneration.

Everyone who knows anything of the conduct of St. Martin's
Hall must be aware that Mr. Hullah's enthusiasm for his art and
for the diffusion of instruction in it among the body of the people
have been the *sole cause of his embarrassments.*

I have had recent personal communication with him. I have
ascertained that he wishes—before all things—to be enabled to
continue his most useful career. This would nowhere be so successfully accomplished as at St. Martin's Hall. I cannot therefore but
entertain a hope that by care and prudent arrangements the warm
support of his friends, by a public subscription, may enable his
family to repurchase St. Martin's Hall and restore Mr. Hullah to
that scene of his public labours to which all his own most earnest
wishes point as the chief object of his life.

If you could read this letter to the meeting [called together for the
purpose of organising a scheme of assistance] of his friends with
propriety, it would be a great relief to my mind, which is burdened
with a sense of obligations incurred towards a gentleman whose
merits have far surpassed his fortunes.

While not in accord as to what he had best do in the
future, both parties kept in sight the fact that Mr. Hullah,
now past his prime, stood a ruined man in the midst of a
large family, some members of which were just approaching
the expensive age of preparation for a start in life. And yet
his advisers as a body did not hesitate almost to congratulate
him on the crisis that had arrived, while deploring the pain
and humiliation which were in such large measure incidental
to it. All assumed with flattering unanimity that with energy
so indomitable, talents so varied, power of work so inexhaustible, for him success was certain in whatever he undertook.
For future consideration was left the choice of what that something was to be. But when the moment for decision arrived
there really was no power of choice, for the sum total of the

contribution (though a handsome amount) being wholly inadequate to the reconstruction of the Hall on an even less ambitious scale than heretofore, Mr. Hullah could but clear himself of his obligations as promptly as possible, and begin life anew as best he could. Commenting on the close of the legal proceedings, the 'Times,' supported by all the leading newspapers, paid him the following warm tribute of respect:

That everything which a high-minded and strictly honourable gentleman could imagine to maintain himself above reproach was proposed by Mr. Hullah, those well acquainted with the whole transaction are ready to attest, and no other proof of it need be cited than the unanimous interest which his temporary secession has elicited.

And the flow of private correspondence, affectionately congratulatory, set in and continued for some weeks.

CHAPTER XIV.

BIOGRAPHICAL.

1861.

THUS upheld and honoured, he could not do otherwise than lift up his head and take courage to face the world, so kindly to him, and begin life again. In his characteristic way, he silently formed his resolution, definitely and definitively, to put his troubles behind him and to throw his full strength into the work that presented itself to be done. He again took up his pen, and when opportunity occurred, sought for new employment.

Though not always successful he did not lose heart, but looked steadily forward, fortunately not foreseeing what adverse fate had yet in store for him. To find a new home was the first and more immediate need, and by no means an easy task, for large rooms were required, it would seem, for the use of the pictorial as well as of the musical artist in the family. 'One of our difficulties in choosing a house,' writes Mr. Hullah to an inquiring friend, 'is to find a room large enough to hold two canvases, each seven feet long,' in order that Miss Hullah—to whose studies in Holman Hunt's studio there are several encouraging allusions in letters to her father from members of the Coleridge and Kay-Shuttleworth families—might execute a commission to paint a large picture on the scale of the original.

In course of time a house, with the one advantage of large rooms, was found in Devonshire Place, at a moderate rental. Into this the family gathered before Christmas, 1860-61, and immediately experienced further proofs of the forethought and generosity of their friends, some of whom had bought back articles of furniture saved from the fire, but given up for the benefit of the creditors; in some instances leaving the things at the house without any clue as to whence they came.

1861. In January Mr. Hullah sought for rest at Sellinge and Stanford. His first daily report home, written before going to bed, says:

> It was a curious sensation to sit again in the Tylden's little drawing-room and think of all that has happened since Patrick last called me out of it to hear of the fire! They are so kind: thinking, I found, the same thoughts as I. . . . We had a beautiful service yesterday: better than ever. I sung a tenor solo in an anthem! It was so odd to sing again. I found my voice fair in quality, but very weak. It was like skating over *very* thin ice; all this morning I have been very lazy, doing nothing but read articles on ' Construction.' Tylden, who is at work at the other end of the table, desires his best regards. I hope you are taking *good care of yourself*; not doing too much.

This is the first note of anxiety heard from him about the state of his wife's health. In her usual unselfish way she sought to conceal her condition from him, and it was long before he fully awoke to the consciousness of the terrible calamity that was threatening him—a calamity in comparison with which nothing that had occurred counted for aught. His own health, too, was somewhat shaken, and he was compelled to admit that rest was needful. But he made light of it.

> For a day or two I only took short turns in the garden, and employed myself chiefly in lying upon the sofa and reading my friend, Viollet-le-Duc. But on Sunday I went a little further, and yesterday did something more, with, I think, some good effect. I have taken to *Port!* so you may look for a certain portliness and rubicundicity when I return. So much for myself. . . . *Take care of yourself, about whom you say nothing.*

When he returned to town Mrs. Hullah took his place in the hospitable rectory. Abandoned to his own devices, lord and master of his own domain, he was ' but a puir thing,' as a Scotch friend once remarked, who happened to alight upon him in that position. During this, his first experience of sole control, he required all the excellent good looking-after his many lady friends considered necessary for him. Every day he had to give an account of himself, and tell how some one had come and insisted on carrying him home to dinner. 'I shall get the gout,' he exclaims in mock despair, after giving a long list of dinner engagements and confessing to a mildly convivial meeting, to which Sir Arthur Helps—never very far off—made exhilarating contribution, accompanied by a formidable outbreak of wrath against biographers.

As your taste and mine are somewhat similar (he says), I venture to send you some wine, which I hope you may like. Debauched fellows, such as we are, like to drink wine out of tumblers. What a sentence for our future biographers to lay hold of, in order to prove that we were both arrant drunkards, which fact they will snuffle over with unctuous and sanctimonious regret, and make a capital paragraph about it.

Another day Mr. Hullah's report is quite businesslike :

We get on pretty well with the class (he assures his wife, who, when at her post, frequently played the accompaniments) ; so well, in fact, that we were all agreed you had better stay a long while in the country, in fact just long enough to get thoroughly fit to come back to us, by which time we will begin to grumble. . . . We had a capital meeting again of the Upper School last night, though the weather was wretched. The new classes opened with twenty-eight gentlemen, but only six ladies.

. . . .

It is consolatory to find that other people's wives do occasionally quit the bosoms of their families, and leave their small children at home. This moral reflection, in the manner of Plato, whom I read continually, is not supposed to have any personal bearing—ahem ! Everybody is very kind—no news *that* !

Dr. Whewell's gift of his recently published translation of Plato, which Mr. Hullah declares he was continually reading, brought about a renewal of correspondence between them. Here is Dr. Whewell's reply to Mr. Hullah s acknowledgment of the book :

It was very gratifying to me to find that my Plato interested you so much. I am very glad that you find anything to approve in the musical part of it, and that you think me right in the main about the modes. As to the expression in page 216 about the efficiency of music in its ordinary sense, and although undoubtedly music included poetry, yet so much stress is laid on the difference of modes and its influence in education, that music in our sense must have been a very effective element in it. But I suppose the Greek boys learnt the words and the music together; this appears, I think, from other passages.

The account of the musical instruments which Socrates would allow in his ideal state, I confess, puzzles me. I translated it as I could from the Greek, not supposing that I had made musical sense of it. I had so many rather bold philosophical interpretations to introduce that I did not wish to venture any such in a field where I was more strange. Nor, in truth, have I anything to offer in the way of conjecture.

I have no special lore about musical instruments. Barnes, Hawkins, and the authors whom they quote, especially the admirable old Kircher, would be the books to which I should first refer. But *you* will easily find better guides. When the ophicleide (was not that the instrument?) was reinvented by copying an old instrument found in Herculaneum there would have been a good deal of erudition brought to bear on the subject. At present I do not know where this learning is to be found, but I dare say you will have no difficulty in hunting it out. I believe that a good deal of the mathematics which you have in the Republic and in the Timæus is introduced for the pleasure which Plato found in working out the mathematics of music. I think that we have evidence of this in the way in which he tries to put down, in page 316, the non-practical musicians who refer to their ears to know whether notes are identical or not. You are quite right about the necessity of beginning the intervals from C, F, G, or D in order to get the [illegible word] natural scale. I know this very well, and ought not to have forgotten it. . . . There are a great many points I should like to discuss with you for which we could never find time except in conversation.

But opportunities for prolonged conversation over these matters did not occur again during the remnant of Dr. Whewell's life.

Somewhat unwillingly Mr. Hullah was persuaded to take his Easter holiday in Paris, but he carried so much work with him that he was compelled for the greater part of each day to sit at his desk. He just contrived to get a flying view of some of his favourite pictures in the Louvre galleries, or to secure a rapid hunt for old books on the stalls along the river parapet before the short days closed in. Many were the purchases he made towards the reconstruction of his library, destroyed or dispersed by the fire. By way of preparation, Mr. Butterfield had designed for him a pair of large bookcases, charmingly proportioned, which filled up the spaces on either side of the fireplace in the drawing-room of the new home in

Devonshire Place, imparting to it an air of dignity as well as of comfort not to be got by any other furniture. To add volume after volume, to fill up the ample shelves, was a source of never-ceasing delight to Mr. Hullah, and what he possessed he read, for his books were his intimate friends—the best loved 'companions of his solitude.'

CHAPTER XV.

BIOGRAPHICAL.

1861.

SCATTERED about in the correspondence of the two or three years subsequent to the fire which laid St. Martin's Hall in ruins, there are traces of renewed efforts made by Mr. Hullah to revive his Singing School. It was not to be expected that the earnest purpose of his best days should die out without a struggle. Eventually the original scheme, as he had worked it out, had to be allowed to slip away in part, but believing that music, as a branch of education, had taken root in popular education in England, he was fain to appear resigned to stand aside and take but little active share in its conduct : *contented* in such comparative inactivity he never was.

Early in 1861 Mr. Hullah had undertaken to give a course of lectures on the 'History of Modern Music' at the Royal Institution, the preparation of which occupied every available moment up to the time of their delivery in May and June. Being musically illustrated, these lectures involved, apart from their composition, a considerable amount of trouble, but were so far valuable to him that the interest of their preparation did more than anything else to restore to him the buoyant tone of past days. They were admittedly a success, fully justifying their publication at the end of the year. The volume was dedicated to Sir Arthur Helps, who, by this time installed in the Council Office, writes his consent :

> Yes, my dear Hullah, with pleasure. You will fancy it mock modesty, but I really do not feel worthy of having the book dedicated to me; but I know you won't think so; and so, deeply feeling the unworthiness, I still say, yes. The pressure here is awful!

So soon as the 'History of Modern Music' reached the

public, many letters, flattering, though often very critical, were addressed to him. Dr. Whewell writes :

> I have been reading your book with great interest, and find in it notices of many important events in the history of music which I never saw so clearly explained before, or indeed explained at all. I would particularly point out, as of this kind, the account of the discovery of the perfect cadence, which is, as you say, the inevitable [consequence?] of a complete revolution in music—one of those revolutions which, when consummated, make it difficult to recall and conceive the previous state of things; like, for instance, the substitution of versification by accent for versification by quantity. About the modes of the ancients I am very curious, because I have had to write about them myself.

'How beautiful a book it is!' exclaims Mr. Craik, and I have already, though I have scarcely been left alone since I got it, examined it sufficiently to have ascertained that you have not proceeded, after the method which Milton conceives to have been followed in the creation of women:

> In outward show
> Elaborate, of inward less exact.

> I have as yet been able to read the first lecture only, for I have lost my evening by having had to preside at a lecture in my own village here. Now, that has so excited me that I shall have no rest till I have got through the others. Nothing, I think, could be better done, but yet I confess I understand but in part. Even that, however, is something. I long to have a talk with you upon some points (connected more especially with ancient psalmody) upon which I have in vain tried to get some light from musical people without succeeding even so far as to get them to understand what my difficulties were. . . . We *must* [also] have a talk on this subject of Greek and Latin prosody. . . . But as for the Church hymns of the Middle Ages, I apprehend that the reason why we find no difficulty with them is simply that they are not at all in accordance with the prosody of the classical writers. They are purely accentual, exactly like our common modern verse, *e.g.*:

> Dies iræ, dies illa,
> Solvet sæclum in favilla.

> In reading this we accent the *di* of *dies* both times; we leave unaccented the *æ* of *iræ*, and the *vet* of *solvet*; and we make a distinct syllable of the *lum* of *sæclum*. But in classical Latin verse the *di* of *dies* is short, and the *es* is long; the *ae* of *irae* and the *vet* of *solvet* are both long; and the *um* before a vowel is elided. No matter how the *dies* or the *iræ* may have been vocally pronounced, whether with the accent on the first or on the second syllable, the fact remains that, generally, in any species of verse where *dies* would be good before a vowel, *fines*, for instance, would be wrong. The question is, for what musical reason ? or rhythmical

in my sense? But no more at present. You shall hear from me again before long at greater length. I am writing by the same post to another friend who has been corresponding with me about some similar points which he has been discussing with Professor Connington, of Oxford. Probably you know Professor Connington; he is a first-rate man, and would probably help us. . . . I am astounded by what you state about the irreconcilable difference of various musical systems. That is quite a new idea to me. The inscription to Helps is as good as possible.

From the Rev. Derwent Coleridge came the following essay rather than letter about the book:

Not only is the book most agreeably written in point of style, but the *exposition*—the flow and intertexture by statement .... is very happily managed. In short, it is the best book, *quâ* book, which I have met with for a long time. I am proud to say that my musical studies, though a little rusty, enable me to follow the argument without any difficulty, and I shall take occasion when we meet to talk over some of the particular points with you. John Phillips tells me that at Grasmere all the old folks used to sing the minor scale without sharpening the dominant, and that they stoutly resisted the innovation. This seems to prove that the old tonality may have prevailed once in popular music. You do not answer the vexed question, how comes it that, if the Greek music were poor and false, it could have more than satisfied so artistic a people? Instances of unequal development in the arts are not wanting, but there is no exact parallel to this. Cimabue's rude Madonna was admired as a miracle of art, but by a public very little in advance of the painting, not so very bad after all. The picture *was* admirable so far as it went, and it was admired for its excellence, not for its defects. I have a little bit of a theory on the subject. The technical definition of music, as distinguished from ordinary speech, is to the effect that music is the orderly [expression?] of measurable intervals, and that the latter, in music proper, conforms to certain fixed laws of acoustics. But this is not the [only?] difference to the [musical?] law. Singing is a simple succession of intervals more varied and ranging at a higher pitch than common speech. Hence lads, without a notion of tune, take a delight in warbling up and down their voice, and receive from their wood notes wild' a sensation of singing. Now, add to this *any law*, however conventional, make it rememberable and recognisable, and we get a basis for intellectual pleasure, which again may be heightened by habit and association almost *ad infinitum*.

Now this, I take it, is Asiatic music. In the case of the Greeks, whether acoustically true or no, [this] becomes exceedingly [probable?] and, we find, accommodating itself in a wonderful manner to the accent of passionate speech. Thus their music became in a high degree *mimetic* and *expressive*, and what the Greeks understood and valued, a true *accompaniment* harmonising exquisitely both with song—*i.e.* [poetry?] and dancing.

I quarrel with your 'epithets' gentlest and humanest as applied
to your art. What do you mean by *gentle*? Soft? If so, this is but an
euphemism for effeminate, and perhaps music is the most effeminate
of the arts, for every good thing has a bad side.

But if by 'gentle' the noble grandsire of a degenerate grandson
—genteel, then gentle it is, like all poesy, but not so pre-eminently.
It is certainly most humane, yet again not *pre-eminently*. It is
literature—*literæ humaniores*, and especially poetry, which holds
this prerogative. I could better excuse a *fanatico per la musica*
calling it the divinest of arts—

> For all we know of saints above
> Is that they sing and that they love.

And [illegible] says that music is next to Divinity, which is not
an art. It is the most religious of the arts, and this because it is
the most sensuous, appealing to body, mind, and spirit. It has the
vague infinitude of religion, [but though] for good [or] for evil—
favourable to religious *recueillement*, it has yet some cousinship
with fanaticism.

R—— P——, of S. S. Coll., a friend evidently not recently
seen, brings himself pleasantly to Mr. Hullah's recollection.

The inscription of [the book] to our dear friend Helps, and your
name in the title-page, turn my thoughts to a period which at this
distance looks all rosy and radiant. I don't know that I have much
reason to complain or to regret, but somehow, as one advances, life
becomes more stern and grim. It is pleasant, however, to find one's
self remembered by those who dwell in one's own memory as
deserving much praise and honour. Pray direct me to the spot in
the 'Divina Commedia' from which your motto is taken.

> [Io non posso ritrar di tutti appieno,
> Perocchè si mi caccia il lungo tema,
> Che molte volte al fatto il dir vien meno.]

Italian was one of my earliest loves; long before I came to
Cambridge I had worked hard at it and reaped the advantage of
its glorious fields. But without practice time wears out knowledge. . .

And his lively friend Mr. Jephson, of the 'Guardian,' sends
a gay and cordial congratulation, as was usual with him on
fit occasions:

If a good digestion wait on appetite and your cup of congratulation be not already filled to overflowing, permit me to squeeze in
my drop. . . . [The book] will sustain your reputation as a
musician and a writer. . . . I heard from Sharpe yesterday, 'acci-
dentally' or 'promiscuously,' that he had sent your lectures for
review to one of our critics. I hope the learned pundit will hit off
the points you speak of as not having been yet noticed. . . . I am
glad it was not given to me, for I should have spoken of the work

only from a literary point of view, and though literary style is much, it is not everything. . . .

Nor were excellent judges and appreciative readers of his book slow to urge him to further efforts.

I hope the delivery of the lectures was satisfactory to you in *every way* and may be useful hereafter. I should not think lectures on subjects of this kind a bad way of preparing a series of essays on them, which might steer clear of being superficial, and give a good deal of sound knowledge in a very agreeable way. For example, to take Handel, Haydn, Mozart, Beethoven, biographically and artistically, bringing out the distinctive character of each, and how it was affected by the circumstances of his life and times, reviewing incidentally some great work of each in his several kinds. I doubt whether this has been done. For myself, I should like to read such a work by you.

Within the last few years Mr. Hullah's interest in the lectures was revived by Signor Alberto Visetti's excellent translation into Italian. In Italy as in England the work has met with a flattering reception among the readers of musical literature.

The book once off his mind, Mr. Hullah recreated himself by writing two songs. Of these, ' The Reverie of Poor Susan ' is perhaps the better, and still holds its own among young people and country audiences, who love a song with a story, such as Wordsworth has told, of a rustic heart perishing in the gloom of the great city and pausing in dreamy forgetfulness to draw a moment's solace from the vision of her distant home and its rural surroundings, called up by the song of the lark—and possibly also by the sight of the sentinel tree— at the corner of Wood Street.

For the midsummer vacation it was agreed by all concerned that nothing would be so good for the heads of the house as a Continental trip. Accordingly, the younger members being safely distributed amongst relatives, Mr. and Mrs. Hullah, accompanied by their elder daughter, crossed over to Dieppe and established themselves there, until, towards the close of the holiday in September, it was decided to spend a few days in Paris, chiefly, it would seem, for the pleasure of hunting up books, of which so goodly a parcel was taken home as to require a whole day—the very last leisure day— for the judicious arrangement of the contents on the shelves

of those capacious 'Butterfield bookcases.' Then Mr. Hullah
fell to work again. The Diary notes many pleasant breaks
in the monotonous round of his avocations. There were frequent social gatherings at which familiar names occur, such
as Helps, Butterfield, Jephson, Chorley, Grove, &c. On one
of these occasions, no doubt, was discussed some very special
Barsac, the coming of which was announced with much mock
pomposity by a donor whose signature, alas! no expert that
ever lived could decipher. It was a pleasant habit some of
Mr. Hullah's friends had contracted of sending him little
presents of wine! And by no means were the delicate gifts
thrown away; for he was an excellent good judge of wine, as
also were not a few of the brilliant talkers who from time to
time gathered about him.

It was at one of these parties that was repeated the
following *bon mot*—a naughty *bon mot*, and yet it came
through a most orthodox source—a dignitary of the Church!
so, perchance, it may pass with a well-merited 'Oh, fie, for
shame!' ——— had one morning racked his brain in fruitless
endeavours to fathom the obscurities of 'Sordello.' Failing, he
had gone out to ease his aching head, and had met a friend,
who in the conversation which followed chanced to mention
that the author of 'Sordello' had a son.

'A son!' exclaimed ——— 'A son! Why then are there
three incomprehensibles, not *one* incomprehensible!'

Among the people of whom he saw a good deal about this
time was his father's only sister, Mrs. Smart. She was connected by marriage also with the musical composer, Sir George
Smart. Ample and comely in person, always carefully and
suitably dressed, bearing herself with a certain severe dignity
even while dispensing cordial hospitality, she seemed never
quite one of the party, but always seemed to impose herself
as a little apart, a little superior, a little wiser than the
younger generation. She was an excellent specimen of an
old gentlewoman of a passed-away style. The appointments
of her house and table were all of a certain ponderously handsome kind, and suggested a system of housekeeping in which
change of any sort was scarcely conceivable. Mr. Hullah's
natural courtesy and tender attention to old people never

showed to better advantage than when he was with this formidable though kindly intentioned old lady. For years she had maintained a certain distance towards him and his belongings, nobody quite knew why ; but his misfortunes at the time of the fire brought her out of her reserve. In letters of appalling length and wearisomely pedantic phraseology she had written to him placing her purse at his disposal.

She remembered his grown-up family in her will, and was helpful to them and kind to him during the remainder of her life, though she resumed at intervals the distant demeanour of former days, which Mr. Hullah found most tedious. The most constant and equable of mortals, caprice was a sore trial to his temper.

CHAPTER XVI.

BIOGRAPHICAL.

1862.

DURING the early part of 1862 Mrs. Hullah was so completely out of health as to necessitate frequent absences from home. Kind friends were never lacking to receive her, tend her, and endeavour to make life pleasant to her. Mr. Hullah, left at home with the young people, was of course very busy, but, however busy he might be, he never failed to write to the invalid wife a few words of news, for which she eagerly looked out every day.

Why (he says in reply to her constantly expressed desire to return home), why do *you* talk of returning ? . . . We are going on very well, and can, I think, do so for a while longer. So pray, dearest, get as much oxygen (isn't that the right stuff?) as you can, while you can. . . . We had a capital muster of the Upper School [it had been recommenced] last night, and they sang famously. We did a new anthem, 'The King shall rejoice,' right through. The new members are excellent. I have been exercising myself on the furniture of my room—setting to rights a bit, as you will see. I meanly took advantage of Mum's [meaning Miss Sampson, the governess of the youngest son] absence and got Betsey [the housemaid] to help. . . . I have told everybody that you were not coming home 'till the weather was warmer,' as Helps would say, of which, at present, there is no sign. The boys are all well. . . . I go to Butterfield's to-morrow. . . . Yesterday I went to B—— and paid my respects to the new Mrs. C——, who seems a very nice person. But a second and new anybody or anything ought to be superhuman or supernatural to stand comparison with what one has known and is used to. . . . The boys are going on very well and the establishment seems to work very smoothly. So pray don't flatter yourself you are wanted; but consider that you are discharging all the duties of life in laying up health and strength and being as comfortable as you can make yourself. Love to Sissy. . . . P.S. Your *daily dish* at breakfast-time is more welcome than ever.

But these encouraging reports notwithstanding, Mrs. Hullah was not at rest away from home and her young tribe of sons and daughters. Mr. Hullah was unavoidably absent from the house the greater part of each day, and no one knew better than she did how little he was fitted by nature or experience to cope with the usual difficulties of family life. It is easy to understand how, in her enfeebled and often suffering state, she probably exaggerated these difficulties and fretted to be back at her post in the midst of her dear belongings. So there quickly came a moment after she had gone down to Stanford, when she turned a deaf ear to all the kind wishes of the friends she was with, and to the advice from home, and announced her speedy return.

I can only write a line (he says, on learning her decision). I suppose a wilful woman must have her way, and that you will come on Monday. But it is really a pity. . . . We have had a capital meeting of class. Everybody is radiant at the idea of meeting you next time. Not but what we could get on very well indeed! I have written to Tylden thanking him heartily for his and Ellen's hospitality to you and Caroline, but especially insisting on their fixing a time for their visit to London.

Mrs. Hullah returned, and family life resumed its usual course. She assisted in the classes when she could, and her very presence lifted a great burden from Mr. Hullah's shoulders, and with a lighter, if not less anxious heart, he went about his avocations, throwing into each and all the fulness of energy which was so remarkable a characteristic of him.

At Easter, according to his now long-established habit, he left town for a few days. His letters are long and chatty, but reveal a constant unrest; he was often wishing he could 'telegraph for instant news,' or ' peep into a certain room.'

I suppose I must take your account of yourself (he writes after receiving a circumstantial and encouraging letter) and make the best of it, though I should have been glad to know what the *doctors* say. This I shall look for to-morrow. . . . It is impossible not to enjoy the sweet country and delicious spring weather and everybody's kindness; but I wish I could have a peep at you now and then. I wonder whether science will make such a procedure possible to future generations? But I shall soon know for myself.

And after a very brief visit he went home, quite unable to bear the anxiety of absence. But Mrs. Hullah's condition was becoming rapidly graver, though what the doctors really said she was careful he should not learn. Again change was recommended, and she left home for Brighton. The demands on his time were too pressing to allow him to accompany her, so his only comfort was in the diary-letter that was daily exchanged. Not a detail was omitted on his side that could give relief to her maternal anxieties or interest her intelligence. Points in her letters about herself, her lodgings, her landlady, were all taken up and commented upon in the effort to cheer the variable spirits of an invalid.

Have you tried any of the celebrated old Tipper ale, patronised by his late Majesty George IV. of Pavilion memory? . . . I have finished the last of the arrangements of Pearsall's part songs this morning, since which I have been to Queen's College, Battersea, and St. Mark's. Everybody [Dr. Watson included] rejoices to hear you have made a *move* and prophesies all sorts of speedy good results from it. . . . The boys are good. In fact we are very humdrum, respectable people, early to bed and early to rise, &c. &c. God bless you and make you strong and well soon. . . . Your cheery letter—quite an old-fashioned letter—produced a wonderful sensation, read, as for the most part it was, in fragments, to an admiring circle at breakfast this morning. R—— and S—— went to a small saltatory exercise (*in vulgo dicto*—hop) last night, so that I did not get your letter brought to me *in my room* as usual. . . . I rejoice over the excellence of the lodging greatly. In future I must have a commission for my *agency*. Gimber seems to be a Brighton word for the perfection of lodging-house keepers. . . . I hold to my plan of coming on Tuesday; but I am invited to dine with the contributors to the Biblical Dictionary at the Crystal Palace on Tuesday, so I shall come *on*. . . . I have been thinking about my Edinburgh lectures [he had accepted an invitation to lecture at the Philosophical Institution during the winter], and I have resolved to take the German and Italian schools of the first half of the last century. These include Bach and Handel, with the influences of the Italians on the latter. . . . This morning *we* had all breakfasted, and *I* had done with the ' Times ' at a little after *nine*. . . . This morning we had a visit at the Charterhouse from the Public School Commissioners. . . . I have planned some more lectures. . . . I am glad you have begun upon ' Fénelon ; ' you will be pleased with that and the ' Life of Vincent de Paul.' I have been utterly *bouleversé* by Victor Hugo, whose ' Les Misérables ' I rejoice to have finished so far as it has gone. As a work of art it is too shocking; but I do not know that one has a right to close one's ears to any utterances of a writer of genius. . . .

Last night I dined at W——'s, and went afterwards to a concert for the benefit of poor Ernst, who is in a grievous state of sickness and adversity at Nice. Everybody did everything for nothing, down to the doorkeepers. . . . I see by Caroline's letter that you are really coming home to-morrow. Had you chosen a later train we might have illuminated; as it is, you must be content with being received by the guard of honour and a great many 'salutes.' Good-bye till to-morrow !

Contrary to the hopes and wishes of her friends, Mrs. Hullah did not grow 'steadily stronger' as the summer holiday drew near. It was, therefore, decided to give her the largest amount of quiet attainable, in country air, and a cottage was hired at Godstone, in Kent. Here Mr. Hullah installed his family before yielding to his wife's persuasion that he should accompany Mr. Butterfield on a short Continental trip. The friends set out at length, and halted, according to their habit, at the Hôtel Quillac, in Calais, at that time in all its glory. Looking out at moments on the rose garden of the great court, Mr. Hullah writes, as he sits waiting for his fellow-traveller :

The morning is beautiful and bright, and they say there is *beaucoup de vent*—a fact altogether without interest to us. . . . Here is Butterfield and also another B., namely, *breakfast*—which will be very welcome. . . . We go to Brussels. . . . To Brussels (he continues) we had as our travelling companions two Germans on their way from England, whom I ventured to address in the language which *we* love so much ! This made a good deal of fun all day, for I had to *collect myself* for every successive observation. . . . The tea is just come, but the lazy B. (not the 'busy') is not yet down, though he should have been in bed (*I* was !) by ten. . . . Here he comes, looking flourishing. . . . We go south into the warm ! not that we can complain of this. My *hair* (my barometer) is as dry as old hemp. . . . *Basle.*—Many thanks for the glad tidings of your well doing ! B. took it into his head that he should like to go to Trèves again, and that we might cut across the country from Saarbrücken to some point on the Strasbourg line, as we had meant to go from Epinal to Thaun. So we went to Trèves, and refreshed our memories on various points, and visited an old and little-known church—St. Mathias—outside the town. . . . On our way to Saarbourg, when the daylight began to fail the driver's courage did the same, and he asked leave to invite a friend to accompany him to show him the way, which *he* had never been. . . . We found that both gentlemen were disposed to recruit their sinking spirits with spirits of another kind. . . . The journey, in many respects delightful, was without many incidents. At one place we saw all the cows, calves, sheep, goats, and pigs of the neighbourhood brought into the village—to bed. The lowing, skipping, baaing and squeaking were beyond conception. . . .

September 7.—This is Butterfield's birthday. . . . Twice we have spent it together abroad. . . . *I* have just been reading *yesterday's*

Times,' which *you* cannot yet have seen! I've been to the post, but could not buy a postage-stamp—all shut up. . . . *Lucerne.*— I am not sure that in my last I said half as much as I ought to have said of yours, more especially about the *bulletin* announcing your stupendous walk, which exceeds, though not in length, in importance any of the feats of the members of the Alpine Club. What are Professor Tyndall and the Monte Rosa to me? You have *done* Tilbaster Hill almost, and perhaps by this time quite! . . . Butterfield is crazy for the Alps; so I suppose we shall sleep at Andermatt on Friday night and spend Sunday in Lugano, then come gently back to Basle, where we shall probably sleep on Wednesday night. Please let me find a line there. . . . Last night . . . a good-natured official actually turned back to his office, being on his way home, to find me two postage-stamps. . . . I have been lounging about a bit, making more sketches. . . . This afternoon we went to the cathedral to hear the organ, which is exhibited on alternate days from four to five. After a succession of operatic tunes played first on one fancy stop and then another, and accompanied by [musical notation] chords, which lasted about twenty minutes, under which I sat as quietly as I could, the gentleman set up a waltz, at which I fairly bolted, with sentiments which, I fear, had they found utterance, would have been unbecoming the 'sacred edifice.' *Hospenthal.*—Such a wonderful contrast to Lucerne, which is ' full of noises.'

Lugano. . . . In spite of all my experience of travelling, I cannot grapple with the fact that it is but twelve days since I left Godstone. It seems an age, and an age during which all sorts of wonderful changes must have taken place. . . . Really your visitors should take a hint from the travellers here, and *telegraph for beds.* . . . The children here are all singularly beautiful, not so fiercely dark as farther south, but often with that *luminous* dark-brown hair that looks gold in some lights. . . . The hotel in which we are is made out of an old convent, which I remember in 1845 as such. It is an enormous building, with huge stone staircases, a large cloister, and corridors and galleries bewildering to the best organ of locality. The chapel (still such) contains the famous fresco of Luini—the Crucifixion—his greatest work, and, to my mind, the noblest piece of wall painting I have yet seen. I have, perhaps, a prejudice in its favour, as being the first fresco I ever saw in my life; but after spending about two hours seated before it this afternoon, I am only more strongly confirmed in my first impression of its grandeur of design and execution. . . . I rushed off [after this] to the post . . . and went and stood under the nearest piazza (this town is full of them), and read your letter through. After that I had another good turn at the Luini. . . . You will all, I fear, have a sad day in parting from Tilbaster. But the best friends must part, and we shall have a glad day very soon after, when we all meet again at D. Place. . . . Butterfield and I are both so much better, that fatigue which three weeks ago would have seemed unendurable proves now of no account whatever. . . . From Lugano we walked out to the Convent of Bigorio, which took three hours (all up hill) out and two hours back. Such a walk! under the shade of chestnut-trees and vines—refreshing ourselves when needful by plucking the fruit of the latter. Love to all. God bless you! We shall meet soon. . .

His heart was gladdened on his return home to find Mrs. Hullah so far recovered that the day after his arrival she was able to pay *her* first visit to the Great Exhibition with him. His sanguine temperament instantly recovered its tone, and he plunged with his accustomed vigour into the vortex of winter work. The classes at home improved and the Upper School also was progressing not unsatisfactorily, though the working of it would seem to have been attended with difficulties, presumably of the old financial nature. Rent in London is so high, and the various attendant expenses of hired rooms so disproportionately great, that in the case of these classes the most unavoidable outlay would seem to have swallowed up all the fees, which were necessarily, the position of the students being the first consideration, very moderate. At the very end of September Mr. Hullah sat down to write the course of lectures he was pledged to give in Edinburgh. Working on the system of *nulla dies sine linea*, he progressed steadily, and was in a fair way to be ready betimes, when Mrs. Hullah's condition forced him to postpone the delivery of them in person. Preparation for these lectures was no light matter. It involved much time spent in the British Museum, and many diagrams on a very large scale had to be drawn. In the preparation of these he was assisted by his eldest daughter, who still adhered to her chosen profession. At the appointed time the lectures were read for Mr. Hullah by Mr. David Boyle Hope, and were so well received as to bring him subsequently into communication with more than one learned body in Edinburgh.

But, though Mr. Hullah would not leave home, he was by no means idle. Indeed, work seemed his only refuge from the misery of the home over which the angel of death was hovering. Throughout the dreary winter he did his work from day to day, from hour to hour, saddened and oppressed by the knowledge of his wife's suffering state, but yet not realising how near was the close. He had grieved over her illness, but

not as one without hope, for his temperament was of the
most sanguine; and her real condition she kept carefully veiled
from his knowledge. That his life should run on smoothly,
all unruffled by home troubles and home cares—that her
daughters and her sons should live their lives of pleasantness,
unchecked by a care, unburdened by a premature sorrow—had
been the habit and rule of her existence in health, and she
strove that in these her last days on earth her sufferings
should disturb them as little as possible. She exacted no
sacrifice of material interests, claimed no marked exhibition
of grief. She knew that when she was gone, he, who had been
her one great study throughout a long married life, would
find hard to bear, and to contend alone against, the many petty
trials which she, in her loving forethought, had hitherto been
able to spare him, and her last anxiety was still to ward off
the dark hour for him and see him come to her bedside with a
smile of hope, whenever he could snatch a leisure moment
between one piece of work and another. Therefore, when
death claimed her, the blow fell upon Mr. Hullah as a terrible,
overwhelming surprise. A very close acquaintance with him
was necessary to a complete understanding of the full measure
of his sorrow and desolation, for marriage meant to him love
the most limitless, trust the most unreserved, and in the
union now severed by death he had found a perfect love with
unison of thoughts and pursuits. He had known in the
highest, fullest, best sense of the word—happiness. Rich
in friends, some of them the very salt of the earth, still he
was in one sense absolutely alone, for, as he had said long
ago, 'the only creature to whom he could open his heart'
was gone from him—for ever! With his rare powers of
self-control—the very essence of courage—he bore his sorrow
silently and went onward, and did the work of his life, following her lead in that he darkened no fellow-creature's existence
by obtrusive display of his grief. Happily—and he had the
comfort of knowing it—his grief was not only understood, it
was largely shared by many outside his own immediate circle.
Traces of this are frequent in the entire correspondence of the
year.

In March, some few weeks after his wife's death, he went

to Stanford for a short rest, and then returned to his routine of work in London ; but soon he began to feel that some of his work he could no longer continue. For a while his courage seemed failing.

The first classes he decided to give up were those of the 'Upper Singing School.' The following letter shows with what regret his decision was learnt:

Music Hall, Store Street, March 18, 1863.

DEAR SIR,—The communication you caused to be made to us at your last meeting, announcing that the relations which have so long subsisted between us are to be immediately brought to a close, although not altogether unexpected, has caused a feeling of deep regret among all the members of your Upper Singing School.

We readily comprehend some of the circumstances which have induced you to come to this determination, and are not surprised that your recent sad bereavement should have operated to that end.

Those among us who have had the pleasure to be members of your Singing School for some years have been enabled to appreciate the unwearied zeal, patience, and ability with which the late Mrs. Hullah co-operated with you in carrying on the classes, and we are anxious as a body to take this opportunity of offering you and your family our sincere sympathy and condolence on the great loss you have sustained. . . . Many thousands of persons have, under your immediate direction or superintendence, received instruction in the system of musical education founded by you, and have been trained in your classes to take part in the performance of choral music ; by means of which the works of the best masters have become known and appreciated, and the knowledge of music of the highest class spread amongst the people. . . . And now, in taking leave, we sincerely hope that you may long be spared, and that the Almighty Disposer of events will cause your bereaved retirement to be one of tranquillity and comfort.

The letter was numerously signed on behalf of the members of the Upper Singing School.

Once again desolation of heart found expression—perhaps consolation too—in his own art. Clough's words, which he set to melody so sad that, when sung by himself, the most indifferent hearer felt instinctively that a heart's experience was revealed in the mournful accents, give so clear a picture of Hullah's inner life at this period that the poem is quoted entire :

> My wind is turned to bitter north
>   That was so soft a south before ;
> My sky that shone so sunny bright,
>   With foggy gloom is clouded o'er :

My gay green leaves are yellow black,
　Upon the dark autumnal floor;
For love departed once, comes back
　No more again, no more.

A roofless ruin lies my home
　For winds to blow and rains to pour;
One frosty night befell, and lo,
　I find my summer days are o'er;
The heart bereaved of why and how
　Unknowing knows that yet before
It had what e'en to memory now
　Returns no more, no more.

CHAPTER XVII.

BIOGRAPHICAL.

1863.

NOT for long, however, could he keep away from his old busy existence. In April his Diary tells how he was much engaged in assisting the Committee of the National Society to arrange and carry through a festival in Westminster Abbey. So successfully did he do his part, that the Committee assured him that, 'had he not worked as hard as he had done, they were aware the festival could not have been held.' At Easter he was summoned by his friends at Sellinge Rectory to help in the management of a sort of miniature choral festival at Elham. During the London season he recovered sufficient outward calm to see a good deal of his more intimate friends, and during the summer holidays he was induced to pay several short visits before going to Eversley. Very delightful and refreshing to Mr. Hullah were the walks and talks in the woods around, amid the sweet sylvan sounds of birds and insects, concerning which Mr. Kingsley had so much to say that was instructive and poetical, especially when he spoke with a listener by his side so receptive and responsive as his musician friend. And one evening the post brought them a fresh subject for discussion in the shape of a letter from Miss Masson, enclosing a translation into French of the 'Three Fishers' which she had just roughly blocked out.

Less than a Victor Hugo ought not to attempt to follow a Kingsley (Miss Masson says when despatching her translations to the 'poet and musician in council'). My sole object was to feel the effects of foreign syllables to music so thoroughly adapted to the impassioned grandeur of the original ones, and it is the quicksilver activity of the French that so stands in the way, robbing us of all that sturdy resistance, that hearty massiveness belonging to our

mother tongue. My poor translation has yet . . . to be rewritten.
Everybody being gone and I left in sole charge of the metropolis,
I've scarcely time to add that your distinguished host has no truer
follower than the poor scribe who addresses you.

Here is Miss Masson's translation of the first verse :

Trois morts se déploient sur la plage luisant
  Au clair du matin, á descente de màrée ;
Et les femmes se déplorent en plaintes amères
  Les âmes chéries qui ne reviennent à jamais ;
Car aux hommes le travail, aux femmes les pleurs ;
  Plus courte la vie, plus vite sommeil (*or* dormir),
Et adieu aux murmures qui jadis faisaient peur (*or* firent frémir).

This is very promising, but whether anything more was
done to it does not appear. Some years later Madame de la
Madelaine made an excellent translation of the ' Three Fishers '
for Mr. Hullah's music, and the song was, possibly still is,
fairly well known in France.

A third very clever rendering of the poem into French has
been done by Signor D. Tagliafico.

With this bright little visit to Eversley Mr. Hullah brought
his holiday to an end, and contentedly joined his family at
Sevenoaks, and lost no time in getting to work over an article on
Lady Wallace's translation of Mendelssohn's Letters. Scarcely
was this sent off to ' Fraser ' than a Grammar of Counterpoint
was commenced. This, again, was barely dry when a lecture
on Handel was begun. London folk came and went, and
doubtless he enjoyed their society, but a very fever of work
was on him, and he never seemed to pause or try to enjoy
that *dolce far niente* possible even in England, with such a
place as Knole Park at hand. When, however, he had worked
several consecutive days at ' Handel,' Mr. and Miss Bellamy
appeared, and when they went back they carried him home
with them to Sellinge, and presently passed him on to Stanford. Thence he started, in company with Mr. and Mrs. Tylden,
for a trip which included Blois, Tours, Loches, Poictiers, the
return to Paris being effected *viâ* Le Mans and his beloved
Chartres, where he had been before, and where he went many
times subsequently, but never found leisure to examine anything but the cathedral, every detail of which was familiar to
him, and of which he made many sketches. It was well that

Mr. Hullah was able to return to London with a large store of health, and some recovery of his naturally buoyant spirits, for he found there was infinite work awaiting him. He had again undertaken to lecture in Edinburgh early in 1864, and having regard to other calls on his time, he had to set to work immediately on his return home. Before Christmas the lectures, diagrams, and all were prepared and despatched to the scene of future action. Mr. Froude had asked for a second article on the Mendelssohn Letters, which he duly received before the year ran out. In this article Mr. Hullah had been somewhat severe on what he considered a too great freedom of translation, whereupon Lady Wallace pertinently required of him a better rendering of the phrases or words criticised. After a rapid exchange of good-humoured thrusts and parries, Lady Wallace and Mr. Hullah met at the house of Mr. William Longman (who had recently become Mr. Hullah's publisher), and the lady allowed herself to be convinced of the justice of her critic's remarks.' The following true, if perhaps a little too severe, remark on English class prejudice brought upon him the pleasant infliction of a long letter from his own untiring critic, Mr. Jephson.

No living English father (says Mr. Hullah), of the status and culture of the elder Mendelssohn, would allow, still less would encourage and help his son—gifted never so highly or unmistakably—to make music the principal business of his life; and a man of lower status and less culture would foster such a son's musical faculty to the neglect of every other.

I have read your article while waiting for proofs in the office of the 'Guardian' (says Mr. Jephson). I need not say that I was delighted with it. I must get the book itself, but I daresay I have got the best of it in the review; at any rate, what you have said will make me better able to appreciate the book. Mendelssohn must have been a most delightful person—an utterly exceptional person—and therefore I do not think one could fairly draw a comparison between English and German education from the one instance of him.

Besides, you know, whether rightly or wrongly, Englishmen do not value accomplishments. Many, indeed, would be ashamed to own themselves accomplished for fear of seeming effeminate. [What changes we have lived to see in twenty years!] This makes society in England much less interesting than it is abroad, but I am not sure that it does not make *life* more earnest and real. But indeed the whole thing is a mystery. What is the object of life? To be happy, and agreeable, and accomplished, and sociable, or to *succeed* at the expense of being narrow and serious? It is hard to say.

... Do you remember my saying that I admire very much the introduction to your book upon the scale ?

It is odd that William Chappell, whom I met the other night at the house of a neighbour, Captain Jesse, without my saying a word about it, instanced that as a perfect piece of writing.

And Mr. Tylden sends a letter on many subjects with a well-turned compliment.

I have read your interesting paper .... Mendelssohn could hardly have found a fitter memorialist. There is one trait given of his character which makes me think that I have at any rate one among my friends who resembles him: 'Nothing will strike the reader of these letters more than the capacity for general appreciation in one so highly gifted with a special talent.'

Mr. Tylden had closed his letter with a reminder that after Christmas Mr. Hullah and Mr. Butterfield were due at Sellinge, when 'other points' could be discussed at leisure. To arrange about the journey Mr. Butterfield insisted that his friend should desert Devonshire Place for a *tête-à-tête* dinner in the bachelor chambers in Adam Street, on the last day of the old year. It is easy to imagine how, as the sad year 1863 died out, the old friends talked of many things, but finance, it is to be feared, did not come on the *tapis*; which is matter for regret, for the advice and supervision of a cautious friend was certainly needed at this time by Mr. Hullah, in whose diaries and notebooks stray jottings about investments are disquieting to the mind of a staid and careful financier. The advice under which Mr. Hullah's extremely small property underwent constant changes was, no doubt, well meant, but these changes became mere dissolving views with inconvenient frequency; all the more inconvenient that, while the domestic expenditure of this period showed no downward, the individual needs of a growing family did show a very marked upward, tendency.

But whatever were the subjects under post-prandial discussion at that *tête-à-tête* dinner, they came to an end with a salutation to the new year, and the friends parted to meet again twelve hours later *en route* for Sellinge Rectory, where a warm welcome and much bustle awaited them; for the little village world was tremendously excited about an imminent lecture, with musical illustration, 'all under the sole management of Miss Bellamy,' the Rector's daughter.

CHAPTER XVIII.

BIOGRAPHICAL.

1864.

On January 10 the long-thought-of visit to Edinburgh was actually carried out, Mr. Hullah being on this occasion the guest of Mr. and Mrs. D. B. Hope. That evening he met a crowd of people connected with the Philosophical Institution, and the next day he made personal acquaintance with Dean Ramsay and Professor Donaldson, and was introduced to many who subsequently became his firm friends.

The first lecture—on Handel—was very fully attended, as was also the second. During the days between the lectures the lionising was stupendous. It seems wonderful that an average man could reserve sufficient energy after such a week of fatigue to lecture at Newcastle, as Mr. Hullah did immediately on leaving Edinburgh. Thence he went to Sunderland, and on to Tynemouth, lecturing at both towns, on vocal part music, to very large and attentive audiences. It must have seemed to him as if life had slipped back to the years 1840 to 1844, when he used to scour the country, now and then accompanied by Mr. Carleton Tufnell and Sir James Kay-Shuttleworth, expounding his then new Wilhem Method. Those who had seen him twenty years before said that he scarcely looked older. As for other sign of age there was none. Decidedly cheered up he returned to home and a severe routine of professional work, the monotony of which was relieved in the course of the year by two or three lively incidents.

For some while back Sir Arthur Helps' benevolent brain had been evolving a scheme for building a school, and he wished for the co-operation of his old friend Hullah. Therefore, so soon as the latter came back from Scotland he was asked, 'Have you ever thought (yes, of course you have) about the building of a school—how it ought to be done? If so, I wish you would give me your ideas on paper in the roughest way.' Sir Arthur was right; Mr. Hullah had, being more rather than less of an architect, ready-made plans in his head about schools as about other sorts of buildings, and was delighted to unfold them and have confabulations concerning them. For some unexplained reason Sir Arthur's *cacoethes ædificandi* took the form not of a school but of an infirmary, 'all about which' a neighbour of Sir Arthur's writes to Mr. Hullah, rightly surmising that in the Helpian pie there would probably be a Hullah finger.

We are in our own little cottage. . . . Mr. Helps is the founder of a projected infirmary, and the young Prince Leopold lays the stone; so, of course, there is to be a gathering and a to-do. . . . It strikes me you might be visiting Vernon Hill, and so I venture to remind you that, whilst sitting with 'Friends in Council,' you should not forget friends at hand, and *we* are close by—only, alas! in such a wee bit of a house that we have no suitable kitchen for a scientific cook. We do contrive to eat, but as our fathers did—under a tent. But such hospitality as is possible we would gladly share with friends who will put up with a scramble. You will see at once my Irish origin. . . . It occurs to me to mention as likely to be useful that *possibly* in connection with this infirmary there might be some opening for your son. Dr. B. told us the other day it would be a good opening for a young man. . . . In conclusion, I must tell you we have our small feeble choral society, originated by ourselves, who would, I fancy, sooner see John Hullah than even—a Royal Prince!

Later on the event to which this letter refers came off with *éclat*. In speaking of this grand day—the opening of his infirmary—Sir Arthur used to lay great stress on the excellence of the arrangements for the reception and departure of those present, and the grouping of the guests which, by cunning social tactics, was so contrived as to bring together persons acquainted with each other, to the complete avoidance of the awkwardness and restraint which follow an indiscriminate herding of people merely for eating' sake. Everyone was pleased because no one seemed neglected, ' and all this was *his* doing,' Sir Arthur would say, pointing an approving finger at his coadjutor and regarding him with a peculiar pose of the head that always made him look like a portrait by Velasquez come to life.

Mr. Hullah had not despatched a full and minute statement of his architectural ideas anent schools many days, when his aid was invoked for the disentanglement of a difficulty which the Dean and Chapter of —— apparently found unmanageable without help.

The correspondence concerning this transaction reveals an amusing state of bondage which would seem to be the occasional lot of cathedral dignitaries. The negotiations with Mr. Hullah were opened through a friend of both sides, who writes :

> You may perhaps remember my meeting you in the street one day in January and asking you whether you would object to help us to get rid of some effete voices in our cathedral at ——. We have the power of calling on any vicar, who from loss of voice or other similar reason is past work, to find a substitute, or to pay an annual stipend to us to find such substitute. Before, however, we call on any one of our present staff to do this, we wish to be fortified by advice on which we can rely, and which, if need be, we can quote. And so I have been desired to ask you if you will professionally advise us in the matter as *amicus curiæ*, and at the same time overhaul our choristers, advising us who ought to be turned out, and whether they are in the right places, according to their merits of singing power. . . . The Dean desired me to say that he should be most happy to offer you hospitality. . . . March 21 : I should be glad to report to the Dean that you can fix a day for coming to him. On a Sunday the whole choir is always present, but on Monday afternoon and both services on Tuesday the three great offenders against the harmony of our choir are all in attendance. . . . You will hear from the Dean, who will most gladly welcome you.

An invitation to stay at the Deanery followed. Mr. Hullah accepted it, and betook himself to the scene of discord, pronounced a decisive opinion as to the incapacity of the inharmonious vicars, and left matters in training for their speedy dislodgment.

' Our old alto has knocked under without a struggle, and we shall soon be quit *of him*,' triumphantly reports the corresponding member of the Dean and Chapter ; ' but,' he continues ruefully, ' I expect we shall have more trouble with our tenor.' On this remark Mr. Hullah doubtless commented by expressing his opinion, not for the first or last time, that for some inscrutable reason tenors always are more difficult to deal with than the owners of other voices. While these differences were being gradually adjusted, Mr. Hullah was steadily getting through his own engagements, and quietly packing up the goods and chattels necessary for his holiday, when in post-haste Mr. Jephson writes to him :

What extraordinary things happen to one in the course of one's sublunary pilgrimage! I have been asked to write a biography of you!!! What am I to do? I know nothing, to begin with, but that you have pursued me with unmitigable hostility for several years, slandered me to my friends as a man who never kept his engagements, and I don't know what else besides. It seems that the photographers have got hold of you among the 'eminent men' of the day. Your face is to be represented to the public looking, as Dickens says, like a newly ploughed field, and a life of you is wanted to match. What am I to do, I ask again? I should like to have an opportunity of cutting you up and paying off all my old grudges, but it is so ridiculous. However, you might perhaps fall into worse hands, and if you will give me the materials I will 'do' for you, unless you can suggest a more promising operator to Lovell Reeve. . . .

Mr. Jephson's letter was carried off as a reminder, and in course of time the necessary memoranda appeared at Brentwood, to be operated on. The preparation of notes for his own, must have set his ideas running on biographies in general, for presently he wrote to propose that he should translate a life of Beethoven recently published in Germany. Mr. Longman, however, improved on the idea, and suggested the preparation of a new life of Beethoven. But for independent researches Mr. Hullah could not command the necessary leisure. He had already, indeed, more work than was good to be done in a time called holidays.

The accumulation of unanswered letters was portentous, and some of them required answers of considerable length— essays, in fact, on the art of teaching vocal music to amateurs of every conceivable degree of aptitude and inaptitude.

The following passages are from the voluminous letters of a zealous disciple who had gone some years before to Australia. One of the letters begins by a warm outbreak of gratitude to Mr. Hullah for some kindness shown to relatives of the writer, and contains curious descriptions of life and the state of musical culture in the colony.

I am going home [to Melbourne] to-morrow with great joy, my brother having induced me to stay down here during his absence since the great flood. The bushrangers are now close to Goulbourne. I am puzzling my head where to put my money; it is no use trying any of the old places of concealment, as hiding in stockings, hats, or bonnets. I think the best plan would be to stuff it all in one's mouth as soon as the bushrangers come in sight. If I were compelled to speak I should resemble the lady in the fairy tale who dropped a pearl from her mouth at every word, but *my* speech would be golden. . . . I wish we could get the Singers' Library here. I imagine my musical society in Goulbourne have made discord amongst themselves and all gone wrong in my absence. I hope it may prove only a discord by suspension which I may be able to resolve by my appearance . . . . *Goulbourne*: A gentleman, master of the collegiate grammar school in this town, came to me yesterday evening to inquire how and where he could obtain all your sheets, manuals, &c. . . . In Sydney they have them not, in Melbourne there are no more. I know lots of people who want the manuals. If they had them at either place the percentage would be enormous. Why is this? Who sends out music? In books and magazines the percentage is not so high. I have known an edition of the 'Messiah' costing [at home] three or four shillings, being charged one guinea. . . . I have partly succeeded in getting together a concerted music society; we meet once a week at my brother's house here. . . . I cannot tell you what patience one has had to practice. At the first meeting every one quarrelled with every one else; at the second no one had any idea of his or her part, and the discord was so frightful that my brother went off into the next room, where he sat with his hands to his ears. Still, one has triumphed. The lazy ones, who did not really care for music, but only for the show and glorification it brought themselves, have fallen off, but we have a few (quite enough) who are really desirous to persevere. . . . Dear Mr. Hullah, I do hope you are well—every way. Often I think of our last ride to Chelsea, when I had the misfortune to say good-bye to you perhaps for ever! I see you still standing in the gateway, and that is a lasting picture in my memory. Once more let me thank you for your recent goodness to ——, and say that if possible it has increased the love and esteem which I have always cherished towards you. . . . —— tells me that he too, like the writer of 'All the Year Round,' saw your manuals in Pitcairn's Island, where men have learnt from them to make the desert blossom with their songs.

No doubt letters like these were pleasant enough to read, if somewhat tedious to reply to, and Boulogne, to which the family had migrated, is not conducive to a calm or industrious condition of mind, especially to any one devoted, like Mr. Hullah, to sea-bathing, and taking a lively interest in the ridiculous side of French seaside life as exhibited on the beach.

At the end of a few weeks Mr. Hullah, accompanied by his second son and Mr. Cock, of Queen's College, set off for an independent tour. At Malines the party stayed long enough to enjoy thoroughly a remarkable exhibition of mediæval metal work, arranged by Mr. Weale with consummate skill and knowledge. Taking Aix-la-Chapelle on the way they journeyed to Cologne, where Mr. Hullah enjoyed a long chat with his old acquaintance, Herr Rheinthaler. While at Cologne he made a short excursion to Rolandseck and Drachenfels, associated with happy memories of other days, and then started off for Bremerhafen, to place his son under the care of a German professor, in order that he might acquire the German tongue, and drift, in a matter of course way, into commercial life. His errand accomplished, he wended his way back to England, and began at once a long list of lectures, for which he had prepared notes during the vacation.

At Bristol, Winchester, Southampton, and various places in and about London, Mr. Hullah delivered these lectures on different branches of musical instruction, and during the evenings he spent at home (not many, certainly) he arranged the 'Song Book'—one of the dainty 'Golden Treasury' series. Towards the end of December Mr. Hullah notes in his Diary a performance of the 'Messiah,' at a small private house, as 'very good.' It would seem to have been exactly the sort of performance which was the expected result of the taste for concerted music which Mr. Hullah's life-long work had revived and fostered in a class possessed of leisure to practise a difficult art—just the sort of performance he had often dreamt of as possible in a moderate space and with moderate means. On New Year's Eve of 1864-65 he was again 'assisting at a musical party at the same house. In the course of the evening he was introduced to a new acquaintance, known for a season as 'The Friend.'

'A concurrence of felicities,' as he puts it, enabled him to improve that acquaintance rapidly. Mr. Hullah's power of entering into all the interests of his friends, his perennial youth of heart, winning refinement of nature, and the sunny moral and intellectual atmosphere in which he enveloped any one whom he much liked, wrought their charm, and exceptional circumstances in this particular case made such a friendship as his most welcome.

'The voices of the dead and songs of other years' still made music in his heart, and still found sad response; but into his life, which had seemed for a while a barren waste, there came a new interest, beneath the influence of which he appeared to gather fresh strength every day, and which did not fail to tell favourably on the manner in which the innumerable lectures of the next year were delivered.

CHAPTER XIX.

BIOGRAPHICAL.

1865-66.

BEFORE Easter Mr. Hullah had given lectures on various musical subjects at Leeds, Newcastle, and some smaller towns; at the College of Organists, and at some less important places in London.

It must have been at one of these lectures that a 'Reverend' chairman, famous for his inability to resist saying a brilliant, even if somewhat profane thing, introduced Mr. Hullah to an audience in this wise:

'Now, then, ladies and gentlemen—you all know Mr. Hullah, and——'

A long pause, during which every eye was bent on the lecturer—

' *Ecce Homo!* ' continued the chairman; and forthwith sat down.

He had also conducted the four concerts of the Philharmonic Society in Edinburgh; and during his visits to the Modern Athens, hasty though they were, he had been made much of, added enormously to his acquaintance and to his stock of anecdotes, and began to find health and spirits return to such an extent that his ordinary London work ' was just nothing at all ' to him, even when certain suburban expeditions on most urgent business were duly taken into account. It is just possible that these very expeditions, made in a style of equestrianism all his own, on the back of a steed of Quaker sobriety, were distinctly beneficial, leading as they did to visits to the studio of ' The Friend,' she whose ' trade was with sticks and clay.' These visits were necessarily many, and unavoidably long. So much was there to talk about ; for in that studio a small statue was in progress, concerning the treatment of which there were discussions, new to Mr. Hullah, about ' lines,' and ' modelling,' and ' draperies,' and ' lights and shadows,' very important points, not to be settled in a hurry, nor, indeed, without protracted consideration. Now and then the late Mr. Richard Westmacott, R.A., would drop in to bestow advice, and opinions were not unanimous on the above-named abstruse matters. It must be confessed a great many hours were passed in this way—hours that were remembered in the coming years as very bright and happy, and of which the after-glow has not even yet died away.

Happily the plastic problem was solved before April, and ' Italia ' gone, asking admission to the goal of all youthful artistic hopes—the Royal Academy of Painting.

At Easter, Mr. Hullah, like all the world, left town, and he went to Winchester, possibly because ' The Friend ' happened to be there. Also, it chanced that Mr. Butterfield was superintending the restoration of the church of St. Cross. This was, indeed, a brilliant ' concurrence of felicities. He was radiant as the ' Three Arts ' walked about the beautiful church, though a listener would certainly have imagined that Mr. Hullah it was who represented architecture, so very professional was his talk thereon.

With a revived interest in life and renewed health came back a strong desire to recommence the old work of public teaching, and in the spring of this year there is no doubt he began to form plans for constructing a new St. Martin's Hall. Fortunately the business negotiations were prolonged into the summer, when a path leading to the ' fresh woods and pastures new ' of Scotland presented itself.

Intelligence of the death of Dr. Donaldson, who had for many years held the Reid professorship of music in the University of Edinburgh, was sent to Mr. Hullah, accompanied by an earnest suggestion that he should become a candidate for the vacant post. Nothing could be more acceptable than the chance of getting into a haven of comparative rest, which offered so much that at that particular epoch of his life he especially needed. It was a most honourable post, fairly remunerated, and offering considerable scope for the exercise of his varied powers as a teacher, a lecturer, and a writer. The social surroundings were interesting and agreeable, and material life not difficult. His visits to Edinburgh had been made singularly delightful to him. He was already appreciated there by the many who had personal acquaintance with him, and by a still larger public, before whom he had appeared as a conductor and as a lecturer. Concurrently with the proposal to stand for the Reid professorship came the certainty that obstacles to his marriage with 'The Friend' would be set aside. Under these circumstances the removal to a new home promised advantages which, perhaps, were easily exaggerated. Migration northward pointed a way of escape from difficulties which were recognised by his future wife as likely to prove very hard to grapple with in London. In Edinburgh she also had friends, so after brief reflection he decided to try his luck, and followed the counsels of his Edinburgh advisers in the steps he took to further his interests. So soon as it became known that Mr. Hullah was a candidate for the Reid professorship, more than one of the gentlemen who had intended to stand withdrew. One did more—he threw the entire weight of his own influence into the scale for Mr. Hullah's benefit. Indeed the amount of assistance proffered or given at the slightest request seemed to promise an election that should be remarkable chiefly for its unanimity.

In London, friends, brother-professors and pupils regarded a separation as inevitable, and expressed in flattering language regret at the prospect. There were moments when Mr. Hullah was half tempted to draw back, but for the reasons given he had set his mind, if not his heart, on going to Edinburgh.

Therefore, when he learnt that at the eleventh hour a candidate had appeared whose merits as a cultivated member of society had succeeded in deflecting the votes of some of the electors who were, by implication at least, pledged to himself, and that the casting vote of the rector—to the surprise of every one—turned the scale in Mr. Herbert Oakeley's favour, Mr. Hullah felt the disappointment a little disproportionately perhaps to the cause.

Some weeks passed before he quite recovered his usual calm and contented condition of mind ; but, as was the way with him, the trouble once got over, he put it from him as if it had never been, and when next he was invited to lecture and to conduct the concerts of the Philosophical Society in Edinburgh he accepted with cheerful courtesy, and was very glad to see the faithful among his friends again, steering his way skilfully amidst the excitement that continued for some time to agitate society in the northern capital. Passion and party feeling were violently stirred by the decision of the rector (Mr. W. E. Gladstone) and the elective body of the Reid professorship—the exceedingly caustic remarks of the 'Athenæum' adding fuel to fire at short intervals. The paper war raged high. Hard words were hurled in all directions. Pens fought fiercely and punctured deeply ; but winter frosts cooled angry feelings, and little by little the combatants recognised the excellent qualities of their new professor, and decided to let bygones be bygones, and to hold out the hand of welcome. Society endorsed that decision—so wise, since it was inevitable—and time has not shown cause for regret.

But, to return to the months immediately preceding the time when he was drawn into the whirl of this disappointing affair, Mr. Hullah went two or three times to Oxford, where she ' of the sticks and clay,' having been successful in getting ' Italia ' installed in the sculpture-room of the Royal Academy, had gone to dream of ' Gibson demolished ' amidst the cheerful surroundings at Lincoln College.

Here Mr. Hullah made the acquaintance of the late Mark Pattison. Mrs. Pattison (now Lady Dilke) he already knew. The rector came out in his kindly aspect, with the inevitable result—he made a deep and lasting impression on the keen intelligence and receptive mind of Mr. Hullah. As years went on he saw Mr. Pattison from time to time, and learned to look forward to a meeting with such pleasure that there were few engagements he would not have set aside for the sake of an evening with the rector, especially if Mr. Pattison happened to drop in at the dinner hour, and stayed just as he was, in walking coat and dusty boots. Dinner over, the rector would crook himself up in the biggest chair at hand, and talk—as so many will recollect he could talk—when the surroundings were favourable.

Mr. Hullah's happiness during these visits to Oxford was quite unmeasurable. There was the charm of the place itself, enhanced by an exceptionally brilliant summer, in full term time, when his own old friends were on the scene. There were forenoon *tête-à-tête* walks in the Magdalen or Christ Church grounds—Dante and notebook in one pocket, a sketch-book, pencil, and indiarubber in the other; the glorious hot sun glinting through the thickly foliaged trees; the warm soft air gently swaying the boughs. With elastic step, slight figure a trifle too small for the head—at that time still protected by a fluffy (real!) beaver hat—beneath the rather broad brim of which looked out a pair of shining eyes and a face so radiant with the inner light, that it was no wonder when a passing young man looked and smiled—or old man glanced back lingeringly—or women's eyes rested with responsive sympathy on that embodiment of content, moving gaily beneath the leafy aisles, wholly oblivious that three-and-fifty summers had passed over him. Well he might forget! for he scarcely seemed to have touched even his own ideal age—thirty-seven! During these forenoon expeditions a good deal of Dante—he had been working on and off at the prose translation of the 'Purgatorio'—got done somehow; but the pencil, if used at all, did not achieve much, for the pictorial treatment of trees was beyond him. He was only able to deal at his best with buildings, bits of carving, or groups of street lines. The morning lounge over, the friends strolled back to luncheon, at which meal some interesting if not always precisely genial guest dropped in. After luncheon came the long dreamy afternoon, spent in college gardens or on the river, till five-o'clock tea reunited the hosts and their guests, among whom on this occasion were a Madame de P—— and two most agreeable daughters, who scarcely shared their mother's stern disapprobation of the freedom allowed in England to young persons, whether about to marry or not. Outsiders, too, came and went within the pleasant house, and so glided away much too quickly this and subsequent flying visits.

As the plans for the coming winter included a Continental

tour, Mr. Hullah resolutely refused to let himself be decoyed to Italian cities, even by Mr. Butterfield, and settled himself down during the summer holidays, when he and 'The Friend' were left in charge of the Metropolis, to getting through the notes to his 'Song Book,' in preparing a lecture to be delivered at Norwich, and in doing a little translation of the 'Purgatorio.' A week or two went by smoothly, when one day it was necessary for 'The Friend' to announce to him that she was required to take her mother abroad. 'I call this a disgraceful breach of contract,' he writes. 'The novel experience of remaining in London in the dog-days is all very well so long as there is some one particular person to whom one can present personally all the luxuriant flowers of thought called into existence by this tropical heat, but if you go away, and don't take me with you, I shall Bohemianise.' . . . Accordingly, no sooner was he 'abandoned to his fate,' than he packed up and resumed the migratory habits proper for August and September. Now these migratory habits made the reception and despatch of the 'absolutely indispensable daily letter' a matter of consummate postmaster-generalship, and caused no small amusement among the various friends with whom he stayed. In some mysterious way he did contrive to keep up a steady communication till the traveller returned. Not long after the important event a day was agreed on for the marriage. Then and there it was decided that the customary festivities should be entirely waived.

In preparation for his new obligations Mr. Hullah did the little he could to set his house in order, and circumstances seemed to favour his efforts. His eldest daughter, about six-and-twenty years of age, was beginning, not unremuneratively, to be known as a skilful illustrator and painter of some promise. His eldest son, of one-and-twenty, was with a country doctor as assistant, and Mr. Hullah considered him as 'permanently provided for.' Concerning the next member of the family, who was two years younger, there were as yet no distinct views. The second son, a lad of sixteen, was to remain for at least a year in Germany, in preparation for mercantile life, for which there seemed reasonable hope of an opening among his mother's relatives.

The youngest boy, between eleven and twelve years of age, had yet, of course, to be educated.

The state of matters gave rational ground for the belief that in a few years a family for whom it had not been possible to lay by a competence would, as a matter of course, leave the parental home to seek a self-supporting career each in the way for which he or she had received preparation.

In December Mr. Hullah was married, by the rector of Lincoln College, Oxford, to Frances, only daughter of the late Hon. Lieut.-Col. G. F. Rosser.

The much-talked-of and longed-for journey to Rome was postponed *sine die* for prudential reasons, and they determined to content themselves with a few weeks in Paris. A small *appartement au troisieme* was taken in the Hôtel Cantorbéry, where, alas! Galimberti no longer presided to feast the guests with macaroni. Madame Erard's generosity contributing a piano, books and music being arranged, a very pleasant but far from idle holiday month began. All the forenoon Mr. Hullah worked at the overture to ' The Gondolier.' All the afternoons were spent in long rambles along the Quais d'Orsay and Voltaire, and the streets round and about the Sorbonne, in search of books not particularly needed, but pleasant to hunt up ; or, while daylight lasted, in dreamy lounges through the Italian galleries of the Louvre, where many an old friend (on canvas) was introduced by each to the other. Then, in the twilight, visits were paid. Dinner came in its course, and the evenings were spent with friends, or at some concert or theatre —this last amusement being Mr. Hullah's chief delight. The weather was often wet and always cold, but the sun shone brightly—when it shone at all—and there was almost always a blue sky far away over head. How different from the horrible fog and smoke that wrapped them round as they came home late on a January evening, 1866, to the ' City of Dreadful Night!' Not that Mr. Hullah was ever much affected by the horrors of the London atmosphere ; he was much too thoroughly well-seasoned a Cockney.

A few days after the home-coming Mr. Hullah was due in Edinburgh, and his wife accompanied him. The Philosophical Society's concert, which he had to conduct, went off brilliantly. There were plenty of people to see every day and all day long during the visit, all with hearty greeting for the old friend and a kind welcome for the new. It was a most gay and gladsome week.

In February and March the conduct of other concerts—of the Philharmonic Society—took Mr. Hullah again to Edinburgh, but he had to go alone, which he did not like nevertheless was able to send a capital first report of himself:

Such a day as I have had! My *bâton* was in my hand for more than three hours . . . . but this year nothing tires me, in comparison with other years. . . . Last year I remember sometimes coming back from rehearsal half dead, and flinging myself on to a bed full length, with a vague idea I should not be able to get up again till the day after to-morrow. Yesterday my inclination would have led me to walk up to Arthur's Seat. . . . The concert has been a great success, such 'entoosy-moosy.' . . . The M——s are charming. I have never been in a pleasanter house, and I have been in many pleasant houses. The doctor is a man of great accomplishments, fine taste, and much humour. . . . Tell Helps to arrive immediately I return. I rejoice you see so much of him.

It was easy to give the message, for that excellent friend had been most attentive in Mr. Hullah's absence, and willingly came the evening after his return to meet, as it happened, for the first time, Mr. and Mrs. Mark Pattison. Sir Arthur was greatly struck with the rector, with whom he had a long *causerie*. Outstaying other guests, as was his habit as long as he remained in health, he remarked : 'Mr. Pattison is the most learned man—Sir William Hamilton perhaps excepted—that I have ever met.'

A brief lull at Easter was followed by a severe London campaign, during the whole of which Mr. Hullah worked incessantly all day, and yet was ready for any number of parties half through the night. In August he insisted on carrying out a portion of the tour which had been talked of for the previous winter. On the way to the coast he 'called in' at Stanford Rectory, and made his wife acquainted with its inmates. Resuming the journey a fortnight later, they passed through Paris, and halted, to their sorrow, at Moret. There was but one inn, and that had but one decent guest-chamber, which was already in possession of three French gentlemen 'out a hunting' and their dogs; so, since there was no possibility of getting away from Moret till the next day, there was no escape from the garret '*à deux lits*' offered with becoming apologies by the *garçon* in charge. Such a garret! The window glass was broken away—there was a fracture in the ceiling above and a suspicious depression in the floor below. As for the furniture, the less said about it the better. Luckily the beds, though coarse, were clean. On the whole, since there was no alternative but the stable, there was cause for thankfulness, the attainable was accepted, and anything available ordered for dinner. A fine melon, pepper and salt, and brown bread first appeared; next came two *côtelettes au naturel* with the regulation six inches of bone to half an inch of meat, and, fortunately, a capital salad to eke out the course. An unexceptionable bottle of Beaune, comfortably clothed in an antique cobweb jacket, and reposing in a *crèche*, made this appear a sumptuous meal and set them up for an hour's hard sketching of a Roman gateway of which the townlet can boast. Darkness drove them indoors—to bed, as the only place there was to go to. The dry warm air made the absence of serviceable windows a matter of no moment, and they soon slept the sleep of the contented, and were only aroused in the early dawn by a gentle continuous sound of dripping water, which must have been going on for a considerable time, for the depression in the floor was a lakelet fed by a gentle cataract coming through the fracture in the ceiling over head! There was no time to be lost if luggage and garments were to be saved from the flood, and no time was lost. Never did two people make a toilette in so few minutes, or crush the *garçon* of an inn more mercilessly than did Mr. Hullah the poor jack-of-all-trades who was whistling gaily through his work below in no costume to speak of, but who showed what a good and forgiving Christian he was by a remarkably prompt administration of capital *café au lait*, followed by the most modest of bills. With unfeigned astonishment and gratitude he took the proffered *douceur* which accompanied the liquidation of it, and bade them farewell without malice as they trudged off to catch the early train for Sens. Here the accommodation, which included a ballroom, presented a ludicrous contrast to that afforded by the little inn at Moret.

There was plenty to see and to do in Sens. The cathedral within and without is most interesting. There are some other churches, a well-arranged hospital, presenting capital points architecturally and artistically, an *archevêché*, and much street architecture of the most picturesque kind, to the sketching of which Mr. Hullah devoted his time, while the rival pencil was contentedly occupying itself in some quiet airy part of the town with the minimum of architecture and the maximum of foliage, as being conveniently vague, with now and then ambitious additions of figures, the approximately successful delineation of these exciting great jealousy in the marital breast. The next journey took them to Auxerre, where they had a letter of introduction to Monsieur D——, the possessor of a large collection of miscellaneous treasures, including a good though small conchological collection, and some most interesting MSS., such as 'The Golden Legend' and an illuminated 'Histoire de France' which had belonged to Marguerite de Bourgogne. Among his odds and ends M. D—— had a cane which François Premier had flourished in his royal hand, and which M. D——, being a Republican, did, as is customary with Republicans in such cases, prize most inordinately. On turning over a portfolio of prints a portrait of Garrick came to view. This M. D—— drew forth, admiring greatly, but regretting that he knew not whose portrait it was, and was made a proud and happy man for the space of a day by being enabled to affix a descriptive label to the margin. In the midst of his heterogeneous treasures trove' M. D—— was spending the hot days *en garçon*, extremely happy and contented. Thanks to his kind courtesy a very agreeable day was spent at Auxerre before going on to Avalon, a quaint but singularly unclean little town, on the way to Vézelay. Here the glorious abbey church amply made up for the utter lack of creature comforts. At Sémur two most delightful days were spent in merely marking out positions for sketches, the only difficulty being [the impossibility of settling on the *most* desirable in a place where everything was desirable from a sketcher's point of view, be his powers great or small. A peep at the forest of Fontainebleau, a day or two in Paris, and the summer trip was over, and home reached late in September. For the next three months there was an unbroken round of work, enlivened now and again by society.

Among the letters awaiting his return Mr. Hullah had found one from Mr. Kingsley, enclosing the words of 'The Knight's Return.' These he set to music which admirably renders the weird, old-world picturesqueness of the poem. The song was sung by no less an artist than Mr. Santley at one of the concerts conducted by the composer in Edinburgh in December, and made a decided success.

CHAPTER XX.

BIOGRAPHICAL.

1866-67.

The events of the latter months of 1866 and the first half of the year 1867 present nothing of general interest. It was a period of deep anxiety, disappointment and grief, on the details of which it is as needless as it would be painful to enlarge. Suffice it to say, that for three or four years back the income had been unduly taxed, and the necessity for retrenchment was somewhat abruptly borne in on Mr. Hullah's mind by the discovery that his own and his wife's means combined were inadequate to a perpetually increasing scale of expenditure, and that, if financial ruin was to be averted, very considerable changes must at once take place in the habits of the family. A system of economy was planned under competent advice, and consistently carried through in course of time. It will be easily understood that this was not effected without the endurance of many small privations and the curtailment of many social pleasures, but the financial problem once worked out, for the rest of his life Mr. Hullah was untroubled by doubts as to whether the year's earnings would cover the year's expenditure, and he was able to meet his parental obligations, as they came upon him during several successive years, to the extent reasonably to be expected from a man whose life had been so chequered, and whose fortunes had been so adverse to the accumulation of wealth.

Looking and feeling ill and miserable, Mr. Hullah went immediately after Christmas to Stanford and thence to Sellinge, where one of the little musical performances familiar to that melodious village took place under his general guidance. Nothing less ambitious than the 'Messiah' had been chosen on this occasion, and so great was the zeal of the singers that many of them came through roads heavy with snow and slush to take a share in the performance.

A little later Mr. Hullah went again to Edinburgh to conduct the first of the Philharmonic concerts. As on former occasions, he enjoyed his visit greatly, and added largely to his stock of those excellent Scotch stories which form so amusing a characteristic of Edinburgh society. Several of these he was learning to tell in capital style with a close imitation of no less than *two* distinct ' accents '—a feat of which he was extremely proud.

On his return to London in March he had to apply himself with assiduity to the preparation of a set of lectures for delivery at the Society of Arts' rooms. The entire illustrative talent of the home establishment was laid under contribution for the drawings and diagrams required. For the further enrichment of the lectures ' some angel ' music that ' St. Dunstan heard them sing and noted down ' was promised by a friend, but it did not arrive in time, apparently by reason of postal disorganisation, caused, it may be, by objections on the part of celestial composers to have their inspirations submitted to the cold criticism of a sceptical age. Who shall say!

Postal irregularity once again, but traceable in this instance to quite mundane influence, nearly caused a case of books despatched to the International Exhibition in course of arrangement in Paris to arrive too late. The case contained a complete set of Mr. Hullah's educational works, which he had been requested to contribute. One of the English jurors writes him a pleasant report of their reception:

> One of the last [French jurors] was M. Rilié, President of the Orphéon, and you would have been interested to hear the really eloquent and earnest manner in which he brought under the attention of the jury the paramount importance of recognising vocal music as an essential province of popular instruction.
>
> Frequent mention was made of Wilhem, and when I briefly explained what you had done—at first well-nigh alone, now with a goodly band of collaborators—in the same good cause, I found no need of many words, for your name and services were as well known to my colleagues as to myself.
>
> Your books arrived just, and only just, in time. Twelve hours

later they would have been too late. I had a little case made for them, and found space[1] for it next to the series of our Reporter's reports.

So you and I together have redeemed the English Department of the Exhibition from what would have been a grievous lacuna. All our recommendations of recompense have gone up to the group jury for approval. The results will be known in a few days I suppose. . . . Don't suppose for one moment that your name needed introduction or advocacy. It is a household word in France as in England.

The result of the jurors' decision in the distribution of medals was the award of one to Mr. Hullah. And the next 'case,' containing a model of the Chevé system of musical notation, also received a medal! It is regrettable that the historical and educational value of the exhibits in question was not completed by a display of the tonic sol-fa notation, and it cannot be doubted that it would have won from so discriminating and impartial a jury yet another medal!

Schools and classes closed, lectures over, and holiday-time being come, Mr. Hullah left town, requiring rest very greatly. When, having arranged for the various members of the household, Mrs. Hullah was able to join him in Herefordshire, she found him amidst pleasant and interesting society, gathered together by chance in the houses in and about Staunton-on-Wye. At Bradwardine, in the loveliest of Rectory houses, were his old friends the late Mr. Samuel and Mrs. Clark, among whose guests was Mr. F. D. Maurice, looking fragile, but full of gentle pleasure at meeting with an old friend, and giving a kindly though scrutinising welcome to a newly presented acquaintance. Then from more distant parts of the country came two great travellers of apparently inexhaustible knowledge and most singularly brilliant conversational powers, making up a delightful society, all the more enjoyable that the weather was just what it should be in the month of August.

The 'lesser holiday' over, Mr. Hullah clamoured for a short spell of 'great holiday,' and as wilful man should sometimes have his way, it was agreed that as soon as the concert of the Metropolitan Choral Society was over (in September) he and his wife should depart to the sunny land of France, furnished with brand-new sketch-books and not much else. This they did, and the history of that delightful tour was afterwards written by Mr. Hullah, and appeared in 'Macmillan's Magazine' under the title of 'Ten Days in the Nivernais.' It sent a number of people on the same track, not all of whom found it quite equally delightful of course, for the excellent reason that journeys are, more often than is acknowledged, what travellers make them, and amusing events will not repeat themselves. For instance, the little incident Mr. Hullah relates in his magazine paper of the *cornemuse* player coming down from the mountains to perform for his edification and setting the entire *personnel* of the inn, even to the cook (who forgot his cutlets) and the Pomeranian dog, a-dancing, could certainly not be 'got up' again, or if got up at all would lack the freshness of an *impromptu* performance. These 'great holidays,' it will be perceived, were very short though very fruitful in enjoyment. This one did but last ten days. Three more were spent, on the way home, in the familiar town of Dijon, and four in Paris, during which a visit was paid to the Exhibition. On the return to the 'Louvre' hotel, an amusing instance of the readiness with which French hotel servants can at need defend the dignity of a guest occurred. The Hullahs had walked back in a downpour of rain, and arrived dripping and bedraggled to meet the English, Jewish, and American guests streaming down to dinner in toilettes more suitable to a royal drawing-room than the public dining-room of an hotel. The miserable appearance of the weather-worn excited the scorn and derision of the largest and most magnificently attired of a particularly gorgeous group of the daughters of Israel. When within a few feet of Mrs. Hullah she drew back her skirts, and, turning to a trim waiter, asked him in a high-pitched nasal voice :

'Who are those persons who traverse the staircase in such a state as never was?'

'De titel I do forget, madame,' smartly replied the little man with a reverential bow to the offenders. The suggestion conveyed was too much for the self-possession of the manifestation from the Jews' quarter of—no matter what town —who, flushed and crestfallen, collectively scuttled away, regardless of the sweep of their long and splendid train gowns.

For a few days after the return to England there was nothing very active to be done, and Mr. Hullah settled down to his desk, and the immediate results of his labours were the 'Ten Days in the Nivernais already mentioned, and 'A Colloquy in Grey Friars —also for 'Macmillan's Magazine.' The last paper was the outcome of one of those dreamy Sunday afternoons in his sanctum at the Charterhouse, where, seated before a roaring fire, he might peacefully evoke the spirits of his predecessors in the office of organist, and go back in imagination to the days of perukes, lace ruffles, and spinets. During these quiet hours also was completed a hymnal, compiled from Roundell Palmer's ' Book of Praise.' The usual amount of ephemeral work—arranging and harmonising—brought to a close a year distinctive in many ways from those that had gone before.

CHAPTER XXI.

BIOGRAPHICAL.

1868.

MIDWINTER of 1868 was mostly taken up, in addition to the usual round of work, with the preparation of examination papers, some articles for the 'Dictionary of Christian Antiquities,' and rehearsals for the Metropolitan Schools Choral Society. These occupations filled up the active portion of each day, but in pursuance of a revised scheme of life, drawn up in the previous year, 'Evenings at Home' were the rule rather than the exception; and Mr. Hullah took very kindly to them, enjoying, indeed, a cessation from his nomadic life in London, as giving him leisure for more systematic reading than had perhaps been possible to him at any other period of his life. Still, though always perfectly happy in the family circle, small social gatherings in his own or other peoples' houses never lost their attraction for him. More especially, perhaps, did he delight in the little unpretending dinners of six or eight at home, at which, among other very intimate friends, Mr. Deutsch—'that dear delightful creature,' as George Eliot calls him—was a frequent and ever-welcome guest. Sometimes he came straight from George Eliot's house while still under the influence of his last *tête-à-tête* talk with her, full of admiration, amounting to enthusiasm, for her genius, and overflowing with gratitude for the comprehensive sympathy of her friendship for himself, ' a lonely exile!' Never, in truth, was lonely exile more welcomed to the hearts and hearths of his adopted countryman (the word ' man ' shall here be taken to include ' woman '), but then, never before or since has exile been as eloquent, in English so brilliant, so picturesque as to be a revelation of the capabilities of the language.

But though Mr. Hullah dearly loved a cosy dinner 'where the mutton was hot and the wine was cool,' and the friends charming and all things as they should be, set luncheon-parties he regarded with a sort of horror, as a something little less than a crime against the working hours. Consequently the inducement had to be strong that took him out to a meal at 2 P.M. Such an inducement, however, came to him this season in the shape of an invitation from Lady Bloomfield, aged ninety, an age at which people may be excused for not receiving late in the day. She had long wished, she had said, to make his acquaintance, and the introduction was to be made by the friend who brought the invitation. Under these circumstances he accepted and went. A tiny figure lost in the depths of an armchair essayed to rise as he and his wife entered the sanctum of the *ci-devant* ambassadress, and the small deeply-lined face, encircled by a closely-fitting cap, lighted up, while in bright brisk tones she welcomed him, drew him into a chair by her side, and was soon in active conversation about his past musical work in the country, in which she showed a most intelligent and enlightened interest. Then, some chance observation having led her to allude to France in the early part of the last century, she delighted Mr. Hullah by recounting many personal reminiscences of the period of the French Revolution, and of some few years prior to it, as forming topics of everyday conversation in her immediate family circles. While talking to Lady Bloomfield Mr. Hullah was able to link himself, as it were, through four or five generations with several persons of note in literature, diplomacy, art, or science, who had lived in the latter half of the last century—a sort of historical chain-making in the manufacture of which he showed great ingenuity, and which always seemed to give him lively pleasure. A long and interesting visit was terminated by a cordial invitation from the aged hostess to 'return again very soon and she would revive her recollections of the Russian Court for Mr. Hullah's benefit.' But soon after this visit she was taken ill, and Mr. Hullah writes to his wife :

Now mind you go to Lady B—— if she rallies, and see her again, as she asked you to do.... It will be something in the next century for you to say that you have talked with a person who was a woman before the French Revolution!

It has been observed that Mr. Hullah accepted a quieter life not only with cheerfulness, but with a due appreciation of its advantages. So far the 'revised scheme of life' was all very well, but to one clause he never could get cordially reconciled, the clause that both heads of the house should not frequently be absent at one time. For both it was an equal deprivation, though he chafed the more openly, and raised a storm in a teacup on every occasion calling for reference to that 'most obnoxious rule.' Every now and then, however, the pleasure of an excursion à deux was made possible by the kindness of Mrs. Rosser, whose affection for her son-in-law, fully responded to by him, increased with the years of their acquaintance. 'The conquest of my mother-in-law's heart is the tallest and proudest plume in my cap,' he used to say. Occasionally she would come and assume the command of the establishment, son-in-law and babies included, and enable her daughter to get a few days' change from the climate of London. The first idea, whenever the chance occurred, was to rush down to Oxford as fast as possible, generally as a guest at Lincoln College, Mr. Hullah going down for a day or two when he could. 'Now mind I get my daily tract,' he would say as the train moved off, and to content him it was necessary to despatch at least once a day a minute and circumstantial report of everything heard, seen, or thought, he on his side scarcely missing a post, lest the continuity of the story should be broken.

June 25.—Just got home from my round [of colleges] (with dashes into Longman's and Clay's) only in time to send a line or two before post time. I got yours last night before I went to the M——'s party... I met the Blunts, he, whom I did not know, and she, an old friend. They are charming, and kindly wishful to know us ... I was telling Doyle about poor Nicholson [a flute-player], when Captain Ottley, who was near us at supper, instantly offered me 5*l*. for him. It was very kindly done, for he does not know Nicholson. ... I look forward to a quiet evening with pleasure, and to to-morrow at Oxford with delight.

And he went, and enjoyed himself as usual, attending service in Magdalen Chapel and getting a long ramble in the afternoon in the warm humid air of the water walks, working out, as he sauntered alone with his thoughts, the anthem, 'Joy cometh in the morning.' The next day he returned to London to keep engagements, to attend an important meeting at which the reconstruction of the constitution of Queen's College was to be considered, and to dine at King's College (probably a dinner given in honour of Dr. Jelf, who left about that time). Of his day's work he reports:

> I hope I was of some use at the meeting [at Queen's College]. Three and a half hours in a stuffy room instead of a pleasant evening, open air and light, with you, the Rector and Rectoress. Oh! . . . Last night the King's College dinner came off. It was very gorgeous, real turtle and all that sort of thing. . . I sat next to Cock and other pleasant people. The speeches were poor, notwithstanding they came from the mouths of great guns. Mr. Gladstone talked away for half an hour . . . fencing himself against giving offence in such a mixed assembly in such a transitional time. As I was coming out of the place where hats were deposited on entering, I came right up against him. I was turning away when he . . . took my hand . . . and expressed his regret at not having seen me so long. I suppose I looked a little odd, for he said, 'You have not forgotten me?—my name is Gladstone.' I am not likely to forget him in a hurry! It would be curious to know what was going on in his mind during those few moments. . . I find this room oppressive at this time of day [he was writing from the British Museum]. I saw Deutsch before coming into the Reading Room. He looks very worked and seedy, but was very amusing. He sent his message of 'profound consideration to you.' I wish I was at Oxford.

Shortly he was able to run down again and stay three days.

In the autumn of the year quite a novel experience awaited him, for he had accepted an invitation to be umpire at an Eisteddfod, an account of which he subsequently published in 'Good Words.' For weeks before he started he was much exercised to get up the Welsh pronunciation, to which end he paid constant visits to an opposite neighbour, Mrs. Gwyn Jeffreys, who took the most lively interest in his progress, and was indefatigable in practising him in uttering impossible-looking combinations of consonants, which, however, when sounded, came out with all the liquid richness of vowels.

Extremely proud he was at finally compassing the correct pronunciation—accent even—of several dozen Welsh words Armed with the new knowledge, he went off alone, but in capital spirits, and became immediately interested in the whole performance, returning with a high opinion of the musical genius and vocal powers of the Welsh people, which made performances, otherwise commonplace, impressive—at least at the moment. The external surroundings were sometimes peculiar and material comforts not always assured; but the weather was perfect, so Italian, indeed, in its warmth and dryness that, as he sat down to his desk he forgot where he was, and involuntarily wrote :

Leone Bianco, Ruthin. . . . As there is no knowing to what an extent Talhairn may hold forth or when we may get back, I begin a letter at once before starting—*i.e.* at 10.30 A.M. I trust you duly received my pencil note posted at Ruabon; whether you have succeeded in reading it is another matter. The railroad was horribly jerky and the circumstances not favourable to penmanship. We got here about six. I found a very fair and quiet room ready for me, from the windows of which I see mountains which run in all directions round the little town, itself built on a considerable eminence. We found everything in a state of frantic excitement, and altogether *behindhand*—carpenters hammering and sawing and people putting up flags and wreaths and decorations of all kinds. The landlady here was, I am told (for she is too busy, hot, and I fear *worried* to be talked to), a member of my classes at St. Martin's Hall! [That should have excited no surprise ; go where he might, people looking twice his age said they had been in his classes when young.] To this I suppose I am to attribute my comfortable room, with even a bath ! Mr. Thomas and two ladies (one a Miss Watts, who is to sing) were relegated to a large house the landlord has taken temporarily, which is large and airy but almost unfurnished. The only drawback here is the noise at night. Last night it was considerable.

3 P.M.—Just back from my first innings. Altogether it was very amusing. But these dear ancient Britons have queer notions of management. However, everybody is good-humoured, and seems very glad to see me. Mr. Cornwallis West, of the Castle here, has invited me to supper after the concért, which begins at six and finishes before nine. *We* dine at *four.* . . I have made five speeches, each longer than the one before it. . . By this morning's post has come an invitation to lecture at Welshpool, not yet, but later in the year. I shall go, for I think I could make something of those Cymry—your ancestors. By-the-bye, I find that Ross means Russ—*i.e.* Northern. I am coming home to-morrow.

Unfortunately, much that was tiresome awaited him on his return, and, as he had a good deal of writing on hand, it was deemed advisable he should go away to a quieter life. Stanford gates immediately opened wide for him, and, accompanied by a gigantic writing-box, his almost inseparable companion, he started off again. Much at the same moment the babies were carried away by their grandmother to Hythe, which, being quite near to Stanford, gave Mr. Hullah a capital excuse for continual excursions thither, and a chance of sea bathing, always an excellent tonic for him, and highly conducive to good work.

His MSS. posted to their various destinations, he writes:

I have done all, and . . . I shall follow this epistle very closely in person. You must forgive me for not telling you about 'Good Words.' I did not like to risk *your* being disappointed in the matter, which might easily have happened, seeing that I do not know any of the people connected with the work. But you shall scold if you can. I have been working a good deal. I send off by to-day's post, to Grove, the article 'Accentus,' which I have greatly extended and all but rewritten. . . .

A few days after his return Mr. Hullah notes in his Diary, as most interesting, a visit paid, under Mr. Constantine's guidance, to some Jewish schools of a very poor class. He was much struck by the intelligence of the children in all the subjects they studied; the bright, rapid way in which they took in the meaning of a question, and answered at once and to the point, being especially remarkable. After listening long and attentively to the singing classes, he observed that it was a new experience to him to hear, in children averaging twelve years, such an *even* quality of voice. He was also much struck by a peculiar softness and sad monotony in the voices of the children as they recited their lessons, like that of the Eastern chant, not heard in the voices of purely European races.

Some years later, when he was in Berlin, Mr. Hullah took occasion to verify the correctness of this impression by several visits to the important schools of the Jewish community of that city, and found it quite confirmed.

In October a summons from an old relative called Mrs.

Hullah out of town, and the home pictures went out daily by post.

> This morning I have been busy on my 'Dictionary [of Christian Antiquities]' articles; in separating my Museum extracts and generally touching them up. . . . I have seen Mr. Blomfield to-day, who showed me the last plans of Charterhouse 'in the fields.' The governors have turned the whole mass of building round, so that everything looks the wrong way: e.g. Dr. H—— B——'s house (dining-room included) to the *west*! Imagine the sloping rays of the sun at dinner time! . . .

The next letter contained an announcement that his second son had passed the final examination for the Indian Civil Service, and soon afterwards Mr. Hullah had the great relief and satisfaction of seeing him well launched in life. Before he could write again his correspondent had gone to Oxford and had probably given, in no unkindly spirit, a sketch of the rector of Lincoln in one of his severer moods, and the effect thereof on some unhappy undergraduates bidden to the breakfast-table. On this Mr. Hullah comments:

> I pity the poor shy undergraduate (I thought the race was extinct, and that the modern U.G. came up knowing, having seen, done, and used up every earthly thing) who tries to eat in the presence of the rector. It is said to take an actor half a lifetime before he can learn to *eat* in the presence of an audience. Each morsel must stick in the gullet of the U.G. when the rector's severe eye is upon him. Why does a man who possesses such limitless power of giving pleasure without the smallest trouble make himself now and then so disagreeable? . . . Come home in time to go to the concert at St. James's Hall on Monday. I should like to go.

It was at this concert that he resumed his acquaintance with the Greek schoolfellows of whom he speaks in the story of his early days. He had crossed the hall to exchange a word with that one of the three whom he often saw, Mr. Ionides, seated this evening between two strangers. As Mr. Hullah approached, both these gentlemen rose and simultaneously greeted him with all the warmth of old friendship.

For a moment he was at fault. The men who grasped his hands were portly in one case and hirsute in both, and it took him some seconds to identify them, even with Mr. Ionides' assistance, with the slender Greek youths of long ago. No sooner was the recognition established, however, than all four fell into that easy flow of reminiscences only possible to those who have been friends in early youth. Several meetings followed this accidental *rencontre* during the time these gentlemen remained in England, two or three of the dinner-parties, when the Hullahs were the only guests not of Greek nationality, being especially entertaining. At moments the conversation was insensibly carried on by the hosts and their guests in their own tongue. With his scant knowledge of the language, Mr. Hullah was of course unable to follow the meaning of what was said, but he fully enjoyed the melodious resonance of the sounds and the rhetorical swing of the phrases, especially as they fell from the lips of the particular guest whose splendid personal beauty and supple grace of movement perpetually recalled the Apollo of the Belvedere. While his ear was still under the spell of what he had heard, Mr. Hullah went to the Westminster play—' Phormio ' for this year—and had an opportunity of ripening his conviction as to the desirability of adopting in our public schools for the Latin and Greek tongues the vowel pronunciation of Italy as likely to be at any rate infinitely nearer the original than is our pronunciation. He was fond of citing an instance which had fallen within his own observation of the practical inconvenience arising to two persons equally acquainted with Latin, but pronouncing as differently as do an Englishman and an Italian. In the sacristy of a Carmelite monastery in Italy he once met an English friend possessing no knowledge of living—other than his own—though well versed in the chief dead languages, and who at the moment was engaged in an earnest effort to make himself understood by the attendant monk through the medium of Latin ; failing utterly, however, until he had *written* his question, when at once the answer was given in Latin as fluent as his own, but to him quite incomprehensible till it was committed to paper.

CHAPTER XXII.

BIOGRAPHICAL.

1868–69.

The Christmas week of 1868–69 was spent in Scotland, for very early in January Mr. Hullah had a lecture to deliver at Glasgow and concerts to conduct at Dumfries; but the intervals between the concerts, it was contrived for him, should be spent in right good holiday fashion in Edinburgh. Thence he writes:

Sunday.—I have your letter, which accordingly will spend the day in my heart coat-pocket instead of in the post. . . . I am so enjoying the quiet and solitude this morning; everybody else is gone off to church . . .

Monday.—This being of necessity a *no*-letter day, I feel myself rather—I might say altogether—uninspired, and 'I take up my pen' (as a schoolboy would say) without any very distinct idea of what I shall do with it. . . .

I called on a great number of people yesterday, and then went and sat for nearly an hour with Dr. Christison, whom I was glad to find much better. He talked of dining with the Royal Society to-night, and would not bid me good-bye. Late in the evening I took a walk with Dr. Maclagan. . . . It was a most beautiful night, with the least possible tendency to *aurora borealis*. H—— leaves to-day and I follow to-morrow. He was horribly in the doldrums about 'popery.' The young Marquis of B——, who is related to him in some way (everybody is related to everybody in Scotland), has just 'gone over.' I should think, if anything in the world were more likely than another to give the last *chiquenaude* to anybody that way inclined, it would be the having to attend the service of the Church of Scotland. . . .

On his way home Mr. Hullah paid the long-talked-of visit to Dr. Carlyle, and received a hearty welcome from the doctor, suffering though he was, and therefore not very well able to enjoy visitors. They had a good deal of talk over the translation of the ' Purgatorio ' and Dr. Carlyle still entertained some hope of continuing his work so brilliantly begun. Mr. Hullah therefore rather put his own attempts aside, in spite of very great encouragement from Dr. Carlyle, who had seen some small portions of what was already roughly done.

Among the letters he found awaiting him at home was an announcement from the Royal Academy of Music that he had been elected a member of the committee of management. There was likewise a considerable correspondence—presently increased by Mr. Hullah's own contributions—on the question of musical pitch, a subject which seems to have greatly exercised the musical mind, wit, and temper at this time, and to have given constant occupation to the pens of musical authorities. Dr. Pole's learned dissertations arrived not infrequently, and the late Mr. William Callcott spent sundry half-hours in inditing, in a delightfully clear hand, quaint little observations set down with the utmost precision in the very middle of a sheet of paper,

' I mean to fight,' he says. Whereupon an amusing vision arises of that gentle knight of music, so like Don Quixote in figure, seizing with nervous, delicate fingers a tuning-fork and *bâton* and setting forth on war intent.

I mean to *fight* under your banner in the coming *pitched* battle, and I shall adopt for my crest and motto

512 FOR EVER.

I have a letter of Dr. Crotch's, in which he says to me, Don't soil your fingers with pitch, a dirt very hard to get out, though excellent as a covering to Noah's Ark and to the foreground of Wilson's paintings.' I hope, in spite of this, you will write something about it.

Besides the question of musical pitch, Mr. Hullah had been for some time giving attention to the causes which prevent English men and women from speaking in such a voice, or a register of the voice as he would have said, as to be audible at any reasonable distance under reasonable conditions.

Few things ruffled his temper in daily life, but one of these few things certainly was the difficulty of at once catching what some people said, owing to careless and inaccurate production of the voice. The first outcome of his reflections was an article in 'Good Words' on the 'Speaking Voice,' followed later on by a little volume published by the Clarendon Press, entitled 'The Cultivation of the Speaking Voice,' which is said by many who have studied it to be a most valuable little book.

The article on the 'Speaking Voice' despatched to Mr. Strahan, the Hullahs secured a few days at C—— A—— in Easter week. The sun shone brightly overhead and the rooks cawed in a distant part of the old-fashioned garden into which looked Mr. Hullah's room, a quaint wainscoted room, in which Chaucer had slept during a sojourn in C—— A——, hung with moreen curtains of vivid red, and having on one side a vast chimney-place which sucked up far the greater part of the heat yielded by the largest of wood fires. Here, having duly stoked up a fire which filled the entire basket grate, he would sit with the winter sun on his back, and spend the long undisturbed forenoon hours. During the visit in question he wrote four motets for female voices, read two or three volumes of French memoirs, and sundry pamphlets on 'Carillons' and 'Carillonneurs.' This latter course of study led him, on his return to town, to a further and more practical investigation into the subject of church bells within the steeple of St. Giles's, Cripplegate, where, in the company of the bell-ringers, he betook himself one evening, coming home with a most unwonted odour of beer and tobacco about his clothing, which, to his disgust, it took days of sun-sweetening to get rid of. He could not endure the smell of tobacco about his person, and for that reason did not smoke at all himself, nor was he able to enjoy the society of an habitual smoker, however brilliant a talker the smoker might be.

So accustomed had Mr. Hullah become to a comparatively retired life, that it was not without an effort that he brought himself to accept Mr. Marwood Tucker's proposal, made at this time, that he should join the staff of the 'Globe' newspaper in its musical interest. His connection with this paper extended over several years, during which he contributed an immense number of articles, usually under the heading 'Causeries Musicales.' Among the occasional papers may be found some excellent criticisms as well on books of general interest as on music. Once launched, his former keen interest in musical performances and his love for society of an evening revived fully, and he greatly enjoyed the frequent concerts and operas to which he had to listen in the pursuit of his duties, though occasionally much averse to putting aside a pleasant dinner-party in favour even of music. The extent of the change in his habits can best be measured by the fact that his Diary shows him to have been at home but five evenings during the months of June and July. When, therefore, the holidays came, they did not come too soon for his health s sake.

The children were again appropriated by their grandmother, and Mr. Hullah saved from the dreaded necessity of taking his holiday alone. One or two visits were first paid, followed by a modest tour in France, to which the Chancellor of the Domestic Exchequer had consented, since on the way through Paris *both* holiday-makers were to do a little work not altogether gratis. So to Paris they presently went, accomplished their respective tasks, and sped away in high spirits to join some friends who had taken a house at Fontainebleau, where they were leading a country life from a Parisian point of view. The house, the tiniest in which grown-up people surely ever thought of living, was entered by a low door which opened direct into the *salon* from a grove of tall lime-trees. A dining-room, with exactly the necessary space for four chairs round a table, led out of this. Across a passage about eighteen inches wide was a kitchen—that is to say, there was a space whereon a table stood, and a few inches of unoccupied floor about it on which the one maid circulated sideways. There was also a niche in which a cooking apparatus was fixed, with all needful appliances suspended round and about it. There being no room whatever for a chair, a settle, a washtub, and the indispensable etceteras of a kitchen, these articles had a place assigned them on the footpath outside, and were screened from sight of the entrance by a laurel bush. An English servant would have thrown up her place and gone off to 'better herself' right promptly, but this maid, clever Gallic soul that she was (or rather is, for she still lives and does zealous service), enjoyed the opportunity of showing off her talents, and cooked appetising, imaginative little dinners, and served them, and ate up the remains, and did her work outside or in, as convenience suggested, with a blithe goodwill that was charming. No sooner were the guests arrived, than the mistress of the mansion had but to turn her head kitchenwards and say, in a semi-tone louder than her usual soft tone, '*Mangeons*,' when the ringing '*Bien, madame*,' was followed by '*Madame est servie*,' and the party sat down to good cheer and fun, got out of every passing incident, of which Constance, the maid-of-all-work (but yet not the less a *cordon-bleu*), provided her full share by her numerous and curious devices for making 'her people' comfortable. Like all good servants, Constance was observant of the individual fancies of her employers' intimate friends, and enjoyed giving them exactly what they liked. Now she had observed that Mr. Hullah ate bread like a Frenchman, and not being able to get at him during dinner comfortably in the tiny room, she had placed by his side an enormous provision of *pain de menage*.

'Constance, you have forgotten the loaf,' observed her mistress, pointing to Mr. Hullah's place.

'*Mais non, madame ; c'est que monsieur en aura besoin*,' she calmly answered, disappearing to the kitchen.

The sort of life led at Fontainebleau was so simple, easy, and complete a change for Mr Hullah, that he soon picked up his strength and spirits again, and was ready in a week for the projected tour which took the travellers to Gien, Blois, Chambord, Amboise, Chenonceaux, Poitiers, Saumur, Fontevrault, Angers, Nantes, and Le Mans. A few days in Paris completed a trip which gave materials for an article written some time afterwards. On the way home it was, of course, indispensable that the friends at Stanford should be made acquainted with all that had happened, and so partake, by force of sympathy, with all that Mr. Hullah had found pleasant in his journey—which was much. Passing through London, he had but time to regain possession of his gigantic writing-box, judiciously, though unwillingly, left at home during the Continental journeys, in order to arrive at Worcester in time for the Festival. There was a family tradition that he could not possibly leave London unaided, so now, as always, he was escorted to the station and seen comfortably off surrounded by his accustomed impedimenta—looking so extremely dejected because he had to go alone, that a kind old lady, who had witnessed the leave-taking, was inspired with a benevolent desire to comfort him by pleasant talk on the way. So soon as he can get out his writing materials he reports:

I have had no end of adventures since we parted yesterday. You remember a stately elderly lady in the carriage in which I had taken a seat. I got into talk with her, and found her very nice, and found she had been all over *our* French ground last year. When I reached Worcester Station, the first person I stumbled on was a very short, very round, very—well, *very* rosy—lady, who burst into regrets *they* could not take me into their house, which was full, but hoped I would come to *breakfast!* luncheon!! dinner, supper, tea; and booked me to go and dine forthwith. She turned out to be a Mrs W——. . . . I tried the 'Star,' where stood at the door Sullivan, on the look-out for Grove and a party of Scott-Russells and Von Glehns. The 'Star' people sent me off to this lodging, which is very nice, clean and *quiet*. I have had charming little rooms, and nice young ladies to wait on me! On arrival at Mr. —— s, Mrs —— met me with the news that the 'stately elderly lady' was their guest. I can't remember her name. She remembered seeing *you* at Biaggi's lecture, and 'had hoped till we started that you were going to get into the carriage.' . . . After dinner I went down to the College Hall, where they were rehearsing, and thence with Blagrove to Mr. Jones'. This morning I went to the early choral service at half-past eight, and now I must be off to the cathedral. Love to the wee things.

Wednesday, Sept. 8.—The life here is very *fast*, though certainly not in the slang sense. I am obliged to arrange my day on a system, which I began to put in practice this morning. I get up at seven [he must have felt sadly pressed for time to do that; early rising was not his strong point], breakfast at half-past, wrote my 'Globe' letter from eight till eleven, and then set off for the cathedral; there I was till four. It is now five, and I have done up the 'Globe' letter, and have yet to dress and get—I hardly know when—to

Canon C——'s to dinner before six. The concert begins at eight So all I can say is that I am very well and that every one is very kind. Loads of people I know are here, among them Dr. Monk, of York, whom you know I like very much. Deacon turned up this afternoon and sat with us during the performance, which was very interesting. My first 'Globe' letter will appear to-morrow. After that every day there will be one. . . .

Saturday, Sept. 11.—I am just off to the dear Phillotts. Things have been very amusing here. Last night was spent in the house of Mr. and Mrs. ——. He is a man of great knowledge on his own subject, archæology, and is very modest about it. . . . All, or at least much of the furniture in their house is of his designing, a habit which, I fancy, archæological pursuits must develop, I cannot say I think always very successfully either as to form or colour. . . . Husband and wife have a curious practice of collecting and writing down any good stories they hear, and some are very good stories indeed, well worth preserving. . . . If enjoyment be measurable by laughter I must have enjoyed myself greatly, but I am very tired and long to be with the Phillotts. . . .

Staunton-on-Wye at last! but . . . the wretched railway people had sent my darling box (I know you'll hope it's lost, but it isn't) off to the Barr's Court Station, while they carried *me* to the Hereford and Brecon, so . . . I took a fly . . *fetched* the erratic box and started at once for Staunton'. . . got in . . . and found everything, even to a *fire*. . . . I had a very pleasant morning at the cathedral library yesterday. Mr. Baxter, the librarian, exhibited as many treasures as there was time to look at; you should have been with me. . . . This morning, having still one more 'Globe' letter to write, I got up at six and had it done before breakfast. . . . I am so glad you like my article on Sullivan; get some copies and send them to the people concerned. I should like the Worcester people, whose arrangements and mode of carrying them out I have extolled (with all my heart) in the last article, to see it. . . . So far from reading in bed I don't even seem to *look* at a book— till the next time. . . .

When he came home he was refreshed and strong after the week's rest at Staunton, and quite equal to his work for the winter. A little dinner-party, such as he loved, had been arranged for his welcome home. Among the friends who came were Mrs. Procter, Mr. Marwood Tucker and Sir Arthur Helps, whom he had not met for some months, and with whom he consequently especially enjoyed a long talk. Time and hard work were telling on Sir Arthur's not very robust constitution, but still he was in good conversational form that evening, and responded gaily to Mrs. Procter's brilliant lead.

So soon as Mr. Hullah was settled in his study again the accumulated correspondence of many weeks claimed attention. An odd collection it was!

There were letters from America about 'Manuals;' large sheets, small sheets (of music); whether two hours a day, or more or less, would suffice for vocal practice; whether it was beneficial or harmful for a class to consist of ten, or twenty, or a hundred; what should be the dimensions of a concert-room; what the position of an organ. From young people all over the country came requests for an opinion on the state of the musical profession, with special reference to their own chances as members of it; they having, according to the highest local authority (whose testimonials were invariably enclosed with a request that they might be returned without delay), voices of quite unusual compass, sweetness, pathos, and power—Marios and Grisis by the dozen. Occasionally the Tonic Sol-faists were unwittingly the cause of his being greatly troubled with letters. They were engaged in their propaganda so actively that it happened now and then that they claimed, or it was thought they claimed, individuals or schools or districts that did not desire to be 'sealed unto the faithful' of that denomination. Forthwith the individual or representative of the school or the district would write to Mr. Hullah and entreat him to arise and fight for fair and honest teaching on the lines and with the symbolism recognised by the past masters of the musical art. But Mr. Hullah was much too thoroughly absorbed in his own work to feel disposed to fritter away time and temper in light skirmishing. When the right time came, as it did subsequently, Mr. Hullah made a forcible protest against the use of quack notations in the elementary schools of the country.

CHAPTER XXIII.

BIOGRAPHICAL.

1870.

In January the Committee of the Royal Academy of Music invited Mr. Hullah to accept the post of conductor to the orchestral and choral concerts of the Institution. On learning his wishes in regard to this offer, his wife not unnaturally inquired whether henceforth the working day was warranted to extend itself to eight-and-forty hours. 'Oh! never mind,' he airily responded, '*do* be glad, for *I'm* delighted, and let us arrange—everything can be arranged, you know.' Like Napoleon, he refused to include the word 'impossible' in his vocabulary if he *wished* to do a thing; so, somehow, the kaleidoscopic engagements did get shaken into closer order, and on January 28 the hours for the Royal Academy concerts were settled.

Before this additional work it was deemed advisable he should be braced up by country air. Accordingly he departed to Pluckley, of which the present Dean of Wells was then rector; thence he passed on to Stanford, returning home with a great batch of corrected proofs for the 'Singers' Library' and two capital little articles on 'Organ Music' for 'Fraser's Magazine,' the result of work done in those mornings he kept 'inviolate' for serious pursuits. Freshened up in body and in mind, he entered on his conductorial duties. The zeal and enthusiasm of former days seemed to possess him when once his *bâton* was in his hand, a full score on his desk, and his band of attentive, eager students before him, responsive as so many instruments to his touch. While he conducted he was unconscious of fatigue, nor required other stimulus than he received each moment in the keen, quick intelligent glances which met his own as the music progressed. He lived in his art and was happy.

In the midst of all his teaching the 'Dictionary of Bible Antiquities' suddenly sprang once more into great activity, the contributors being called upon at very short notice to finish off old material. Mr. Hullah had long been waiting for 'revises,' which arrived just at the most busy moment, but had nevertheless to be dealt with expeditiously. Then, as the press of engagements grew closer and closer, came a copy of 'Casimir Maremma' and a note from Sir Arthur:

> You deserve not only that your friend Arthur Helps should send you his productions, but that all authors should, for you are a model reader of a book—that is, of course, of a book you take to. No skipping or scamping of any kind! You decline your nouns orderly, as Charles Lamb's grammarian said.

Before there was time to cut the pages of the new book Mr. Macmillan asked Mr. Hullah to write a review. 'By all means,' he replied, but how was he to get time to read the book? How, after it was read, was he to find time to *write* a review?

Impossible it seemed; but, by dint of increased compression of the engagements in hand, by reading in hansoms, and making notes as he took his indispensable walk home before dinner, and by sitting up late of nights, the required review was written, and approved by the author of 'Casimir Maremma.' The Diary tells of only four evenings passed at home between January and April. No wonder then that his excellent health showed some signs of failing. He became himself aware that something was amiss with him that was aggravated by too prolonged deprivation of exercise and fresh air.

With some difficulty he consented to take medical advice and to allow himself to be examined. Valid reasons were found for placing him under immediate treatment for the removal of an internal obstruction, the existence of which he had never suspected. Easter presented a convenient opportunity for the slight but necessary operation, which was quickly and successfully performed, but for a time Mr. Hullah was confined to his room, much to his own disgust. During the period of convalescence he distinguished himself as the most utterly unruly patient that ever fell to the lot of a guardian angel.

So unaccustomed was he to illness, that the first drive out was deemed worthy of entry in his Diary. At the earliest moment possible after this he broke away from the trammels of the invalid condition, sent off the doctor's fee, and vigorously returned to his six colleges, the Academy of Music, his desk, and his parties at home and abroad till the autumn, when, as musical critic, he had to attend the Hereford Festival, but as he did not go alone his letters are few. One day, however, it happened that Mrs. Hullah, having gone to Charlton Kings, did not return in time to hear 'The Storm' sung by Madame Patey, so Mr. Hullah tells her all about it as an item of the 'daily news.'

After all *I* am to accompany Madame Patey in 'The Storm' to-night. The band did not go with her one bit, and there is no possibility of another rehearsal. She sang it with me this morning very finely.

He had been induced to contribute a trifle to the popular excitement about the Franco-German War, which was furiously raging at that time, by writing the music to some words persistently pressed on his notice by a clever but not successful verse-writer. Sensational writing, whether of words or music, was not much to his taste, and he had but a poor opinion of his own music to the 'Message from the War, even when sung by Madame Patey. However, it was considered a 'telling' song.

It seems she has taken immensely to the 'Message from the War (continues Mr. Hullah). Proofs of it have come to-day, and I have just finished looking them over. . . . Now I am going with Mr. Wren Hoskyns to luncheon at the Bishop's.

And a final line is added on his return:

It has been very pleasant. I wish you had come back, for there was much talk about the war. I do pity the poor dear French. I shall join you to-morrow.

Together they went to Staunton-on-Wye; and soon afterwards, accompanied by Mr. Phillott, they joined the Archæological Association in exoursions, altogether delightful, to Kenchester, Weobly, and Llantony Abbey, not as yet colonised by Father Ignatius. A few of the remaining spare days were spent at Great Malvern, where he imbibed as much as possible of his native air and made acquaintance with various people staying at the hotel. Among these was a Mr. T——, a civil engineer, who, in spite of being a hopeless invalid, was planning and carrying out works all over the country, which his wife from time to time inspected and reported upon with a minuteness and precision which enabled him to judge accurately of the progress of the undertaking, whatever it happened to be. When Mr. T—— himself mentioned this fact, the conversation turned on women's work generally, and on the difficulties they especially experience in life from lack of systematic training, such as boys are put through as a mere matter of course. Mr. Hullah maintained, as the result of his own observation, that with equal advantages women would do most things quite as well as men. This view Mr. T—— combated, denying to women at the same time the right to equal educational advantages with men, on the ground not only of their mental inferiority but also on the commercial ground that, in their case, there would be no certainty, scarcely indeed a chance, of any 'return on money expended.'

It was strange to hear such opinions thus openly expressed and advocated by a man daily receiving and profiting by the great capacity, energy, and industry of a woman in the admittedly indispensable assistance rendered him by his own wife. Mr. Hullah was quick to seize on this weak point in his antagonist's argument, and silenced, if he did not convert him to his own more just and generous views.

Before returning home Mr. Hullah had again occasion to expound his chivalrous opinions on behalf of the women during a visit to a friend at Blackheath, in whose house Dr. Guthrie, the Scotch minister and famous preacher, was already installed. Controversy was in the very air of the house, though now it ran chiefly on social ethics. To dinner arrived several guests, Dean Alford being of the number. Among the subjects more or less discussed was the question, raised by Dr. Guthrie, of legalising marriage with a deceased wife's sister. The challenge was immediately taken up by the Dean, who was one of the strongest and most prominent advocates of the proposed change in the marriage law, and was wont to express his opinions very freely and forcibly. He did so on this occasion, and, moreover, laid especial stress on the *expediency* of such marriages, minutely and openly pointing out in how many ways the man would be the gainer thereby, apparently to the entire exclusion of any consideration for the woman's view or position. Indeed, it did not seem to have occurred to the Dean that a woman could have independent wishes and opinions on the subject. To Mr. Hullah the doctrine of *expediency* as ruling in the choice of a husband or wife was abhorrent, nor could he be induced to tolerate any of the arguments advanced. The Dean, of course, held to his own views, which were not, however, without effect, for they sent Mr. Hullah into the ranks of the active opponents of the measure, though the multiplicity and absorbing nature of his own pursuits prevented him from as public a participation in the organised opposition to the Bill as he could have desired.

Indeed, it was with the greatest difficulty that he was able twice or thrice to get a free hour for aiding in the more immediately pressing movement for getting women elected as members of the London School Board, in process of formation in November 1870.

The influence of his name, however, enabled his wife to gather in many a vote as she canvassed her ward for the benefit of Miss Garrett, M.D., now Mrs. Anderson. Not seldom it happened that some master tailor, or other employer of a large number of hands working in one room, would suggest to the canvasser that she should herself make known her errand to the men—some of whom might be voters—collectively. He would lead the way to the work-room and introduce her by name, perhaps adding, ' Some of you, I dare say, have heard of Mr. John Hullah.' Whereupon some one was sure to look up and ask, ' Of St. Martin's Hall ? ' ' Yes.' ' I knew him.' ' So did I,' voices would be heard to say, and the most genial, respectful attention was at once secured. A very short experience taught the canvasser that, when such an incident occurred, her candidate might safely count on most of the votes asked for in John Hullah's name ; and when, very near the election-day, some of the householders in the Portland ward were visited, perhaps for the *third* time, not a few suggested that Mr. Hullah's wife should herself become a candidate, ' for it is a name that ought to be on the Board,' they said.

Miss Garrett's brilliantly successful election an accomplished fact, congratulations exchanged all round, and thanks received by the fifty ladies who had worked for her, the *quondam* head of the Portland ward was free to superintend the removal of the bearer of that useful name of Hullah, with goods and chattels and children appertaining thereto, to a nest of rooms at the top of the Grosvenor Mansions, up to that time—Hankey's Folly not being as yet in the air—the highest dwelling-house in central London.

Fate decreed that Mr. Hullah should escape the horrors of a move by providing him opportunely with lecture engagements at Hull and elsewhere. Being so near Edinburgh, of course it was just as well' he should go there; so while in mid-winter the family was getting itself, its general impedimenta, and his ' three tons of books ' transferred to the flat, he, lucky man! was doing the work he delighted in, and revelling in the anecdotic society of Auld Reekie. But then he wrote twice every day and told all the news, and ' bottled up no end of good stories to let off, to do which effectively there must be no end of little dinners.' This at a time when to get a dinner at all of the most modest pretensions was as nearly an impossibility as can be imagined. No kitchen—no cook! All unconscious of the family plight he writes cheerfully:

> And now that you are going to set up a French *menage*, and we are going to live delightfully on nothing a year, please let us have some close imitation of sundry little dinners we wot of, the *menus* of which are stored away, I know, in your treasure-box. And to that end take care Mariette's Médoc does not take cold.

By Christmas Day the two small people, their nurse, and a quaint old Irishwoman, untainted by Fenianism, who had elected to share the fortunes of the family in a greatly reduced establishment, and to try how it might feel to live among the ' chimbley pots,' were all housed and Mr. Hullah came home

immediately after New Year's Day, and had to labour right
hard to get his books set up in the Butterfield and several
other bookcases before his full complement of work began.
Thanks to the persuasive eloquence of the late Dr. Charles
Appleton, his tasks were further increased by weekly contributions to the 'Academy.' So soon as the new home was
habitable, and the dinner-table usable for its legitimate purpose, a tiny house-warming had to be arranged. Mr. Butterfield, of course, was present, and fortunately approved of the
new abode; Charles Appleton, who had rapidly fallen into the
groove of an old and much-loved friend; Miss Jewsbury, and
a few others. Over Sir Arthur Helps' defection, by reason of
Privy Council Office overwork, there was great lamentation,
and he had to come soon afterwards alone by way of compensation. Mr. Hullah joyfully 'let off' a good many of the
'bottled-up' Scotch stories, duly appreciated by the aid of
the Medoc, which, far from having taken cold, was in splendid
condition, and very conducive to narration and to late sitting
up. A night or two later Mr. and Mrs. Pattison ascended
'Mount Grosvenor,' when more Scotch stories were told,
much relished by the Rector, who, in his turn, capped most of
them by something equally good. Yet a little later there was
a musical party, which went off with *eclat*, thanks to the
kindness of Mr. Hullah's tried old friends Mr. Henry Deacon,
Signor Pezze, and his younger friends the Misses Farrari and
Mr. William Shakespeare, then a pupil of the Royal Academy
of Music. The house was now felt to be 'warmed,' and life
went on its usual course till Easter, when Mr. Hullah went
to C—— A——. The greater part of this visit was spent
by Mr. Hullah in the open air with his active host. They
even made an excursion to Nottingham to see the last of St.
John s House, which was in course of demolition, much to the
disgust of the conservative archæological baronet. Great
batches of letters awaited his return home, among them one
from Mr. Marwood Tucker, announcing his resignation of the
editorship of the 'Globe.' In conclusion, Mr. Tucker says :

> Let me take this opportunity of thanking you for your very
> valuable assistance and very agreeable co-operation in putting the
> paper (*quâ* circulation, at all events) in literally close on *ten* times

as good a position as it held when I was bold enough to take it up two years ago.

It was now hoped by the folks at home that Mr. Hullah would consent to retire from newspaper work as too fatiguing. But not so; indeed he would have accepted two or three more posts similar to the one he occupied on the staff of the 'Globe' had the day been long enough. Pen work seemed urged upon him from every quarter. Principals of training colleges had long been anxious for a Government Inspector of Music, and clearly felt that if such an appointment should be made—and the project was much in the air—Mr. Hullah was the right person to have it. At any rate, many of the heads of colleges turned to him as the recipient or exponent of their own views.

I am very anxious (wrote the head of one of the most important of the Training Colleges) to obtain your consent to the printing of your admirable criticism of the Government Musical examination, in order that all Training Colleges in the country may have an opportunity of seeing the arguments in favour of urging the Government to make a radical change. I have sent a copy to the Education Department, and am now appealing to all the other colleges to make an outcry on the subject.

For months past Mr. Hullah had been called upon to go through the verb 'to examine' in almost all its tenses. The Royal Academy had had examinations. The City of London College, whose classes for vocal music had been under the charge of Mr. Constantine, one of Mr. Hullah's old assistants in the halcyon days of St. Martin's Hall, wished him to become honorary examiner. It seemed as if he were in training for the special work that was coming to him. All this was pleasant but very exhausting, as he began to find towards the end of July, when he mutinied altogether for a 'great' holiday. He would not be put off with a mere run round England.

Prudence must hold her peace. Glad to be silenced, Prudence held her peace, and packed up her travelling trunks. Just at the moment of starting came a quaint note from the late Mr. William Holmes, a Professor at the Royal Academy of Music, wishing Mr. Hullah 'might take the air with all its little variations by St. Swithin.'

. . . In every way this note is unanswerable. Men must not always work. It would make the earthly angels among 'The Village Coquettes' weep and raise a 'Storm' of indignation. . . Mrs. Holmes played and sang such a lovely song of yours to me the other day! I tell you there is a great power of concentration in all those songs of yours.

The song to which Mr. Holmes had listened with so much admiration was 'How shall we flee sorrow?' published some months before. The words are a translation from lines by Victor Hugo, and had been found by the Rev. Reginald Haweis at the bottom of an editorial basket, and brought to Mr. Hullah, who, under the influence of a peculiarly soft, lovely hued September evening, had married them to music most dainty and delicate. To return to the moment of departure. The Franco-German War was just over and Paris open to travellers. Thither therefore they went. The weather was very hot and the city far from agreeable—a sad spectacle, with the bullet-holes still unmended in the walls, many a shutter still hanging by one hinge, and a portentous number of houses still closed. Strange figures, not commonly seen in the more fashionable parts, flitted in and about the Rues de Rivoli and de la Paix, starved and hungry-looking beings with the light of mischief still unextinguished in their eyes. It was a relief to get into freer air as the train rolled away to Troyes, and thence to Langres. The pretty little town lay in the midst of ruins, scarcely a yard of its wall left standing. Belfort, too, was terribly battered and was still occupied by German troops. The pale straw-coloured young privates, mere boys for the greater part, were quiet and meek enough, poor lads, but the officers, most of them big burly men, bore themselves as conquerors, neither gentle nor generous. At no time partial to the loud-voiced German race, the sight of these domineering warriors, puffed up with success and champagne, was unendurable, and Mr. Hullah hastened away to Italy. The Hullahs travelled by Lucerne to Hospenthal, where they took the diligence for Bellinzona. Having secured places, they were seated in the *coupe*, impatiently awaiting the moment of departure, and wishing that the babel of tongues without would cease, when athwart the polyglot din came a cross-fire of expletives in Italian. With a jerk the carriage door was flung open, and, muttering most uncomplimentary nothings concerning all other languages, the speaker, of brigand-like aspect so far as the darkness permitted a view of his conical hat and ample cloak, plunged in across legs and bags and wraps, and sank exhausted into the vacant seat at the farther end. '*Ah, scusi!*' he said urbanely, as soon as he realised he was not alone.

'*Diverse lingue, orribili favelle,*' responded Mr. Hullah sepulchrally. The quotation acted like an electric shock on the new-comer, who sprang bolt upright and peered through the darkness to discover what manner of man it might be who saluted his ears with the sound of the '*benedetta lingua,*' not heard nor spoken for five years, he explained. As regarded the speaking, he made up considerably for lost time, by pouring forth hour after hour an unbroken stream of Tuscan delightful to listen to, and, as Mr. Hullah said, as good as fifty lessons. Then, as morning dawned, his journey came to its end, and bidding an effusive adieu he went on his way to the home he had left so long before.

After several stoppages at small towns, full of interest, Milan was reached in a week. Mr. Hullah knew the city well and was a capital cicerone, but, thanks to the courteous kindness of Professor Ceriani, the treasures of the Ambrosian Library were made more easy of access to him than on any previous occasion. Several days were spent at Brescia, where Mr. Hullah passed a good deal of his time in the churches, listening to the voices of the choirs. He was greatly struck with the universal beauty of the Brescian voices, all untrained and undisciplined though they were.

From Brescia the journey was continued to Verona, and being at Verona it was irresistible to run down to Venice, the ever-delightful city. Some time had elapsed since Mr. Hullah had last been there, and the light, the colour, the silence of the place affected him as freshly as if he had never felt their charm before. It was a new experience to his companion to watch the changing expression of his face as, gliding hither and thither, the scene momentarily changed and the indefinable charm of the city stole over him. One wondrously lovely

When

And,

> We bade the gondoliers cease to row,
>
> Looking upon the evening and the flood,
> Which lay between the city and the shore,
> Paved with the image of the sky.
>
> . . . . .
>
> Dark purple at the zenith, which still grew
> Down the steep west into a wondrous hue,
> Brighter than burning gold, even to the rent
> Where the swift sun yet paused in his descent,
> Among the many folded hills.
>
> . . . . .
>
> Dissolved into one lake of fire, were seen
> Those mountains towering, as from waves of flame,
> Around the vaporous sun, from which there came
> The inmost purple spirit of light, and made
> Their very peaks transparent.
>
> . . . . .
>
> And from that funereal bark
> He leaned, and saw the city, and could mark
> How from their many isles, in evening's gleam,
> Its temples and its palaces did seem
> Like fabrics of enchantment piled to heaven.

Rousing himself at length, as if slowly set free from some influence he could not resist, he gave the signal to proceed.

A life did not seem too long to spend in Venice, and they had of it but ten days. Bidding a loving adieu to their last gondolier the travellers turned back to Verona, through which it was necessary to pass on their homeward route. The intention was to sleep but one night in Verona, but as they re-entered the *Due Torri*, a friend crossed their path with whom it was pleasant to think of journeying, so, while he went for a whiff of Adriatic air to Venice, the Hullahs made themselves more than happy by renewing an already close acquaintance with the picturesque streets and the lovely buildings. In due time Mr. Price (of Exeter College, Oxford) returned, and the party set off for the Stelvio Pass with the further project of dropping down to the Bagni di Bormio *en route* for the Engadine. The project was carried through with satisfaction not quite unalloyed by suffering, thanks to rapid changes of temperature.

At Poschiavo Mr. Price started the idea of walking over the Palu to Pontresina, and Mr. Hullah agreed; and next morning, while the lazy member of the trio got sleepily into the diligence at 4 A.M., the gentlemen started off on foot with knapsacks, provisions, and a guide to walk to Pontresina. Hours after the diligence had deposited its freight at Pontresina the walkers came in, very tired, but having had a most successful day, Mr. Hullah being especially pleased with himself, for years had passed since he had done anything so fatiguing, and he was delighted to find he bore it so well. When, a few days later, Mr. Price suggested the ascent of the Piz Languard, his former companion was charmed to join in, and a pedestrian party was made up which again did not include the 'lazy person,' to Mr. Hullah's disgust, for ladies often go up the Piz Languard. The weather was splendid, and the ascent was considered successful, but the feat proved a much stiffer affair than Mr. Hullah, at any rate, had bargained for, and he returned silent and weary, and required a considerable administration of beef-tea, fortified with cognac, before he could get up and enjoy a copious dinner, after which he said he was 'all right.' However that might be, he never found the weather—and he had become such a judge of mountain weather!—exactly propitious for further ascents during the remainder of their stay in the Engadine.

At Chur Mr. Hullah got possession of the great organ in the Domkirche, and at Zurich also he was lucky in picking up a chance of exercising his fingers on the keyboard.

Homewards the route chosen took the party to Mayence, where Mr. Hullah s youngest son came from Gotha to meet and spend a day or two with him. *Viâ* Liege, Noyon, and Amiens, London was reached only the day before the *baton* was resumed at the Royal Academy. Towards Christmas the pressure of work became so great that he was fain to exclaim, in writing to his wife:

> Oh, for *every* morning to write in. Heaps of things come in: proofs, music, letters, &c. . . . People, it seems, are crying out for copies, now that they are all gone, of my 'History of Modern Music.'

I cannot have it printed again as it is, and to get out another edition is out of the question. Oh! for leisure!

By which he only meant, 'Oh that the day had forty-eight hours of daylight!'

Of all his Christmas correspondence the pleasantest to him was the letter in which Dr. Bellamy announced his own election to the Presidency of St. John's College, Oxford, ending with:

> And now you will have a choice of houses. . . . Mrs. Hullah, I know, has a liking for Oxford.

CHAPTER XXIV.

BIOGRAPHICAL.

1872.

MR. HULLAH preferred congratulating the family collectively in person, for which purpose he went on New Year's Day to Stanford, carrying with him unanswered letters and Helps' 'Thoughts on Government' for reviewing.

Here we are in the dining-room, Tylden and I (he writes). Tylden has his Hebrew books on one side and a case of formidably antlered beetles on the other. I am supported by Helps on my right and my darling box on my left, but I can't write, for Tylden will talk. Everybody is enchanted about the appointment at St. John's. . . . It appears my 'memorandum' about examination in music, addressed to the Council of St. Mark's, and afterwards printed, has had some effect. H—— has been busy about it, and I am to see Sir Francis Sandford this week. If anything is done with *me* it will remove me, of necessity, from St. Mark's and Battersea. But it is all in the clouds as yet.

It was not long, however, before the scheme descended from cloudland. On March 23, some weeks after the above letter was written, the post of Musical Inspector was offered to Mr. Hullah. Acceptance involved not only the resignation of his appointments at St. Mark's and Battersea—which was inevitable, since one and the same person could not be teacher and inspector at one time—but it also involved giving up a great deal of remunerative work, the loss of which meant an appreciable diminution of income, for the salary of the new inspector was to be but 200*l*. per annum. In all he could but draw 400*l*., from which would have to be deducted travelling and hotel expenses while he was out on his rounds. Had the salary, however, been but two hundred pence, Mr. Hullah would still have been ready to take the work, for he believed that in doing so he would be able to advance, perhaps even to carry out to their realisation, the dreams of a life.

His views on the importance of popular instruction are known to the reader, and do not need to be recapitulated. The time had come when he, who had done so much to spread a love for and a knowledge of music throughout the country, might hope to see its consolidation on a scientific basis in the educational scheme.

At home his satisfaction was fully shared, but somewhat dashed by anxiety as to his physical ability to stand the wear and tear of much travelling, especially in winter. Though alert, full of energy and life, it was impossible to forget that he was touching his sixtieth year, and was in a remarkable degree sensitive to noises such as are inseparable from railway travelling conducted on its present barbarous system. It was worse than useless, however, to advance objections.

He did not know what quantity of work there might be for him to do, and he did not care. He wished ' to wear out, not rust out.' The work that had to be done must be got through at any sacrifice of time, or strength, or comfort, or pleasure.

Like an old war-horse, he fretted at the curb and longed for the signal to dart forward. In the meanwhile, he had many congratulations on his new appointment from strangers as well as from friends.

I congratulate you, hearty, earnest worker as you are, in being placed in a position in which your powers for good are vastly enlarged. Was there ever a time in which a Hullah was more needed as Inspector-General of Music ? Short hours coming in and no fitting amusement at hand for the pleasant and enjoyable employment of those extra idle hours. I feel in my heart that the angel Music can alone exorcise the demon Drunkenness from the very marrow of the nation. A glee class for every schoolroom, a choral society for every town, is surely the real temperance movement. Sweet sounds poured out of, instead of vile beer poured into, man's mouth. It is our motto. And really I do not think we half realise the amount of music that might be had for the organisation.

. . . Last week I made a visit with my wife to five centres of choirs in Cleveland. I am sure you would be delighted with the musical intelligence, capital ears, and fresh, full voices of those stalwart Yorkshiremen. . . . I think even you would have been satisfied with the delicacy and brightness, the exactness as to time, and the purity of tone. . . . Some walk eight, ten, twelve, fourteen miles to rehearse. If you can find anything for me to do in the great, good cause of *Temperance, Soberness, and Chastity*, rely on my being a hearty workman. At any rate, if your duty calls you to York, I trust you will give my wife and myself the pleasure of welcoming you at our small rectory. We shall feel we are doing something for music if taking care of you. Yours,

J. P. M——.

This letter, written by one to whom Mr. Hullah was not as yet personally known, represents the pleasant side of the correspondence which followed the new Inspector's appointment. Other communications came in shoals which had no element of pleasantness in them. Applications for help to obtain teacherships, organistships, assistant inspectorships, and what not, from people manifestly incompetent, but to whom the writing of a refusal was necessary, however disagreeable; and there were not a few obliging communications from Tonic Sol-faists concerning their 'new notation,' which Mr. William Chappell's erudition described on one occasion as 'that exploded system of tablature for music which began in the second half of the sixteenth century and was universally discarded in the seventeenth century.'

But private correspondence by no means satisfied these improvers of a symbolism which has sufficed for the needs of a Beethoven, a Mozart, and a Mendelssohn, and which does not seem inadequate to the more involved and complex musical phrasing of a Wagner. They resolved to strike at once for an equal position with the old notationists, and in addition would seem to have claimed the right to *choose* an inspector. The deputation instructed to represent their views met with a reception from the heads of the Education Department which sent them on their homeward journey individually and collectively more enlightened than pleased.

But while the Tonic Sol-faists were hysterically agitating themselves with imaginary grievances, Mr. Hullah, after supplying required memoranda to the Council Office, was using his temporarily increased leisure to get comfortably ready for his autumn tour of inspection, by no means neglecting a good deal of pleasure as it came in his way at home or abroad.

We had a very pleasant party at home last night (he reports to his absent wife); Appleton and Ralston came in addition to those you invited. Some of the talk was really good. Appleton is full of a new book on 'Philosophy' by a young Italian, which he is pounding away at with great interest. He says it is very good. We shall soon see the Italians doing themselves more justice than they have done for ages past in a hundred different ways. . . . I should so like to have a peep with you at your sea-wall and have a share in your prospects of sea and sky now and then. . . . Take the opportunity, while you have it, of reading *great* books—even bits of them if not the whole. . . . I went straight from the Academy to a Mendelssohn concert, which lasted till after post time. On reaching home at about seven, I found two tickets for Drury Lane for to-night. Campanini plays. The excitement about him is very great. . . . I went yesterday to the Derwent Coleridges' concert at Hanwell. It was very pleasant. I wish you had been back in time for it. I accompanied all the vocal pieces but one—about twenty—and sang, 'by especial desire,' 'The Storm,' which resulted in a storm. This morning I was, at ten o'clock, at the South Kensington Museum to meet a party for a private view of the ancient instruments. It was great fun, playing on the old spinets and harpsichords, some of which are beautiful. . . . I long very much for the next ten days to pass, but don't spoil your visit to your old aunt by coming away abruptly. I want you to hear Campanini He is the most interesting singer that has appeared in my time . . . Last night I heard Prince Poniatowski's new opera—trash! This morning I have finished my Thursday essay for the 'Globe,' of which (did I tell you?) Dr. Granville is now editor. The Duke of Edinburgh has summoned a committee for to-morrow.

The important meeting in question was convened for July 1, at Clarence House, by H.R.H. the Duke of Edinburgh, for the purpose of considering the position of the Royal Academy of Music and the possibility of amalgamating it with a new scheme which by-and-by took shape as the Training College for Singing, though without the co-operation of the older institution.

Mr. Hullah began his inspection at Bristol, where seventeen students presented themselves for examination. It was his custom to comment in his letters on the students' work as he went on from day to day, the substance of these remarks being a part of the material whence he drew up his annual reports. From Bristol Mr. Hullah passed to Carmarthen and spent his first Sunday at Borth. Writing thence he says :

After a week of work, which *was* interesting, and *would have been* easy and pleasant but for the incessant noise I seem to have been in since I left, I have at last got into a place of rest, in which,

at this moment, I hear no sound but that of the calm sea, on which I look when I raise my head from writing. I allowed myself an extra day for this part of the country, determined to get my Sunday, if possible, by the seaside. I never even heard of this place till Friday, when it was recommended to me by Mr. Morris, the Principal of the Carmarthen Training School. I stayed on half a day longer than was absolutely necessary at Carnarvon; the place was so pretty and the inns so nice—to say nothing of broiled fresh salmon and the best *tea* conceivable. (I have given up wine as a bad job, and drink only ale and tea!) This place is *delicious*. It consists chiefly of rather a large hotel (with very few people in it) and a few new lodging-houses joined on to an old fishing village. I have a capital large room overlooking the sea, and in it a *table to write at*! You may imagine how nice it is to have all my papers about without the chance of being overlooked in a ' coffee-room '— that wonderful institution! Truly the British hotel is an abominable invention. Its resources are still limited to chops, steaks (sometimes) and bacon [his experience of inns during the previous days had left a bitter memory]. From my window I see almost the whole extent of Cardigan Bay—the land stretching away towards St. David's on the left and to Bantry Island on the right. Behind the house, at the end of a large plain, rise the hills in amphitheatre form. I had a dip in the sea this morning, and, as usual after that performance, feel a good deal less than that thirty-seven at which, you know, I *stopped* some time ago. After another dip to-morrow before I leave I shall, no doubt, come ' of age.' Did I tell you that I saw at Bristol Canons Wade and Norris, H.M.I. ?
. . . He [Norris] is doing—indeed, has already done—a great work at Bristol. He has been the principal means of completing the cathedral by the addition of a nave, which was left undone at the rebuilding in the 14th century. It will be *vaulted* in this year— before the winter. With the exception of Cologne, I do not know of a similar achievement. There has been plenty of restoration, but no such work as this. . . . I go to-morrow to Carnarvon. . . . This I send to Rouen.

His wife and children had crossed over to France for the autumn holidays. He resumes from Carnarvon :

. . . I found the Training School people very nice. The principal has a large boat and a crew (of students), who took me half way to Bangor, along the Menai Straits, in sight of the Snowdon range all the way. . . . The garden of this little inn is full of *tropical* trees and gay flowers, and commanding a glorious view. . . .

Dumfries, Sept 9.—I cannot bear the idea of your coming back to London again so soon and so long before me. . . . Could you not stay at Havre, or at one of the quieter watering-places in the neighbourhood ? There is Fécamp, for instance, with a most grand church ; and Etretat is not much farther off. . . . However, whatever happens, you must come away with me on my next journey. . . . How I should like to be with you at Le Mans! Mind you go and see the *other* great church there—I never have. And then Chartres! that is really too bad! I had so hoped always we should go there together, with plenty of time. Don't be annoyed with the horrid modern jubé, which disfigures the cathedral horribly. The proportions of the interior alone would make amends for anything. The sculpture will enchant you. And be sure to go up the tower.

. . . My adventures have lately been interesting; more especially my visit to the college at Liverpool, all managed by the Roman Catholic Sisters. We struck up an eternal friendship!

Chester.—Yours of the 27th from Coutance has come. It was an immense comfort and consolation—not unneeded; for, though I meet with every possible kindness from all kinds of people, they are not like certain kindnesses I know of, that come occasionally. . . . After six hours of examination I have been again to the cathedral. Hearing sounds of practising, I sent in my card to the organist. In a moment out came Mr. Gunton with open arms, accompanied by an old student from St. Mark's, who is master of the choristers. . . . It was very nice to be sung to by a very good choir of about twenty, and to hear such fine music in a vaulted room (13th century) all to one's self. . . . How I should have enjoyed seeing all these noble things with you! . . . How those dear little creatures must have enjoyed the *coupé* after the train! . . . *We* will find out some places to which diligences go when next *we* travel. One gets so sick of railways—and the noise! . . . Such an outpouring of enthusiasm as that you have sent me from Chartres, which I found on coming down to breakfast this morning, is not merely refreshment but rejuvenescence. After all, I can *almost* forgive you for going to Chartres without me. To have gone by it a second time, as it were, *blindfolded* would have been too bad. And you will not like it any the less, but all the more, for having seen it once, when we go together to see it again. Is it not glorious? What an age! what a race! to have put forth such a multitude of works of which, though undoubtedly the finest, Chartres is only one. . . .

Edinburgh.—For the first time for many days I have a room I can sit and write in and the view is enchanting. . . . I enjoy my work very much. Principals and committees receive me well, and I contrive soon to dispel from the minds of the students the terrors inspired by my advent. . . . I am sorry you are come back so soon for your sake, though glad for my own; seeing that, in all probability, I shall have to be in London on Saturday, the 28th, for . . . the Metropolitan School people. . . . The journey to and fro is considerable, but the temptation to run up is great I do so long to see home again. . . . Tinling [Canon Tinling had been examining at the same time, to Mr. Hullah's infinite satisfaction, for they had been companions frequently] is gone, but I shall pick him up again at Durham. . . . My work has been hard—fifty-four students yesterday, but they were of the better sex.

He came back on the 28th, was met at the station, and looked so radiant as he got out of the carriage that guard and porter smiled sympathetically as they helped him down with his numerous impedimenta.

On the following Monday he was off again to Ripon. From York he writes:

. . . I have just got some letters—one, an invitation from the Bishop of Lincoln (Wordsworth) to dine and spend the night at Riseholme on Friday. I have accepted the invitation to dine, but not the bed. Fancy! there is a dinner going on at the hotel of old St. Peter's scholars, at which Elwyn is present. I am coming home.

During the days he was at home examinations in London were daily carried on. He next went to Winchester and Salisbury.

I got pleasantly and soon through my work at Winchester (he writes), and had time, under the escort of the principal, to go and see Butterfield's Hospital, a new and really fine thing. I left Winchester at three and got here [Salisbury] before five. My host, the archdeacon, is a charming old gentleman, upwards of eighty, and, barring a little failure in eyesight, as young and bright as need be . . . you must come if we are asked again. To-morrow I have the Training College to examine here, and the next day I go on to Exeter, and thence to Truro.

The next journey out took in Cheltenham, Birmingham, Derby, and Oxford, where his wife joined him, and an evening was spent in Lincoln College.

One more *sortie* from London and the work of inspection was over for the year. There remained a report to be written, and formidable piles of examination papers came from and went back to the Education Department, duly corrected, in course of time.

He granted himself a very brief period of rest, and refreshed himself with a little dinner-party, made up on his home-coming, at which his health was drunk with effusion in some choice Château Yquem—a wedding present kept as a great treat; and he told some of the Scotch *Märchen ohne ende* (acquired during his last visit to the Land o' Cakes) with a nice Scotch accent, as was acutely surmised by Sir Arthur Helps, unable, by reason of 'cattle plagues and other bothers,' to come and hear them on this particular evening

The very next day he took in hand his Report for the Committee of Council on Education. In this Report he says:

Between the end of August and the beginning of December I visited all the Training Colleges receiving grants from the Committee of Council on Education, and examined individually more than one thousand five hundred students, of either sex, in the practice of singing from notes.

Of his method of examination he says:

Of one of the [simplest pieces of music] I put into the hands of the student before me the part suited to his voice, playing (myself) at the pianoforte or harmonium the other parts necessary to complete the harmony, but never that which he was to sing. If he sol-faed (or any method) or sung this fairly, I applied a somewhat severer test; never dismissing him till I had fully satisfied myself as to the extent of his capabilities. . . . When time allowed it (he adds), I had the second-year students reassembled, and by way of revising my judgment of their powers I wrote on a board various passages, generally involving some common modulation or rhythmical succession. These were sung by volunteers; almost always, it proved, those to whom I had already given the best marks.

Writing of the general impression received from these tests, Mr. Hullah continues:

The organisation of most of the Training Colleges is not favourable to the study and practice of choral music. A college composed exclusively, whether of female or of male students, can only furnish each an imperfect choir. The stock of existing music, whether for female voices or for male voices *only*, is not only limited, but inferior to that for the full and therefore mixed choir. It is impossible for either an exclusively male or exclusively female choir to make more than a partial and therefore unsatisfactory acquaintance with the music of all others best fitted for their study—the choruses of Handel and other great masters of sacred harmony and the *best* glees and part songs of contemporary composers. The very natural desire to overcome this difficulty in any degree has, in some colleges, induced a practice which it is to be hoped will not be persisted in, that of singing soprano parts (in male colleges) an octave too low, and tenor parts (in female colleges) an octave too high. Both these practices will assuredly prove injurious as well to the voices as to the ears of those who are concerned in them. . . In consequence of this incompleteness of their choirs, it is only in the mixed colleges, Cheltenham, Edinburgh, Glasgow, and Homerton, that *general* effects at all commensurate with the pains brought to bear upon the instruction of those who produced them can be realised.

Concerning the reading in class 'at sight,' the Inspector remarks:

The piece of music, a copy of which in the tonic sol-fa notation is also subjoined, was attacked by the second-year students, under the direction of their own teacher, in every conceivable fashion It was sung, sol-faed—here on the 'fixed,' there on the movable principle—to syllables, figures, letters, and inarticulate vocables. The result was generally unsatisfactory. The students in the Training Colleges have evidently not been sufficiently habituated to dealing, well or ill, with fresh music. Their reading is, for the most part, marked by the hesitation which results from an inability to take in more than one or two notes at a time.

After making due allowance for partial failures attributable to timidity, Mr. Hullah reiterates his well-known opinions on vocal incapacity:

My recent inspection has simply confirmed what, if once only an hypothesis, is now a theory deduced from many years' experience, that the number, even of adults, who, were they to take sufficient pains, could not be made to appreciate time and tune is very small indeed. . . .

He calls attention to the absence of feeling for *time*:

I attribute this (he says) in a great degree to the insufficient attention given to 'beating time' with the hand. The indisposition of *English* students to do this, and their clumsiness in doing it, are the best possible tributes to its usefulness.

In a word or two he brings forward the complaint of principals and teachers, that 'In no subject do students enter our college so ill-prepared as in music.'

On the question of compulsion in the use of any particular system, Mr. Hullah says:

I desire most earnestly to deprecate any attempt to enforce on the musical instructors in training schools, directly or indirectly, the adoption of any particular method of instruction, books, or exercises whatever.

And farther on he notices, at the end of a long technical passage on methods of instruction, how a particular 'difficulty is met in the *tonic sol-fa* notation by a very ingenious contrivance, the "bridge-tone," which gives the name of a note, not only in relation to what has gone before, but to what is about to follow it, the key just quitted, and the key already entered upon. It seems, however, that even this contrivance is not to be carried out to its utmost logical consequences.'

The following remarks commend themselves to writers on education :

Writers on education, those at least who are not musicians, frequently confound the *study* of music with the *practice* of it, and treat both equally as ' recreation,' ' relaxation from severer studies,' and the like. I have often heard school managers and even masters —those, I repeat, who are not musicians—draw a distinction between music and those subjects which they are pleased to call 'intellectual.' The practice of music on the part of the most accomplished musician calls into requisition a larger number of faculties—*e.g.* power of sustained attention, quickness of eye and ear, readiness in turning to account knowledge already acquired—than almost any other pursuit or series of acts in which he could possibly engage. No doubt this practice is attended with a great deal of pleasure to the practitioner as well as to the auditor. But the exercise of a power already attained and the process of attaining it are very different things. Assuredly the latter as well as the former can be made interesting, and the degree in which it is made so will depend on the method and tact of the teacher. But that it can be carried on without trouble, as a kind of play; that the acquirement of anything worthy of the name of musical knowledge or musical skill can be ' made easy,' is an ignorant misapprehension or a wilful misrepresentation.

On the completion of the inspectorial tour came a number of letters from various schools Mr. Hullah had visited, assuring him that his presence among the students had given an impetus to their musical studies which promised well for future improvement. On the other hand, he learnt that in one place in Scotland his opponents, the tonic sol-faists, were busy sowing tares among his wheat, which proceeding was duly notified to him by a member of their own staff.

I will consider it a special favour if you will kindly send me a sol-fa copy of the musical test you put to the students of the Free Church Normal School at the last examination. I venture to make this extraordinary request [for] it is said that the test you gave in the Free Normal [school] was full of transitions, and that the transitions were not only unnecessarily but incorrectly printed or rather written in the better method. Now whatever the ' better method ' of making transitions may be in theory, all good practical sol faists hold it to be the wrong method when it introduces greater difficulties than those intended to be removed. In bringing the matter before your notice I think it but fair to state that I have not heard the slightest murmur against you as examiner; on the contrary, all who have spoken to me on the subject expressed themselves as thoroughly satisfied that you acted impartially in the matter of method and notation. I am, as you know, an out-and-out advocate of the tonic sol fa notation, and it being openly reported that your sol-fa test was in one respect an unfair one, I wish to satisfy myself that the transitions in the piece you gave were really written in the form best suited for sight-singing.

A pleasing correspondence was evidently within his grasp if he chose to profit by the chance.

CHAPTER XXV.

BIOGRAPHICAL.

1873.

MR. HULLAH had been reflecting for some months on the desirability of retiring from his post at the Royal Academy of Music, and before Easter he brought his reflections to a decision on that point, not without sincere regret at giving up the guidance of a band of students all of whom seemed to like him, and some of whom were devoted to him. Many poured out their lamentations at his departure in language too simple not to be heartfelt.

The usual invitation for Easter having duly arrived from C—— A——, Mr. Hullah gladly availed himself of it, all the more readily, perhaps, that there was a prospect of a form of dissipation totally new to him—steeple-chasing !

Friends were scandalised ; especially scandalised was his staid old friend Mr. Callcott, who hastened to admonish him in Dickens's striking words : ' You didn't ought to have nothink to do with a steeple-chase—wery dangerous for a married man ! ' All heedless of this unanswerable advice, Mr. Hullah unhesitatingly announces his share of the exploits in his first report home.

My host, Captain ——, and *I* are going off to D—— to a steeple-chase.

Having by good luck come back intact, he continues his letters :

The expedition was very diverting though rather tiring; but, being all in the open air, I think it has done me good. We were from half-past one to five on the course, and only got home at a quarter to seven. . . . Some very nice people have arrived ; a Mr. S——, a great naturalist and antiquarian. He is rather broken down in health but very agreeable; Mrs. S—— much the same.... I have been working quietly in my room, amusing myself with translating the Wilhelm Meister Song, 'So lasst mich scheinen, bis ich werde' [for Miss Eleanor Grove's translation of Wilhelm Meister in the Tauchnitz Edition], which I have got in *en bloc*, I think pretty fairly. *Le voici:*

Mignon's last Song.

Such let me seem till such I be :
Take not the angel robe away !
I haste from the earth, so fair to see,
Down to the narrow house of clay.

There for a silent hour I rest,
Till sight and sense renewed I find ;
And doff the veil and candid vest,
And leave the golden crown behind.

In these angelic forms around
Are he and she all undescried ;
Nor robes *conc̒eal*, nor girdles *bound* (a tiresome bit !)
The body—sexless, glorified !

Free have I lived from sordid care,
Yet have I known still sharper pain ;
The weight of age too soon to bear,
Make me for age a child again !

.... A Japanese and a Chinese have just come.... The Japanese is most entertaining, not to say instructive. I have learnt no end of things about porcelain, which I hope to let off in London with immense effect ! Did you know that the Chinese took to imitating French patterns in the days of Louis XIV. ? ... I return in time for the Appletonian gathering....

By which was meant a gathering together of some two hundred persons on alternate Monday evenings for the purpose of getting up a *bonâ-fide* club for ladies as well as gentlemen. The idea originated with Dr. Charles Appleton, and eventually developed into the highly respectable and useful Albemarle Club of the present day.

In his portfolio Mr. Hullah had carried into the country some verses entitled 'Former Days,' which Mr. Marwood Tucker had sent him with the explanation that the original poem, 'Les beaux Jours d'Autrefois,' was by Philippe Theolier. 'I don't think,' adds Mr. Tucker, 'the original is in any collection. I found it by chance among some ballads which my young French servant was reading one day in my ante-room.' Conning these lines as he sauntered up and down the formal walks of the old-fashioned garden of C—— A——, he composed the suggestive music of 'Former Days' in the spring time of the year.

June brought with it much hard work, for the Metropolitan Choral School choirs had to be rehearsed into efficiency for the public performance of July 1, which when it took place was, on the whole, excellent. Immediately following on the concert came many successive days of work at the Crystal Palace, while the voice competitions were going on under the jurorship of Messrs. Ganz, Leslie, Barnby, Arditi, the late Sir Julius Benedict, and Mr. Hullah. By working 'double tides' he got himself free in August, accompanying his wife to Oxford on his way to Malvern Wells, beneath those hills which never failed to fill his soul with joy.

This is the most beautiful place that can be conceived (he exclaims on his arrival). We look over the Cotswold Hills and Gloucestershire. Last night we saw the Black Mountain beyond Phillott's. . . . After dinner, when it got a little cool, we went up to the top of the Herefordshire Beacon, the last great hill at this end of the Malvern range. . . . I find that, among folk we know, Sidney Colvin is stopping in Malvern. The W——s are most anxious that I should invite anybody I fall in with, that I know here, to their house. They are most kind. . . . I began an article yesterday about Mr. Bosanquet's harmonium. . . . I suppose you are enjoying the *dolce far niente* of a guest's life at pleasant Lincoln College; but you *will* come here? An itinerary is sent for your guidance. . . . Before closing I must send you a suffrage story. *Eccolo.*

At a F.S. meeting at Scarborough two or three ladies, not remarkable for comeliness, planted themselves on the platform. The first speaker began her address with this question, 'Can you tell me—why was I born?' which being followed by a solemn silence was repeated, 'Why was I born?' on which a big Yorkshireman rose and said, 'Wall, marm, if that's a conondrum I give it oop.'

A few weeks later and the 'traveller's letters' were resumed. The first start was always a cause for a grumble and a protest against being allowed to go alone, but after a while, as journeying from place to place he fell in with old friends or made new acquaintances, he dropped into a more contented vein and became chatty. From Bangor he writes:

The students (girls) wanted a great deal of encouragement, which took up much time. . . . I travelled with two Orientals who are visiting in these parts. They are very interesting, speaking most beautiful English, though only just come to England. [At Exeter he had sundry pleasant *rencontres*.] On turning into the close I caught sight of a whisker at the door of an hotel there which seemed to be familiar. On a nearer approach the owner proved to be Dr. Maclagan [of Edinburgh], who was waiting for Mrs. M. Shouts of astonishment and gratulation, with numerous inquiries, all in a breath. . . . At the Training College I had already had two visitors, one of them Mr. Marwood Tucker. Then, just as I got into the railway carriage [he was at Bristol when he wrote] there was another pleasant surprise, the cause of which was the Rector [of Lincoln, Oxford]. He was, as ever, very interesting and altogether very genial. . . . I dine presently with Mr. C——, and then go on to Canon W——'s. As I have a day on hand I shall spend it at Shrewsbury, which I have never seen. . . . There are some Italians staying here, with whom I have had a chat. It was nice—a great relief from the German I have been grinding at.

The silence and bracing air of Borth, which had so taken his fancy in the previous year, delighted and refreshed him equally on this occasion. Having finished up his round to Carmarthen and Swansea, he returned home for two nights, conducted another concert of the Metropolitan Choral Society, and took a most vivacious share in a lively little party at the Groves' house at Sydenham, where several capital talkers were present. He next turned his steps to the north. Writing from Warrington he says :

Having the carriage all to myself the whole way I was able to read 'Wilhelm Meister' and do a bit of Bernay's exercises undisturbed. I think I am at last beginning to know something of this horrible language, or at least to read it with a little less difficulty than I have had till very lately.

He took an odd pleasure in this yearly autumnal revival of the old habit of 'his life's morning march when his spirits were young,' and rejoiced in discharging, like Sir Arthur Helps, 'undeclined nouns and unconjugated verbs' at the heads of the unwary. The next letter is from Liverpool, written after his visit to the Training College of the ladies of N. D. de Namur.

Liverpool, Sept. 25.—I have had two long days at Warrington and expect two ditto here. What a horrible district I have just traversed! The sky hidden by volumes of smoke, the air loaded with horrid smells, and the roads and paths made of cinder-dust. London is purity itself to this. . . .

Chester, Sept. 26.—Having nothing more to do in Liverpool, I got out of it as soon as I well could this morning, after another visit to my ' Sisters ' in search of letters which they had already sent on here, where they will not come, I know, till night. . . . I am going to dine with Gunton. . . . What a jolly old place this is ! . . . I had a tiresome, though not very long, examination this morning at Derby. I shall have a long, but I hope not tiresome, day to morrow ; and then a rest on Sunday ; then home ! Hurrah ! !

Eleven days, or rather fragments of days, passed at home refreshed him for a longer absence. When once more on the wing, Mr. Hullah made his way to Ripon, Darlington, and Durham, and on to Scotland. The interim between the last examination in England and the first in Scotland was spent at no very great distance from Glasgow, at the house of a friend, whence he gossips cheerfully :

My three days were rendered as pleasant as can be imagined by the heartiest of welcomes and some very pleasant company, and two or three beautiful walks in the brilliant weather, possible at this time of year. We have dinner-parties Saturday and Monday, and a luncheon-party on Tuesday. . . . I was kindly pressed to dine at —— with the M——s Tuesday, but the prospect of getting up *this* morning at six was too terrible at this time of year, with the additional prospect of such a day's work as I have sustained. I did not leave the Training College till 5, after seven hours of examination of forty-five students. Everything here. I foresee, will be much the same. . . . Mrs. —— is more wonderful than ever ! What a clever, purposeless little creature it is ! On Saturday night a certain Captain —— did me the honour to sing my ' O doubting heart,' which I accompanied. No sooner had he started than Mrs. —— came and seated herself at my side and proceeded to *fan* me ! Conceive having to preserve one's gravity with the gallant captain on one side uttering sounds too terrible for recollection, and Mrs. —— ' supporting ' me in this preposterous manner on the other. . . .

Examination among Scotch students, especially on the Glasgow side, would seem to have been very tiring, and an exceeding trial to patience. Mr. Hullah used to say it invariably took him many minutes to get a student to understand that a direct plain question should be met by a reply as direct and plain instead of by evasion or circumlocution. Every now and then a student would persist in giving—or endeavouring to get a hearing for—a biographical notice of himself in regard to his earliest musical teaching, before making any effort to answer the questions put to him by the examiner.

Well might unfortunate examiners feel with Mr. Hullah when he said:

> I have rarely spent a more wretched day than this, professionally.
> *Edinbro'.*—I have had a very hard week's work, having examined just two hundred students, and having seldom got away from a training school till nearly five. It is, as usual, charming here. . . . Mr. B—— is anxious you should meet me in Derby, though somewhat nervous about his bachelor quarters.
> *York.*—I fell in with Dr. Monk and Sir Frederick Ouseley, with whom I dined in the evening very pleasantly. . . I had a long day at the Training College yesterday. Afterwards, having learnt that your people, the D——s, were at home, I went up to call on them, and was detained by Mrs. D—— to dinner; the captain having gone up to the station to meet *another* captain and Mrs. D—— who were coming by the train from Scotland. They came back together, the poor senior captain complaining of violent headache and all kinds of physical woes. . . I long to get home again, more than I have ever done.
> *Norwich.*—It was a very pleasant meeting at Peterboro'. The Dean [Saunders] and Mrs. Dean both kindly glad to see me again. They hope you will be with me next year. . . . Poor Deacon is only just come, quite knocked up, and I must leave immediately and get home and examine [the Home and Colonial, Westminster, and Hammersmith schools].

For London and suburban work he usually started from home at 9.30, rarely getting back till between 4 and 5. His next and last *sortie* took him in due course to Salisbury, where he again stayed with Archdeacon Honey and dined with the Dean, whose charming conversational powers had a great attraction for Mr. Hullah. Coming home 'for good,' as children say, he felt tired, but not knocked up, and considered that, on the whole, the result of his examinations was satisfactory. Active work at an end he sat down to his report.

Mr. Hullah begins by deprecating, in terms stronger than he had used in 1872, any compulsion in respect of *methods* of instruction:

> I expressed a strong opinion, formed long ago on theoretical grounds, and subsequently confirmed by observation in respect to them [methods of instruction], and a still stronger one against 'any attempt to enforce on the musical instructors in training-schools, directly or indirectly, the adoption of any particular method of instruction, books, or exercises whatever.' The goal of every honest and intelligent teacher is the same, but the ways which lead

to it are various, and the most familiar is likely to be the safest, if not the shortest.

He reiterates an opinion, expressed elsewhere, of the uselessness of *collective* sight-singing :

When there was time for it (he says) I again applied to the students of the second year the ' ear tests,' which was formerly the only form of practical examination they had to undergo. . . . To the ' ear tests ' I am disposed to attach their full value ; for, if I cannot lay claim to their invention, they were, I believe, first applied at my recommendation in cases where no others were applicable. For many years they were the only tests of practical skill, or rather of the connection in a student's mind between notes and sounds, applied in the Training Colleges. The all but universal objection to them on the part of the authorities of these colleges was one of the causes which led to the creation of the office I have now the honour to hold. As a supplement to the practical examinations lately introduced they may be applied with much effect, and I have contrived so to apply them where I have had to do so. The worthlessness of the results obtained from them as a *sole* gauge of musical science or skill is shown in the fact that some of the best ' readers ' whom I have examined have failed under their application. . . . I drew my tests for individual singing at sight from Mendelssohn's oratorio, ' St. Paul,' which I selected because it could be obtained in the tonic sol-fa as well as in the established notation. To this work I confined myself, because a very reasonable wish had been expressed that the students of all the colleges should be tested ' in the same music.'

This year he had again occasion to note the deficiencies of students on entering the colleges :

Of no subject but music is a Training College called upon to teach the very elements. At the very lowest the candidate for admission to Training Colleges must be able to read and to write. and he must know something of the powers of numbers. Why should he be ignorant not merely of the powers, but even the names, of notes : or, worse, unable to imitate correctly a musical sound, not, as is too often absurdly supposed, from natural deficiency, but want of a little pains given to him in childhood ?

And again he urges the need of a ' perfect choir :

The want of these opportunities has led to the adoption of the objectionable expedients to which I called attention last year—the singing of soprano parts an octave too low, and even of bass parts an octave too high. The latter seems to have been given up everywhere, but not the former ; indeed, to one of the questions I had to put to every student—' What voice have you ? '—I received from many a young man, whose bearded lip or chin formed a ludicrous commentary on it, the answer, 'Treble.' In some few places, eminently at Peterboro', my representations on this matter have resulted in a twofold gain—the cessation of a bad practice and the formation in the practising school of a class of boys who, under the excellent instruction of the normal master, Mr. Seabrook, have been qualified thus to complete the college choir. At York, I may remark, this has long been done.

His strictures on the irregularity of attendance had borne some fruit, but he finds that the matter

still admits of improvement. The music master in one college complained that his pupils were withdrawn, sometimes in considerable numbers, for rifle practice and drill. If these pursuits form part of the work of a college, surely a time should be found for them other than that nominally appropriated to another pursuit.

In the practice of *beating time* he also finds room for still further improvement, adding

that practice should begin in the elementary or even in the infant school, not in the training college.

He next calls particular attention to one of the main features of the Wilhem-Hullah Method—sol-faing. He says:

My principal reason for advocating this practice so strongly is that it presents to the teacher the only possible guarantee that his pupils are studying, or, indeed, looking at the symbols from which they are supposed to be singing. A student with a quick ear may, under the influence of those about him who are more attentive or more apt than himself, sing a passage with approximate, nay, with perfect correctness, without understanding or trying to understand anything about the characters in which it is written, but he cannot possibly assign any names to these characters; he cannot sol-fa ' without looking at them.

The verbosity of the students meets with a sharp rebuke, and a few other points are touched upon before the closing paragraphs, as the inter-dependence of theory and practice, which is given in full :

I have found in some of the music teachers in the colleges I have visited a want of recognition of the inter-dependence of theory and practice, exhibited in a disposition to treat them as things to be considered and dealt with separately. Nothing could be more false in principle or more mischievous in application The value of theory should be estimated according to its bearing on practice, disconnected from which it is wanting in life, purpose—I had almost said, meaning. In the degree in which the student realises to his ear—knows the sound of—what he sees, talks about, or writes, he is *a musician*, and no farther; and to enable him to do this should be the end and aim of his musical instructor. His theoretical knowledge, apart from his practice, will be as useless as his practice, apart from his theory, will be empirical. The best illustration of a principle of harmony—for instance, the doubling in or omission of notes from a chord, or the resolution of a dissonance —is the practical one of playing it or making the student take his part in it; and the true mode of correcting practical error is not the tempting because ready one, so 'wise in show,' of example, but the more laborious, and it may seem tedious, one of analysing the structure of the passage in which it has been made. As a rule, teachers sing too much and talk too little in a practical lesson; and they talk too much and play and sing—or make their pupils do so —too little in a theoretical one. In a word, no so-called theoretical lesson should pass without practice; no practical lesson without theory.

With the report his official work for the year closed, and Mr. Hullah resumed the routine of his life, taking part, on December 12, in the functions and pleasant gatherings of Founder's Day at the Charterhouse, and on the 18th participating in the ceremony which attended the laying of the foundation-stone, by H.R.H. the Duke of Edinburgh, of the Royal College of Music. The Christmas festivities of 1873 closed with a dinner, given on December 27 at the Battersea Club, at which were present Sir James Kay-Shuttleworth, Mr. Edward Carlton Tufnell, and Mr. Hullah. For the last time in their lives the three principal actors in the opening scene of the Training College Movement, which began in 1839, were reunited. Of Sir James Mr. Hullah saw a good deal, and many a pleasant chat they had over the labours of old times, their present results and future prospects. Occasionally Mr. Hullah assisted Sir James with notes on the musical section of any scheme on which the latter was employed. Foremost among these schemes was, for the moment, the Girls' High School Company.

The very last incident of the year brought Mr. Hullah the opportunity of pleasing his old friend Sir Arthur Helps, the latest effort of whose pen had just appeared. An early copy of 'Joan de Biron' was despatched to Mr. Hullah with a few lines from the author:

I hope you will like the book. It is not what I would have wished it to be, but it is the best I can do now. This last year has been a year of fearful work for me.

Very gladly Mr. Hullah read the book, and reviewed it to the satisfaction of the author, who thus acknowledges it :

The review is a very thoughtful one. There will, I imagine, be few reviews of the book that will tell so much about it in a few words.

Before closing the chapter with the year, it will be interesting to touch on a difficulty the treatment of which shows how tenderly anxious Mr. Hullah was to ensure for his children, to the best of his ability, a career satisfactory to themselves. To do so it is necessary to go back for a moment to the month of October, when, in the midst of his work, Mr. Hullah was much agitated by hearing of the 'break down' —happily not so 'utter' as was at first supposed—of his youngest son, who, having begun life in a mercantile house, after some preparation in Germany, had so disliked it that his father sacrificed the premium which had been paid, and obtained for him a clerkship in the London and Westminster Bank, where the young man had been but a few months when he became ill. The matter so preyed on Mr. Hullah's mind that most of the letters to his wife, who was absent from home at the time, treat of little else :

With your letter came this morning one from Mary, giving the most deplorable account of Frank, who, through the long hours at the Bank, has utterly broken down for the present. He seems to have been kept till 10 and 11 o'clock at night. In any way it is an anxious business, and has much distressed me. Dr. Fagge, who is connected with the Bank, has got him three weeks' leave of absence. I shall try and learn more about the poor boy's state from Dr. Fagge. Perhaps something is due to rapid growth. . . . He (Dr. Fagge) speaks seriously of him, though not without hope of a better account of him after a little rest. Yesterday . . . I saw Mr. Shipp. He . . . introduced me to the head of the department . . . They spoke in the nicest way possible about Frank, and said they could not attribute his over-hours to any errors or inaccuracies in his work, save on one or two occasions. Touching these same over-hours, there must be a little exaggeration somewhere. It is very difficult for me to see anybody just now that I am at work all 'business hours.' Pray do not, for a moment, think of coming home. Nothing is yet to be done. It is a grievous business to have come upon us, so far apart as we are, and for so long. I shall be off again before you get back.

His anxieties about his son did not end till May in the following year. The Bank clerkship slipped away, and there was doubt and perplexity as to what should next be done. The colonies were of course thought of, for it was about this time that so many young men of gentle birth, but otherwise unblessed by Fortune, were going out, with neither calling nor capital, to seek the one and realise the other, courage and cheerful endurance of hardships incidental to colonial life aiding them. Friends were assisting in more than one way. While Sir Arthur Helps was endeavouring to come to the rescue with his usual inexhaustible kindness on the one hand, Mr. Julian Marshall was using his influence with the late Mr. Crawley, and had succeeded in securing a chance for Mr. Francis Hullah in Mexico, when further exertions were rendered unnecessary by his appointment to an office under the then Solicitor-General.

CHAPTER XXVI.

BIOGRAPHICAL.

1874-75.

A GREAT event opened the year of grace 1874—no less an event than the taking of the children to their first pantomime! on which grave occasion it would have been difficult to decide which took the deeper interest in the adventures of 'Little Red Riding Hood,' the father or the children; or which re-enacted at home with the greater zest the thrilling scenes between Little Red Riding Hood and the terrible wolf, whose deep chest growls (method of production can be evolved from the depths of the 'Speaking Voice') never failed to awaken a sense of delicious awe in the small actress and smaller spectatress, albeit the latter was careful to view the drama from an elevation presumably safe from 'Mr.' Wolf's guileful overtures.

The vacation frivolities over, from Christmas to midsummer life ran on with scarcely a break in the usual course —much work and a little play. Of the former the most important to Mr. Hullah was a little book called 'Time and Tune in the Elementary School.' Of the latter he notes a delightful day spent in the Royal Library at Windsor under Mr. Holmes' guidance, and some musical 'evenings at home,' to one or other of which came Miss Antoinette Sterling, Miss Krebs, Mr. Henry Holmes, with his namesake the late Mr. William Holmes (great as a pianist), Mr. Henry Deacon, and Signor Papini; one and all surpassing themselves under the influence of a kind desire to please a most enthusiastic host and appreciative audience.

At midsummer Mr. Hullah, after much reflection and

hesitation, decided on resigning his post at King's College—a post which he had filled for thirty years, but to which his duties as Inspector of Music prevented his giving any longer the necessary attention. The Governors at once elected him an Honorary Fellow of the College, and gave him the satisfaction of seeing his place filled by his fellow-worker, Dr. Monk. Of all his old colleges there remained now to Mr. Hullah but Bedford and Queen's. To the Council of Queen's College he had long advocated the admission of ladies, and this year he had the pleasure of assisting at the introduction of six to places on the Board. Much about the same time his turn for election to the Athenæum Club came round, and would seem to have tempted him for a short space; but he writes to his wife at Oxford:

> It is an expensive club, and, for an occupied man like me, not worth the cost, so I shall not stand.

He then turns to what he is doing in regard to another matter, to which, in chronological order, brief allusion has already been made—the ungenerous attempt of the Tonic Sol-faists to discredit him at the fountain-head:

> You remember my letter on the Curwenites? . . . I saw Sir Francis Sandford yesterday, who seemed pleased with my reply. The Ministry will probably go out to-day, so Mr. Forster will have no further concern with the matter, though I hope he will *see* my 'state' paper. The memorial of the Training Schools will be just in time for the new people. . . . The Mr. Schultes who called the other day was a 'deputation' from the *Religieuses* of 'the Convent of the Sacred Heart,' who are going to set up a training school, and want advice about the music. . . .
> *Saturday.*—I have just returned from my visit to 'the Convent of the Sacred Heart' at Roehampton, which, as I expected, turned out a most delightful one. Time passed quickly inoculating the worthy *Religieuses* with orthodox notions about music. . . . I am coming down for a night. Will the Frau Rectorinn have me, think you?

Being duly permitted he came, and the same afternoon was presented to H.R.H. Prince Leopold, with whom he had rather a long conversation on the educational aspects of music. In common with most observant people who came across the young student-prince, Mr. Hullah was struck with the concentrated attention with which he listened to an explanation, whether on a subject he had himself started, or on any other which might be in process of discussion among the company present.

When the time for starting on his official tour, towards the end of August, approached, Mr. Hullah urged many excellent reasons why he should not be allowed to go alone; but again it was impossible to bend family arrangements to suit his wishes, nor did it become feasible during any of the following years. He and his wife could but secure a week for paying visits together before he turned solitarily towards Exeter, and she took one child, whose health required complete change, abroad. There was one consolation in separation; he could receive frequent, and write daily, letters, to which he was by no means averse. From Exeter he writes:

Anything like the heat of the weather I never before have experienced in England, and I have only brought two white waistcoats, of which I have to-day put on one.

Weather as hot as he describes always delighted him, and the donning of a resplendent white waistcoat was a joy. Besides, as an Irish member of his extensive family of adopted 'sisters, cousins, and aunts' admiringly assured him, a *white* waistcoat 'suited his complexion; so it did!'

I have been to the cathedral (he continues). The restoration works are all stopped, I suppose on account of the row about the reredos, a feeble thing enough but involving 'images.'

... 27.—I have grieved over your misadventures. I had consoled myself with the thought that you must have had a lively passage; for the heat and want of air on Saturday were fearful, and I was told on Sunday that a sailing match had been postponed because there was absolutely *no wind*. You, it seems, have had it all! ... How I wish I could be with you in Bruges, which I do not know at all. Of course you are drawing! and Millie should try. Do ... I *was* writing downstairs, when at the moment of inscribing the last word, the most horrible of wind bands burst out under the window, and I was obliged to take refuge in my bedroom, where I still hear the horrid noise, but not with the same intensity. To resume: do not be in a hurry to leave Bruges or any other place wherein you are comfortable, as you seem to be in your little lodging. ... Now for my adventures. ... I fell in with Mr. B——, who took me off to dinner. There were two ladies who live at Simla (isn't that where you used to go as a child, say a hundred years ago?) . . . On Tuesday, on coming down to breakfast, I met my co-inspector, Tinling, . . . and—good fortune, like bad, never comes single—at Plymouth we picked up Warburton. . . . The consequence was we made a lively trio, took a long walk, and dined together. I had a most social instead of, as it might have been, a most solitary evening. Yesterday we were all three at the Training College, and . . . went by invitation to dine with Dr. B—— (the band is excruciating). This morning Warburton and I left Truro at 7.30. At Plymouth who should get in but Miss J—— and her brother, who came on to Bristol *en route* for home. . . . At the cathedral I fell in with Plumptre and Mrs. P. They (oh! that band!) . . . and this brings me to the time of the present writing, of which (under the accompaniment) I must postpone more.

Many of his letters were quite excellent guides to places he had not visited, but about which he knew more than half the people who had 'done them,' for his memory was a wonderful storehouse of facts about things, places, and people interesting to him, and he was almost invariably accurate though more often than not quoting from books he had not opened, or an illustration he had not seen, for years. To keep him, however, in letter-writing condition it was indispensable that he should receive full and frequent reports of his correspondent's proceedings :

Your account of your doings is most interesting; your *weather* excites envy! . . . I've just come back from the Training College (it is five), where I have been, since half-past nine, hearing forty-five students. And it is pouring. To-morrow I have a day's work nearly as long. . . . I lead a most primitive life when I am by myself— going to bed at nine and rising at *six.* ahem! This morning I did a long examination paper before eight. I get proofs almost every day from Savile, the correcting of which takes a good deal of time. The only thing I most object to is the rain, which prevents my taking any exercise, without which life's a vapour—just now a vapour-bath.

. . . *S.-on-W.*—I found Phillott, George, and Mr. M—— (M.P. for Oxford, who is staying here) waiting for me at the Moorhampton station, from which we walked over to Staunton. I am sitting with the window open, looking, when I raise my head, over to the beautiful Moccas woods, with no more serious disturbance of my thoughts than is created by the twittering of swallows, an occasional 'moo,' and the crowing of a very remote cock. My time since we parted has been chiefly spent in towns . . . and the quiet of this place is delicious. I wish I could have a few more days of it. The Phillotts are *furious* at my early departure!! The M——s are delightful, he full of knowledge of life and literature, and she very intelligent. . . . We are going this afternoon to Weobly.

Doubtless I shall get news of my nomadic darlings to-morrow, but I don't like to wait till then, especially with this opportunity of writing so peacefully and comfortably.
 . . . Oh! this quiet! I mean to get out the last five chapters of my book ['Time and Tune in the Elementary School'] while I am here. . . . I have had an old Worcester cup and saucer *given* to me! A capital specimen!
 . . . Captain V——, R.N., asks me to stay with him at B—— to-morrow night. I am perfectly well; much stronger than when I left London. The P——s send their love to you, and reproaches for not coming with me. Mrs. P. paid you *such* a compliment last night! which I shall *not* pass on. It is well to keep down the conceit of some people.

He thus describes the house to which he had been invited for the first time :

This house is a sort of French château, very well planned and in some respects very handsome—full of panelling, tapestry, and china! . . . It was designed, down to the minutest details, by its present occupant. It belongs, I find, to Lady S—— W——, a charming old lady . . . I have just returned from the Training College, which, though exactly opposite to us, is on the other side of the strait, and practically four miles off! . . . How I should like to have been with you at Aix in that queer cathedral of which, in spite of its Louis XV. treatment—since, I believe, removed—I used to be so fond. . . . The book is getting on famously . . . *Confidentially* I quite agree with you about Treves. It is overrated The 'basilica' is horribly 'made up.' But the 'Porte' is fine. Did you see St. Remi (at Rheims) and the sculptures (mediæval) in the Hospital?

Lancaster, to which he had gone, not liking Liverpool on a Sunday, was the first place, after some days of very hard work, where he rested—or rather *tried* to rest—unsuccessfully, he has to say :

Two bands, one of fifes and drums, have just passed my window, accompanying troops returning from church, followed by half the population—not favourable to epistolary or any other composition. I met with the most kind reception on Thursday from the Sisters of Notre Dame, and examined sixty students. Canon Chapman, as usual, came to meet me and keep me company at dinner, which, though it was a *jour maigre*, we enjoyed very much. . . . I have got here into a most quaint old house, with an Elizabethan stair case, and full as it can hold of ancient furniture—some of it very good. In my room is a bed which belonged to James I., one of the finest things of its kind I ever saw—not a scrap of it *made up*. . . . This afternoon I mean to walk to Morecambe Bay, which I have not seen for years [probably not since '42]. . . . I have just done correcting proofs of Time and Tune in the ' E. S. the announcement of which has, I find, created curiosity in the training schools. . . .

Glasgow, as usual, turned out far from pleasant in any way, the weather being most especially unpleasant.

Of course it rained when I arrived (he says) and it rains now, and I believe it always does rain. My few days at O—— were delightful. Mrs. H—— sang 'O that we two were Maying,' after about ten minutes' study, really exquisitely.

Having finished his school inspections, Mr. Hullah spent an afternoon

at Paisley to see the old abbey and hear a new organ of much interest; H—— having arranged for the organist to meet us. . . .
On Thursday I went to the *soiree* of the Social Science Association, which was at Glasgow all the week. It was held in the new University Museum. Here I fell in with a lot of people I knew— the Stevensons . . . and Mr. Tufnell, who introduced me to Miss Carpenter, with whom I had much talk, and who invited me to come and see her next year when I go to Bristol, where she lives, and has a school of her own. . . . I rather like this place [he writes a part of his letter from Aberdeen]. It is new and without historical interest, but the granite, of which it is *entirely* built, gives a dignity even to much very bad architecture. It is beautifully clean, which, after Glasgow, is a great recommendation. The air seems to me some of the purest I ever inhaled, and the atmospheric effects, especially in the evening, are very beautiful, the sky presenting that *opal* tint one so seldom sees in England. The examination yesterday went off very well. . . . I am going to see Professor Black, a friend of Dr. Maclagan's, presently. He lives at Old Aberdeen, where the University is, and he is to show me all about. . . . The new book is nearly all printed. To-morrow I go to Edinburgh, when I shall be at Heriot Row till Tuesday, the 13th, when I strike south to Durham.

A few days later, and he was able to announce his return home within three days. Everyone had been most kind at the places he had visited. He had seen all his old friends, and made not a few new acquaintances; but to get home was a most unqualified delight to him, and he would willingly have been relieved from the necessity of again leaving town, but, in addition to the suburban schools, Salisbury and Winchester had yet to be examined. At Salisbury, where he was again the guest of the archdeacon, his wife joined him for two days, and shared the kindness of his host and hostess; but the severity of the weather brought on her an illness which caused Mr. Hullah some days of such intense alarm that he never again urged her to quit home in mid-winter. For others besides his wife he had cause for anxiety during this exceptionally severe season. His two most valued and best-loved friends among men, the Rev. William Tylden, of Stanford, and Sir Arthur Helps, were in failing health, and early in 1875 both passed away within a few days of each other, neither having completed by many years the allotted span of man's life.

To Mr. Griesbach and Sir Sterndale Bennett, with whom he had been long professionally associated, the winter proved also fatal.

Excellent obituary notices of these last, from Mr. Hullah's pen, may be found in the 'Globe' newspaper, while on Sir Arthur Helps Mr. Hullah contributed an interesting paper to the 'Athenæum for the week ending March 13, and another to the April number of 'Macmillan's Magazine.' From these sad tasks it was well for him to turn to help Sir James Kay-Shuttleworth with hard practical suggestions on a more extended scale than had sufficed for the schemes of the preceding year, and to be forced back to the work-a-day world by the necessity for preparing vast numbers of examination papers for the ensuing school term, and to the writing of his report on the work of the past year.

It will be remembered that in 1873 Mr. Hullah expressed a very pronounced opinion on the uselessness of collective sight-singing as a test of knowledge. In the Report for 1874 he reverts to the subject:

> Two years' additional experience has led me to value, less even than before, collective musical skill, however exhibited, as evidence of individual. Indeed, last year I made a point everywhere of cautioning students against the danger, inseparable from all musical teaching in class, arising from one student's singing helping another's too much. Paradoxical as it may sound, I have repeatedly found individual power, especially in reading, least satisfactory among students the results of whose combined performances were the most agreeable. M. Guizot, after hearing (in the capacity of Minister of Public Instruction) some music classes in Paris, is recorded to have said, *C'est très bien,* and then, after a moment, *C'est trop bien.* It proves that M. Guizot's keen perception had led him to detect, beneath the polish which came immediately under the eye or the

touch, the flimsiness of the material to which it had been applied
To students honestly prepared for their consideration, the refinement or *nuances* of musical performance will commend themselves
soon enough, and their attainment prove a matter of little labour.
Over attention, or, more properly, premature attention, to them can
answer no purpose but to encourage self-satisfaction among incompetent students, and win the applause of visitors ignorant of music,
or not in a position to estimate at its true value the sham put before
them. I shall hardly be suspected of a wish to discourage the correction of bad habits in the utterance of words or of notes, but I
protest against anything like an hour's practice (I have known this
done) being spent on the delivery of a single passage so softly as to
be hardly audible ; only perhaps approximately so delivered at last,
through half those concerned in it being silenced entirely.

Mr. Hullah's remarks on a bad method of holding the
mouth and the results therefrom will arrest the attention of
readers who are in any way engaged in teaching the young to
sing :

To the prevalence of one bad habit in training schools I take
this opportunity of directing attention—a habit which would seem
to have been found easier to imitate than I find it to describe. It
consists in preceding the issue of a sound, by throwing the mouth,
after every inhalation, into the position required for uttering the
liquid M ; giving an effect, for example, to the sol-fa syllables like
MDo, *MRe*, and so on, and actually falsifying words beginning
with vowels ; making *e* into *me*, *a* into *may*, and so on.

But if quick to point out a fault he was at all times ready
to hold out encouragement :

Students with the best voices and ears have by no means always
passed the best examinations, and *vice versâ*. This is a hopeful
sign ; showing, as it does, that those students who fail have no right
to attribute their failures to natural inaptitude.

Of the 1,840 students whom I examined last year not two, I
think, can have failed from any cause they themselves could not
have made inoperative. If every pupil-teacher at the end of his
course of five years could, on a key-note being given him, sound
when named, or name when sounded, any other notes in the same
key, and a few altered notes inevitable in common modulation ; and
also sing or recite a few measures in the two principal kinds of time,
or conversely describe them when so sung or recited—accomplishments which an intelligent child of, say, ten might easily attain in
a twelvemonth, with about a quarter of an hour's instruction a day ;
if, I say, every pupil-teacher entering a Training College could do
even this much, changes in the habits of our labouring classes
would be brought about in a few years, by the command of one

humanising recreation, which would assuredly add as largely and permanently to their own well-being as to that of the community at large.

The next extract is valuable for two reasons. It shows how impartial in regard to *methods* of instruction was the Inspector, and it recalls that keen feeling for discipline which had made him so eminently successful as a leader of great choral classes :

> Whatever be the method of instruction in a Training College, the students should be required during their term of studentship to adopt it; first, for the sake of discipline, which the student surely must conform to before he can enforce; and, secondly, because the method which the teacher thinks the best *is* the best *for him*, simply because he believes in it and is most familiar with it.

At considerable length Mr. Hullah insists on inspection in elementary schools, and deprecates forcibly the so-called ' teaching ' ' by ear ' :

> Hitherto singing 'by ear' has been accepted as 'singing,' and the preparation of twelve songs as 'teaching singing.' It is to be hoped that this obviously provisional, and for a time inevitable, condition of things will soon be brought to an end. Whatever its value as 'a means of moral discipline,' singing ' by ear,' regarded from a musical point of view, is simply worthless. That the possession of ninety-nine songs, got ' by ear,' will not enable the possessor to add another to the number by any independent effort of his own is obvious. The process of learning them in this way adds nothing to the power of the learner. It is absolutely sterile, and ends with itself. On the other hand, the least skill in reading music, and the least acquaintance with musical science—and some of both may be given to every child who remains even a year at school—might easily, with subsequent opportunity, be developed, and has often been developed, into a means of innocent and even ennobling recreation. The natives of some parts of Great Britain—*e.g.* of Lancashire, the West Riding of Yorkshire, and South Wales—have shown that musical skill and science are not unattainable for those whose means and whose leisure are alike limited, and, which is even more satisfactory, that this skill is as a rule brought to bear on the noblest music—the concerted music of Handel, Haydn, Mozart, Mendelssohn—uniformly illustrative of and connected with the noblest themes.

Teaching songs ' by ear,' whatever it may be, is not teaching music. On the contrary, it is a serious hindrance to doing so, both as respects scholars and schools. As respects the former, experience shows that those who have been longest in the habit of singing by ear are the slowest to apply themselves to singing by note, while, as respects the latter, the preparation thus of any considerable number of songs, absorbing, as it often will, the whole time available for music in a given school, leaves none for dealing with the subject thoroughly.

With the expression of an earnest hope that the Lords of the Committee of Council on Education will see their way to instituting inspection in elementary schools as soon as possible, the Inspector of Music closes his Report for 1874.

CHAPTER XXVII.

BIOGRAPHICAL.

1875.

DURING these peaceful forenoon hours of the early part of 1875, Mr. Hullah achieved a large number of articles, some for Grove's 'Dictionary,' some for the 'Globe,' the materials for these latter being gathered in the course of evening visits to concerts, operas, and occasionally to theatres, when any actor as good as Salvini attracted his notice, and impelled him to write one of the analytical critiques, excellent of their kind, which appeared from time to time in the course of the spring season of 1875.

He also saw through the press the little volume 'Time and Tune in the Elementary School' (more recently known as 'Hullah's Method of Teaching Singing'), with the accompanying exercises and figures. A new feature in this book is a table of inflected syllables, which the author believed would greatly increase the interest and precision of sol-fa practices. To some of Mr. Hullah's most faithful disciples, this table of inflected syllables was, for the moment at any rate, a sore trial which they could not adopt without a preliminary protest. Indeed, his veteran assistant, Mr. May, fairly rebelled, and said roundly he didn't like the innovation, and would only teach it because he was a true disciple. At least he says so in a letter written in January; but in October he has to say:

I am anxious to let you know that, in thinking over 'Time and Tune,' I am becoming a convert! The truth is that, when first I opened the book and glanced at it, I took a dislike to it because I fancied it was a concession to the Tonic Sol-faists; the inflection of the vowels seemed to me at the *first* glance to savour of the *sect*, and in consequence thereof made me feel *ill*. . . . Observe, it was the inflection of the *syllables* that angered me. I have been mentally sol-faing scales, and am becoming a convert to your system.

A decided triumph this for the inflected syllables, for Mr. May is a master of his craft. Later on the inflected syllables were introduced at Bedford College, and elsewhere in England; in the course of a short time finding their way also to the notice of the master of the choir of St. Peter's, Rome, and other continental teachers of position.

Before Easter Mr. Hullah had begun a new edition of the 'History of Modern Music,' much needed, since, though in good demand, it had run out of print. Having at length taken it in hand, he pressed on steadily, and rather knocked himself up, for his desk work had to be mainly carried on late of nights, the daylight hours proper to work being absorbed by frequent attendance at committees, including some at the new College of Music. Of this institution he had also been made an examiner, which, in respect of that sort of work, had rather the effect of the proverbial last straw on the camel's back. As a new departure in his rhetorical performances, fairly numerous on his own subject in and about London, must certainly be mentioned an introductory speech as chairman of a woman's suffrage meeting held in his wife's drawing-room, on which occasion he was gallantly supported by Miss Anna Swanwick and other friends, who considered that he acquitted himself excellently, and quite secured the approving suffrages of the ladies in that future age of justice and enlightenment when women shall have votes and the country be educated up to the point of requiring that harmony be granted a seat in the Lower House at least.

As the summer advanced Mr. Hullah sadly missed the accustomed visit to Stanford. nor had he heart to go to any other friend, and as from a variety of causes there came an unwonted gap in his engagements, he decided to fill it by taking a trip to France. Nothing better could be decided, for nothing ever set him up in body and mind like a Continental tour. Accordingly, map in hand, he planned a journey of vast extent, which, however, in consideration of his tired state, was cut down to singularly modest dimensions, but yielded, even thus curtailed, a large crop of pleasure. His wife, set free for the nonce, accompanied him, and the journey was taken with safe deliberation.

A preliminary dip in the sea at Boulogne, and total abstention from the merest pretence of work—he said even from thought—for ten whole hours made a new man of him, and after ten more hours spent in sound sleep he was 'as lively as a bird,' and journeyed off to Beauvais, viâ Amiens, en route to Gisors, Les deux Andelys, Louviers, Evreux, 'Chartres the beloved' being the goal aimed at. Here a week's stay was spent almost wholly in and about the cathedral, so that every priest and every townsman knew the travellers by sight, and smiled and chatted on occasion in a way that made them feel as if they left a town full of friends rather than strangers behind when they took train to Versailles.

Here, *not* in the Hôtel des Réservoirs, a suite of three rooms was taken, and a quiet, regular, well-nourished existence greatly enjoyed and profited by for the remainder of the holiday, *less* three days, which Mr. Hullah had bargained should be spent in Paris in order that he might go at least once to the theatre—to the Théâtre Historique. He went, was aware that 'Latude' was being played, but could not attend to a word, so suffocating was the heat; for though indubitably Mr. Hullah had close kinship with the salamander, such heat even he could not endure, so Paris was quitted for once with a sigh of relief, and the homeward journey effected with a good deal more than the average discomfort. But now, as always, the holiday journey had its accustomed effect. The delight of lingering about French cathedrals and quaint streets, the good dinners, the dry light air of France, the general pleasantness of life, had renewed the elasticity of his mind and body, and he was as well and as cheerful as could be desired till the train bearing him over the last stage of the journey came in sight of Stanford Rectory. Then, as he looked out, he grew depressed and sad, and fell to thinking of the dear departed friend whose welcoming face and gentle cordial grasp had made a break in the homeward journey delightful for years past. The weight of mournful memories was increasing rapidly, and as age came upon him began to

tell a little more than formerly on his spirits. This time he
could not shake off his depression, even in the hurry of
preparation for his autumnal tour of inspection. The first
journey was to keep him two whole months from home, so
Mrs. Hullah decided to take the children over to France to pro-
secute in easy colloquial fashion their linguistic studies. The
only drawback to this scheme was that it added to the distance
between Mr. Hullah and his belongings. Nevertheless a most
active correspondence was kept up. Mr. Hullah's letters
present fewer new facts in regard to the educational work,
though they are full of touches, sometimes keenly critical, in
regard to persons. He was travelling over the same ground,
staying in the same places, visiting the same people, and
continually adding to his provincial acquaintances. His
genial, pleasant, facile adaptability and bright conversational
powers

> Accordant to a voice which charmed no less,
> That who but saw him once remembered long,
> And some in whom such images are strong
> Have hoarded that impression in their heart.

Everywhere he was a welcome guest, whose annual return
was, in many a home, looked forward to with an affectionate
interest which found further expression in letters written by
his hosts to his wife after the visits were over, giving all
manner of little details of his doings, health, strength, and
spirits.

His first letters home are altogether clouded and unhappy
in tone:

> I have seldom left home in worse spirits than I did yester-
> day . . .

he begins from Bristol, but for him everything had interest, and in telling his own adventures he regains a more
cheerful frame of mind. His first visit was to the cathedral,
where he was comforted by hearing 'a noble anthem by
Goss,' and then goes on to lunch with Mr. Corfe, who has

> a portrait of an uncle in the Chapel Royal Boys' state dress, red,
> with gold lace on it, which I think must be by Sir Joshua. . . .
> Have you begun the 'Do-do?'

This mystic question refers to the daily five minutes' sol-faing, called by the children the 'Do-do lesson,' which he much wished carried on, and to that end had done his best to 'coach' his wife up to the level of an elementary teacher. On this journey Mr. Hullah had taken by way of literature nothing but Italian books, and it happened that the revival of the language in his memory came in usefully, for on one subject or another there was much communication with Italy.

I have two Italian letters (he has to tell), one from Signor Fano, the editor of the Milanese journal the 'Mondo Artistico,' asking leave to print my last report [translated by A. Visetti]; the other from Signor Visetti, wanting to translate other of my things.

Late in September Mr. Hullah, being at Oxford, is very cheerful and chatty:

This morning I was occupied from ten till three in issuing notices, making my weekly diary, and writing letters, chiefly business. . . . I went out after three and called at Lincoln. No rector! I then made my way to Magdalen. No service! Then I called on Miss Eleanor Smith. No Miss S. till to-morrow; then on Parratt. At home!!. . . He is wishful that I should lecture here. . . . I mean to think of it. . . . Herewith I send a groundplan of my longest foot [to facilitate the purchase of a pair of thick felt shoes till lately only obtainable abroad]. . . . Your account of your supper after a long walk is very classical. It brought to my mind directly Milton's sonnet to Mr. Lawrence. . . .

What neat repast shall feast us, light and choice,
Of Attic taste, with wine——.

. . . Love to the Dodos; and *do do you* get better. . . .

His visit to Liverpool, though most distasteful by reason of the dirt and gruesome squalor of the lower population, all the more terrible by contrast with the evidences of boundless wealth around, was full of interest, because the work of the Female Training College was so efficiently done, and his examination of the results made so agreeable, thanks to the refinement and cordiality of the ladies in command. Nor were incidents wanting to relieve the tediousness of solitary travel. At one moment he fell in with a friend home on leave from India; at another with an American, who, it turned out, had a letter of introduction to him in his pocket.

An hour or so after his arrival he was passing the town hall, and looked in 'just in time to hear some children sing two pieces of music with more vigour than sweetness.'

Then (he continues) I made my way to Mr. Best, the organist, who took me to his room, gave me some grapes, provided by the municipality! and finally introduced me to Mrs. Best . . . who is an Italian! so I aired my Italian. . . . I attended Mr. Best's weekly performance on the town hall organ. I have often heard him before, never with more pleasure. He is really *stupendissimo*—the greatest player in the world.

By the time Mr. Hullah reached Glasgow he was so wearied that the fatigue told on his handwriting. The climate of that part of Scotland and of that particular city disagreed with him, the grime sickened him, and the work was extremely hard; in addition there were unpleasant surroundings and associations. From first to last Glasgow was, on the whole, the one place he entered with repugnance and left with delight:

Are you coming north—will you be in Edinburgh (he asks, in the last letter he writes from Glasgow) ? To see some friendly faces will be a gain, to see a loving one would be a greater. . . . What a relief it will be to leave this place you cannot conceive. . . . I rejoice you are at last come back to this side of the Channel, but not surprised that you find Tunbridge Wells uninteresting. . . . It does not do, stopping about in this country, unless with friends, and not always then.

To add to Mr. Hullah's depressed condition, he began to receive disquieting news of his only brother's condition, to which he makes allusion several times in the course of his letters:

Edinboro'.—I have just finished at the Free Church Normal School. The work has been hard but very pleasant. This afternoon I made an address to the students in the presence of a number of the committee. . . . Every day now brings me nearer to London. I suppose *you* are beginning to think of moving homewards. . . . Home! home! that I pine for again, and that I shall see again (D.V.) this day fortnight! . . . *Durham.*—I am staying with the Arnes, who live in a quaint and also comfortable house, and do all that is possible to make life pleasant. I left the Maclagan's with great regret this morning. . . . I did not say anything to them about my brother's illness, though it would have been a comfort and a relief to do so. . . . *Oct.* 27.—The news of my brother's death has come this morning.

Mr. Hullah came home immediately to attend the funeral. The last link with his own generation was now broken, and more than ever he turned for love, and clung for sympathy, to the ties of more recent years.

The work of inspection thus sadly interrupted was resumed after a brief pause, and the daily communications went on as before, only that Italian being the language specially under study, a portion of each letter was devoted to 'a practice,' to which a due response was expected. At length from Winchester he was able to write:

I have this afternoon brought my inspection work to a close pleasantly. The last student I examined was a capital one. I did not get here till six o'clock yesterday, for I went and called at Salisbury on the Dean and the Bishop [died July, 1885]. The Dean and Mrs. Hamilton only came home a day or so since. They were most kind and cordial, inquired after you. . . . and he talked with his usual spirit and brilliancy. He is a wonderful man—eighty-three!. . . . Warburton is as delightful as ever. I am installed and writing now in the most charming bedroom, with a lovely fire—no unwelcome companion when the snow is on the ground.
. . . I fell in this morning with W——d . . . . who took me about to see all Butterfield's new work, which is capital, especially a tennis court. St. Cross looked lovely. The painting has a good deal toned down.

Just a day for rearranging his books and putting things straight was all the relaxation he secured on his return home before his pen was again taken up. The Christmas season was passed very quietly at home, work, of course, largely predominating over play. Two articles for Grove's 'Dictionary,' several for the 'Globe,' and an immense mass of correspondence were disposed of. There were many inquiries from America as to the best mode of using his inflected syllables. From Rome and Florence also came letters full of admiration of their ingenuity and practical utility. The official report of 1874 was alluded to by all these writers with interest and commendation, accompanied by a request that future reports might be sent. Examination papers next called for attention. These disposed of, the Report for 1875 was written.

The tables of percentages show that a larger proportion of students than heretofore have obtained '60 per cent. and over' of the utmost number of marks attainable, whether for theoretical knowledge or practical skill. . . . Of the 1,672 students I examined individually in 1873, 923 had, before their entry to their several colleges, received no instruction, even in the elements of music, and many had never sung, even by 'ear.' Of the 1,807 (second-year students) presented to me for examination last year, 731 were in like predicament. Relatively this is a very small number, absolutely it is a very large one. . . .

Of pupil-teachers, Mr. Hullah says that:

As a rule, they enter on their term of apprenticeship at the age of thirteen, an age which, besides being five years too late to begin the study of music to much good purpose, is just the age at which the voice, both of boy and girl, is often on the point of undergoing a change, during which it should be exercised but little, or not at all. The years of a pupil-teacher's apprenticeship, from thirteen to eighteen, are exactly those during which his or her voice should be least exercised. . . .

Once more Mr. Hullah speaks of the collective singing as in some few cases ' too good.'

To occupy the time of beginners, often as yet practically uncertain of the most simple melodic or rhythmic relations of notes, with the consideration of any but the broadest distinctions of *effect*, if even with them, is to sacrifice the indispensable to the desirable. As the poet has it in relation to the starving—

> Such dainties to them their health it might hurt,
> It's like sending them ruffles when wanting a shirt.

In the combined singing of the first-year students, whom, though I do not examine individually, I hear always together, a curious result sometimes presents itself. I find it occasionally superior to that of the students of the second year. For instance, at Saltley, Derby, and Cheltenham I have this year noted the latter as merely good, or even fair, and the former as very good. Now and then this result may be attributable to the accident of a higher average of voice as well as of general power in the one body than in the other ; but it is only another proof of the musical inequality of the students on entry into the colleges, generally a constant source of inconvenience to the musical instructors, a disadvantage to the better prepared of those they have to teach, and not an inevitable accident, but a quite evitable cause.

In the individual singing of music already practised, a gradual improvement is to be noted. On this the training of the students in other subjects tells favourably indirectly, and in one especially, reading aloud, directly. Their enunciation in singing is, as a rule, better than that of many amateurs who have studied music apparently under more favourable circumstances. I wish, however, that this improvement could be extended to the choice of subjects on which students exhibit their individual powers. At some colleges—*e.g.* Bangor, Borough Road, Darlington, Lincoln, Peterboro', Ripon, Wandsworth, York—the solos were generally well chosen ; but in some others I was favoured with a variety, or worse, a repetition, of the poorest vocal compositions I had ever before listened to under the same circumstances. The time of a student in training is his best, often his only property, and he should be prevented wasting it on the consideration of trash, literary or musical. I am sure it can only be needful to call the attention of the musical instructors to this matter to have it set right.

In the power and facility of reading fresh music, or, as it is commonly called, 'singing at sight,' the past year's examination has revealed great, and, I believe, unprecedented improvement. Of this the extent, in comparison with that of former years, will be easily gathered from the subjoined table of averages of practical skill; since I have, from my first examination, assigned no less than half the marks attainable to this subject only. Its importance is paramount. It represents both theoretical knowledge and readiness in applying it, habit of attention, quickness of eye and ear, in a word, to what extent the reader or singer is a self-dependent *musician*, competent, unaided, to set others on the right way and to tell them where and how they have departed from it.

The number of students who have undergone the 'ear tests' satisfactorily in the course of the last examination is again somewhat greater than at any previous one. This is one of the subjects wherein the first step seems everything. I find, as a rule, that students can either tell sounds played or sung to them readily and certainly, or not at all. This might suggest the conclusion that the power of doing so was a natural gift. That it is largely dependent on race and family is certain, simply, as I believe, because among certain races and in certain families music has long been cultivated. Among varieties even of the most musical races with whom this has not been the case musical aptitude will be found to die out. Thus the Celts of Wales are, perhaps, the most musically apt of any people in Great Britain; on the other hand, those of the Highlands of Scotland are the least so. I have never met with a Welsh student with what is called a defective ear. I have taken the utmost pains to get a Highland student to imitate even approximately the simplest succession of musical sounds, quite unsuccessfully; and this not in one instance only, but in half-a-dozen consecutive instances. The cause is not far to seek. Music is an imitative art. From time immemorial the Welsh ear has been formed, consciously or unconsciously, by the harp, an instrument not merely refined in its quality, but an instrument of harmony, and, therefore, of necessity tuned on the system which, with Europeans, use has made into a second nature. The Highland ear has been formed on the coarsest variety of one of the most imperfect even of monodic instruments, the bagpipe. I do not give these as the only causes of the musical inequality of these two varieties of the same race, but as one of them, and that of itself a sufficient one.

I have already on two occasions called attention to the teaching of the pianoforte in the Church of Scotland Training College of Edinburgh. The exceptional method employed there and the equally exceptional results obtained from it must be my excuse for doing so again. Between forty and fifty of the female students of this institution are distributed into six classes, in each of which not fewer than seven, or more than eight, receive instruction from Mr. Mackenzie, an eminent Edinburgh professor, assisted by a resident governess, Miss Hart. For this and the use of music they pay a small fee. Some previous preparation is a condition of entrance even into the lowest of these classes, which, of course, are in various stages of progress. Mr. Mackenzie's method is simple, whatever musical science and skill, energy and quickness of observation may be needed to make it effective. When he has occasion to introduce a new composition to his pupils he collects them round one pianoforte, plays it, marks and gives reasons for the choice of the 'fingering,' and then hands them the copy thus marked, that they may transfer his fingering to their own copies. At the end of a few days, during which they are expected to have given it some study and practice, the class reassembles and simultaneously practises it under Mr. Mackenzie's direction. It is obvious that such instruction, in such a subject as pianoforte playing, can only be efficient in very competent hands. It is not enough that the teacher know whether what he listens to is right or wrong; he must know what it is that is wrong, and who is the wrongdoer. Moreover, his eyes must be as actively employed as his ears, that he may note and correct at least the most glaring instances of clumsy manipulation. That individual correctness may be attained by instruction thus distributed I was enabled to ascertain by calling upon individual students, at Mr. Mackenzie's invitation, to play any of the major or minor scales, which they did generally readily and correctly.

The closing passage of the Report merits consideration from others besides the Lords of the Committee of Council on Education, to whom it was addressed. Mr. Hullah's views on the necessity of a ' perfect choir ' have been given at length elsewhere :

Is it to be argued from their action or inaction in this matter that the authorities of the Training Colleges are of opinion that the only adult persons who can safely be trusted to pass an occasional hour, every moment of which would be occupied, and this under surveillance, in company with those of another sex, are the future instructors and instructresses of the people of Great Britain? It is impossible to believe that the subject has ever been seriously considered by them.

CHAPTER XXVIII.

BIOGRAPHICAL.

1876.

DREARY winter, cold and dark, was made as endurable as possible by an unusual course of sociable parties at home, in which Mr. Hullah at all times and seasons rejoiced. A flying visit to Lincoln College, Oxford, Mr. Cotter Morison being a fellow-guest, gave but a fresh impetus to these pleasant social meetings at home on Mr. Hullah's return. Now and then Sir James Kay-Shuttleworth came, or the Hullahs dined with him, and there were long *causeries* over the 'Reminiscences' that were to be written some day. Sir James was anxious Mr. Hullah should begin, promising help in the way of material and counsel; as interested, in fact, as though these 'Reminiscences' were to be purely personal to himself.

In March, Dr. Maclagan, of Edinburgh, ascended 'Mount Grosvenor,' remained a day or two, and departed, leaving behind him a mysterious expectation of some pleasant surprise being imminent—an expectation realised shortly by the arrival of a formal intimation that it was the intention of the Senatus of the Edinburgh University to confer on Mr. Hullah in the following month the degree of Doctor of Laws, 'the highest honour we can confer,' says the corresponding member.

In April, therefore, Mr. Hullah went northward to undergo the 'pleasing pain' of being for a few moments a very prominent figure in an august assembly.

Looking in on friends as he journeyed north, he arrived in Edinburgh a little buoyed up by a hope that somehow he should find his wife had 'contrived to get herself packed up and comfortably labelled, care of John Hullah and the other occupants of 28 Heriot Row.' He took consolation for his disappointment, however, when the weather became absolutely atrocious:

> In case of *not* seeing you this evening, I send off a line just to say I am safe and sound. . . . The Arnes [at Durham] were disappointed yesterday at the sight of one *solo*—a sort of O without a figure before it. . . . *The* 18*th*. . . . I am not very sorry you are not here; for anything more dispiriting than the weather it is hard to conceive; and there is a very determined east wind ' which blows nobody any good.' . . . Indoors it is much more cheerful. There was a very pleasant party last evening, joined after dinner by [the late] Lord Ardmillan [a *raconteur* of great humour], who stayed after the rest of the company was gone, and was very amusing. The Dumfries folks are coming in for Thursday's ceremony. . . . I have not bought a single English book! Yesterday I got a good spell at Italian. . . . 19*th*.—The Italian studies have been broken in upon by a most interesting lecture of Professor Geddes on the Celtic tongue. . . . If you go to the Club [the Albemarle], look out in this week's ' Saturday Review' an article headed ' An Exploded Idol—Blake!' As Deutsch said of him, ' How he wallows in misery!'
>
> *April* 20. . . . I have just got back from the Assembly Hall, in which we have been shut up some hours, assisting at, I must say, a most interesting ceremony. There were degrees of all kinds given; *honorary* ones in divinity and law. The candidates for the latter were presented, one at a time, by Maclagan, who spoke admirably, and altogether acquitted himself of his task with much elegance and consummate skill and tact. . . . I have taken possession of my *hood*, and been already addressed by all manner of people as ' Doctor;' witness the enclosed letter which I found waiting for me on my return home, enclosing a parcel of books from Professor Blackie, whom with many other well-known people I met at dinner last night at the Principal's [Sir A. Grant]. . . . I send a full account of the ceremony. . . .

In presenting the gentlemen on whom the Senatus of the Edinburgh University had agreed to confer the degree of Doctor of Law, Professor Maclagan said:

> Chancellor, I appear before you somewhat unexpectedly, and on rather short notice, on behalf of my colleague, the Dean of the Faculty of Law, who is understood to be detained by adverse meteorological conditions in an outlying part of her Majesty's dominions situated somewhere between the coast of Argyllshire and the United States of America. . . .

Professor W. D. Geddes, of Aberdeen, was then presented . . . and ' capped.' Professor Maclagan next presented Mr. John Hullah.

> The University of Edinburgh (continued the Professor) has had many opportunities of enrolling on its list of honorary graduates the

names of those who have been distinguished in literature, science, philosophy, and politics; but it must be confessed, with some compunction, that it has done nothing towards recognising those fine arts which are at once the source and the evidence of the civilisation of any country, and which furnish us with some of our purest and most elevated enjoyments. It is fitting, I think, that the University of Edinburgh, which alone of the Universities of Scotland possesses a chair of music, should show a practical acknowledgment of past musicians by recognising one of the fine arts in the person of this most adequate representative.

Professor Maclagan then lightly sketched the main facts of Mr. Hullah's educational career, and named most of his important compositions and educational works on music, with a few special remarks on Mr. Hullah's ' " Treatise on the Human Speaking Voice," a work of much physiological and practical interest to all who are disposed to make at any time full use of their " parts of speech." '

But (he adds in conclusion) Mr. Hullah's writings have not been limited to the department of musical literature. He has contributed to our periodical literature many most interesting articles —critical, descriptive, and biographical. He is an accomplished modern linguist. . . . As an admirable musician and a literary man, we request you to confer on him the degree of Doctor of Law.

Mr. Hullah was then 'capped.' In succession, Dr. Maclagan presented Mr. W. S. Jevons, M.A., F.R.S., and Professor of Logic, &c., in Owens College, Manchester; Mr. J. T. Mowbray, W.S., Sir Noel Paton, R.S.A., and the Rev. Colin Valentine, F.R.C.S. Edin. A goodly gathering! A most enjoyable graduates' dinner, given by Professor Masson, completed a rather eventful day in Mr. Hullah's life. He writes:

I sat next to Professor Blackie, who was more poetic than ever. Sir A. Grant too is very agreeable. But the most interesting man I have made acquaintance with this time is Professor Geddes. . . . There is to be a dinner-party by way of *finale* to the week's proceedings.

His wife was not at home when Mr. Hullah returned, so the final report had to be sent to her. He says:

It is disgusting that you won't be home in time to fetch me from the station. . . . The dinner [in Heriot Row] was most pleasant. . . . I am charged with all manner of messages to you. For myself, I seem to have been overwhelmed with 'benevolences' of all kinds. A week of such hospitality and glorification I do not remember.

My host and hostesses expressed *great regret* at my departure!
There!! Hark to the trumpet!

[musical notation] &c.

The most important musical event of the spring of this
year was the opening in May of the National Training College
of Music. But, though the preliminary examinations were
over and the first batch of students chosen, for Mr. Hullah,
as no doubt for the other examiners, there was but little rest
or peace. Day after day disappointed and distressed relatives
of unsuccessful candidates sought personal interviews, using
every conceivable pretext for getting access to him with no
less an object than to upset the verdict already pronounced
on the luckless sons or daughters. Each individual had some
reason to offer in extenuation of voicelessness, hopeless nervousness, or ignorance. Each seemed to think that his or
her reason was quite unanswerable. Here, an ex-housekeeper
complained that all her savings were gone in the training she
had given her daughter. Here, a mother of twelve or more
children urged that if only her daughter 'had received a
chance, a real chance, to become a music teacher,' what a
benefit for the whole family! One poor soul gave as a reason
for her daughter's failure that the baby of the household was
'that fractious' that no one in the house had slept for a fortnight. Not unreasonably Mr. Hullah rejoiced when in July
his colleges and classes closed, and he was able to begin his
holiday by a visit to friends in Hertfordshire, with whom he
stayed till his wife could join him. In an undated letter
written during this or his next visit to Ware Priory, he says :

I've brought down the Dante translation, and this morning I
took my work into the garden and did half a canto (roughly) in a
short time. Not far off, in the shadow of the cloister room, sat the
Professor [Sylvester] a-making of rhymes, measuring his 'feet' the
while by more or less prolonged backward tilts of his chair, which
at moments made me quite uneasy for the safety of his unprotected
head should he miscalculate their length ; but body and metre preserved their balance all through, tilts and 'feet' coming to a satisfactory close when the gong sounded for luncheon. . . . Hungry
work is versification, I can tell you!'

For three or four pleasant weeks he and his wife wandered
from friend to friend, including a few days at Malvern Wells

for a draught of the 'native air,' and then the Dante translation and other such matter was put aside for a season, and the inspection of Training Colleges commenced once more. Much the same route as in previous years was followed.

Recounting the incidents of his Liverpool visit from Chester, he says, after his work was over, he listened to a 'concert offered' to him at the training college of the sisters of N. D. de Namur, and in return sang to them his ' Storm ' and made them an address. 'I then rushed off,' he continues, ' for half an hour's exercise before dressing to be with Mr. Best at seven.'

You know Mrs. Best is Italian. *She* had prepared the most wonderful macaroni!—with chopped things—you ever eat or dreamed of. I all but dined on it. Then there were other Italian things, but the macaroni overlays them all in my memory. . . . The next day I left off at three and returned to the hotel for my things, crossed over the Mersey, left the aforesaid 'things' at the station, and took a cab to the house of Mr. Reay, the possessor of the Rossettis. . . . The principal Rossettis are the 'Beloved' (of the Song of Solomon), and a sort of pendent to 'Adam's First Wife,' a type of moral and intellectual beauty, as the former is (I was told) of physical. The ' Beloved ' is assuredly very splendid in colour and in arrangement, the work of a man with a noble intention, a little kept down in realisation by sensuousness and—imperfect training. The defects of drawing in the second picture are glaring. . . . Altogether I should not care to be surrounded by Rossettis every day and all day long. Did you ever hear of Davis, a landscape painter, who died not two years ago ? [Mr. Hullah had seen some of this painter's work in a country house in Wales the previous year, and had already spoken in high terms of his talents.] I should say that he was the best landscape painter we have at present, equal to, though very unlike, *our* favourite Frenchman [Lier ?]. It is not merely that his trees are individuals, and his turkeys instinct with life, but that he gives to every scene, large or small, open landscape or shut in pool, the same charm, the same poetry. In fact he has found Ste -Beuve's 'talisman.' These landscapes are really worth a pilgrimage ; I don't think the Rossettis are, though I am glad to have seen them. . . . I have discovered at Chester a genius [Tinworth ?], a wood sculptor, who has done all the repairs of the tabernacle work in the cathedral. He is a man who has educated himself in all kinds of ways—history, general literature, and the like. . . . Love to the Minims [his latest pet name for the children].

September 22.—The Dante translation does not progress at present, but I work at the grammar at odd moments, and read nothing but Italian. . . . I read 'Olanda' and *learnt* Dante all the way here [to Truro].

Having made his way round to Brighton he announces his return, adding:

Provide nothing on a large scale, only let us have a quiet banquet together after all this dreary time of separation.

And he came back, very, very glad to rest under his own roof. He was, of course, full of news, and concerning his own special work his enthusiasm had in no way flagged. The improvement was not as great as he could have wished, but progress was 'marching on,' and marching on steadily and surely. During the only quiet forenoons he could secure at home an enormous mass of correspondence was cleared off by the joint efforts of himself and his wife, and then he fell to work on the London District Training Schools and Colleges, going steadily on till the end of October, when he took wing for Scotland. From Dumfries, where he enjoyed three days of complete rest in the midst of 'goodly company,' he writes home:

Many happy returns of the day to you. I am not clear in remembering birthdays, but yours I put into my book at the beginning of the year, and I shall continue the practice so long as I am with you to do so. . . . Accept ——'s offer and go to Paris. . . . . Do change your latest mind and *go*; and *write* and afterwards tell me by word of mouth all about the Architectural Exhibition. It would delight me very much if you would. *Glasgow.* . . . I found Dr. Carlyle at Dumfries on Monday. He seems much better than at our last interview. He will not do any more 'Purgatorio,' even if he has really done *any*, which I cannot quite make out that he has. He says he ought to have done the whole 'Commedia' at once— when he was in the vein and in practice. He showed me all his Dantesque curiosities again. . . . It seems he lived eight years in Rome—*i.e.* he passed the winters there, leaving it in the *very* hot weather. He enjoyed the most perfect health there, as anybody may do (he says) who will take reasonable precautions, which English people are apt not to do. He recommends starting in February. I am now going for the first time for many weeks to *look* at my translation. . . . This abominable Fast gives me the four hardest days I have ever had. I *did* fifty-six students yesterday. Last evening I was talking to a Frenchman—in French. . . . He asked how long I had lived in France—ahem! I wondered to myself what somebody, who shall be nameless, would have said had she overheard praises of somebody else's *accent*! It is curious what a varnish of refinement is thrown over very commonplace thoughts and statements by a foreign tongue—especially when contrasted with the 'd——d Scottish brogue,' as Goldsmith—not I—calls the north-country sing-song. . . . I have seen a review of a book called 'Rahel.' It should be worth reading. I wish, too, you would do some reading about Rome. Clearly *I* shall have but little time. . . . Your musical news are very amusing . . . especially about the children. Fancy their wanting to learn those songs of mine! So, too, is your social news about A. B——'s marriage. I give her up! Never could I have guessed what she would do.

This was a very genuine expression of astonishment at the desertion, from the noble army of spinsters, of one of its most ornamental and admirable, if not most youthful, members. Mr. Hullah quite believed that England would be a much less pleasant and prosperous land if that national institution, the 'old maid,' were collectively absorbed into the married state. Sometimes he would go so far as to declare that if he had had an 'old maid' sister he would never have married at all himself! About which, perhaps, there may be a diversity of opinion.

At Aberdeen, whither Mr. Hullah betook himself after expressing his amaze at the beautiful Miss A. B.'s conduct, he was the guest of Professor Geddes. He writes in the most enthusiastic terms of his host and the incidents of his visit, 'wishing a hundred times a day' that his wife could have shared his 'whirl of enjoyment.' He saw a number of new and interesting people, and was much struck with the work of a portrait painter, since become well known—Mr. Reid—of whom he says, 'I can scarcely think of anyone better, Watts only excepted.'

As soon as Edinburgh was reached, and he was established in his 'home in Heriot Row,' his letters became journals, whatever he had leisure to jot down being put into the post in time for delivery at the breakfast hour:

We dined last evening at Sir Wyville Thomson's. The party was small but very pleasant. Sir Wyville has brought home the most wonderful collection of Japanese things that can be conceived. To-morrow I have promised to go out to dine at *Joppa* with Mr. L——. . . . I cannot get to see many people, for my work takes me every day (and will) from ten till four or five. . . . I have a lot of proofs ('Musical Dictionary') from Grove, which I must look over. Good night. . . .

From Durham.—I have just returned from the cathedral, which has been reopened entire after repairs extending over many years. It is truly splendid! Though anxious to be getting homeward,

I left Edinburgh with regret. . . . I took a little recreation in the way of going to hear their greatest preacher here, a Dr. McGregor. He is certainly very great in ideas, expression, and delicacy—a fiery-eyed little Celt. . . . I must keep a good deal of my news till I return home.

Lincoln.—Before leaving York, I saw Monk and the D——s. . . . . I met a Dr. T——, who knows Rome very well, so I gathered hints. Home! home! Three cheers!

Before Christmas the Report was written. Mr. Hullah began it by calling attention to the addition of a new college (at Aberdeen) to the existing list. Next he says:

> The difficulty of attaining musical skill, altogether unconnected with the particular symbols employed, increases with every year of our lives; (adding) I only quote an observation made to me recently by an experienced musical instructor in a Training College *à propos* to it, 'What our students *begin* here, they generally learn with difficulty, do badly, and forget soon.'

He is glad to be able to note that complete 'failures' are few, numbering indeed but sixteen, of which fifteen occurred in Scottish Training Colleges. But he hastens to add:

> Music is an imitative art, and in the remote and thinly populated parts of every country musical performance is rare. Many of the students in the Edinburgh, Glasgow, and Aberdeen normal schools come from districts answering to this description. 'Till I came here,' said a Glasgow student to me once, 'I never even saw a piano.'

At one of the Female Training Colleges Mr. Hullah learnt that an offer, made by the musical instructor, to 'enable a certain number of those who had learnt something of the pianoforte before their admission to continue or resume their practice,' had been at once declined, on the ground 'that such practice would not only interfere with their other work, but did not become persons of their station in life.'

On this experience Mr. Hullah comments:

> We have learnt from Mrs. Malaprop that 'thought does not become a young woman.' It is new to hear—from an educated committee too—that to accompany a school song, possibly even to play a pretty tune to her scholars now and then, 'does not become a schoolmistress.'

With evident satisfaction he reports that on two occasions first-year students said to be 'voiceless and earless' were discovered under examination to possess *contralto* voices, though 'as yet in unformed conditions, and that consequently they had great difficulty in using their "second registers" at all, and greater in passing from one register to the other.'

In a tone of quiet amusement and banter the students are reported to have been singularly free from 'colds,' it being 'now generally understood that the worst cold need never affect a student's "marks;"'

for it cannot possibly prevent his knowing the fourth of a scale from the seventh when both are sounded, nor even so thoroughly disguise his 'style' as to prevent its recognition for more than a few moments.

As regards style, he has to say that there is marked improvement, and that the choice of music 'in some colleges might have satisfied the most critical taste.' In the Free Church Training College, Edinburgh, a student sang a *French* song, the first he had ever heard in a Training College. With an expression of satisfaction that combined practice of male and female students was at length being tried successfully, Mr. Hullah passes to the subject of musical instruction in elementary schools, which he may be said to have considered as not taught at all, since he does not recognise as teaching of *music* a parrot-like preparation of some half-a-dozen songs. Of the 9,000 students he had in the course of five years examined, the 'great majority,' says Mr. Hullah, are 'schoolmasters and mistresses,' of whom a large number would be capable, more or less efficiently, to 'teach children to sing from notes.'

. . . . Every class of the community has directly or indirectly profited by the impulse given to musical instruction by my Lords in 1840–41, except that particular class which it was hoped and believed would profit most largely from it.

In conclusion, Mr. Hullah says:

Musical examination in elementary schools would seem to be the natural sequence of musical examination in training schools. Of the value of musical instruction in both your Lordships have repeatedly shown your recognition. To put within reach of the people innocent and cheap recreation is an object confessedly worthy of the attention of an enlightened government. Music, at the lowest estimation, is one among the most innocent of recreations, and of all recreations assuredly the cheapest *to those who can make it for themselves.*

CHAPTER XXIX.

BIOGRAPHICAL.

1877.

IT will have been noticed how much Italy—its language, literature, and art—had been uppermost in Mr. Hullah's mind throughout the whole of the past year. Great was the joy, therefore, when, after infinite planning, it was found possible to secure a three or four months' absence during the spring of 1877. With renewed vigour he applied himself to getting through his various engagements, even to the contributing of a little volume, called 'Music in the House,' to the 'Art at Home' series. Then, the time of departure drawing near, he went to Cheltenham to bid adieu to the 'Minims,' who were to be under their grandmother's fostering care during the grand tour.

Packing finished, letters of introduction collected, the flat carefully shut up, the long-looked-for journey at last began on Friday, of all days in the week; but, in spite of the well-founded popular superstition concerning undertakings commenced on that day, no mishap whatever befell the travellers. On the contrary, the sun shone, the Channel passage was less horrible than usual, the restorative *bouillon* at Calais was better than usual, the trains were punctual, fellow-travellers cheery and courteous, hotels clean, their *personnel* alert and positively grateful to have to minister to the needs of the early travellers. The Mont Cénis route afforded infinite delight at a season of the year when, though mornings and evenings were chilly and nights even cold, the midday sun poured down warm floods of golden light over the soft tender green of coming spring. As far as Sienna the route was fairly familiar, but that city was new to both, and a halt of some days was decided upon. Thanks to the urbanity and kindness of the Canonico Bandini, all things beautiful within and without the city were seen under especially favourable conditions. Chief among the new interests presented to Mr. Hullah was the institution so ably managed by the late Padre Marchio for the instruction of deaf mutes. So soon as the Padre discovered an intelligent interest in his *sordo-muti* he unfolded all the resources of his system, nor was content till Mr. Hullah had himself tested the knowledge of the young pupils, happily with perfect success. What Mr. Hullah saw and heard in Padre Marchio's school touched and interested him greatly, and he never afterwards lost an opportunity of visiting similar institutions. Vaguely a scheme of musical instruction for persons so afflicted began to occupy his mind, and would undoubtedly have taken a practical form had he been destined to enjoy a longer life and more unbroken leisure.

But one night was given to Orvieto, on the journey to Rome, which was at last reached towards the close of a beautiful day. Rome was reposing after the excitement of the Easter ceremonies, and the comparative quiet of the streets was particularly favourable to the first ramble through the Eternal City. Mapless and guideless—what did they who had dreamt of Rome for years want with either?—they took their way across the Piazza Barberini, through the Via Sistina to the Piazza della Trinità down the great *scala* to the Piazza di Spagna. Midway on the stairs they halted, and looked back at a tall pile of houses which have their basements in the little Piazza Mignanelli far below and their entrance doors in the Piazza della Trinità far above, when Mr. Hullah's attention was caught by a little window from which it would obviously be possible to look right across Rome to Sant' Onofrio far away against the western sky.

'Oh, that we had that window!' he exclaimed, as they recommenced their descent to the Piazza, crossed it for the Via del Babuino, beloved of artists, and so entered the Piazza del Popolo. They took just one peep through the Porta out into the open country beyond, stretching away solemn and silent far as the eye could see; noted where the road curved round to the Borghese gardens, and, retracing their steps, lingered along the Via di Ripetta to the bridge of St. Angelo, and onward once again till they stood opposite St. Peter's. They paused a moment before entering, then, advancing slowly, they heard an organ pealing. Very remote it sounded; yet presently they became aware that a full service was going on in a side chapel, and were enabled to realise the vast size of the church, which at the first moment of entrance had not seemed so very large.

In the gathering gloom they moved from pillar to pillar, and passed out into the Piazza again just as the last rays of evening light faded quite away and darkness fell upon them. Enough for one day was the impression received of Christian Rome. Scarcely a dozen words had been exchanged, yet they found, when they talked the day's incidents over after dinner, that both had observed the same things, noted the same picturesque points here and there.

'Sleep if you can, but I believe you've deceived me and been to Rome already,' each said to the other by way of good-night. But it was useless to court sleep that first night in Rome. Morning was longed for exceedingly, and came, as it seemed, too tardily; yet it was still very early when they reached the Piazza della Trinità, and knocked at a small door which seemed likely to belong to the 'house of the window,' as the coveted abode was promptly christened. In response came a solid figure with a bust and head like the Fornarina.

'Was there aught to let?'

'Some twenty rooms—for next winter. Would their excellencies walk in?'

'Certainly.' Leading from room to room the Fornarina presently brought them to *the* window. Rome lay stretched out before them, clear and luminous in the morning light. While they stood in admiration, the Padrone came in, saluted, and handed chairs.

'What might be their pleasure?'

'We want this room and three more for three months. The price?' they explained and queried with unpolished brevity, necessitated by a scant vocabulary of common words.

'Ah, a bagatelle—six thousand lire, but for *six* months.'

'Three months—two hundred and fifty lire,' they persisted, while hope all but died in their hearts.

'Impossible, *impossible*,' the Padrone said, bowing himself out in a polite rage.

'This is hard,' Mr. Hullah moaned, as the Fornarina, with speculative wonder in her eyes, led them back to the entrance door.

We'll return to the charge—let us yield for to-day. *Avanti !* '

Down the steps of the Trinità del Monte they meditatively went, and before taking a carriage to convey them to a distant part of the city they stayed a moment to discourse with Mr. Shee concerning that house up yonder. What he said in reply was forcible and picturesque, but calculated to damp the ardour of less self-willed travellers.

' " Nil desperandum ! " be our motto,' they exclaimed, as they climbed into a carriage and the skeleton steed flew over the rugged stones towards the Vatican, where the day was passed in pleasure deep, lasting, but indescribable.

With unshaken determination a second visit was paid to the Padrone of the ' *casa della finestra*,' with no better result, however, than a considerable diminution of the original price asked and a firm adherence to the price offered.

' Nil desperandum ! ' they reiterated, and addressed themselves to the pleasures of the day, remarking to Mr. Shee, who was ' taking the air,' that they yet hoped to sit at yonder window. With a smile of pitying wonderment Mr. Shee returned their salutation and withdrew to his sanctum, while his would-be clients sped away to the Palazzo dei Cesari, and lived out a long day, which seemed yet all too short, among the ruins of ancient Rome.

' And now for a final attack and victory ! ' one said to the other on the third morning, as, unfurling large umbrellas, they marched resolutely up the Via Sistina, crossed the Piazza della Trinità, bathed in golden sunlight, and halted at the little door in the shadowed corner. Mr. Hullah raised his hand towards the bell. The door flew open ere he touched it.

'*Ecco gl' Inglesi!*' shouted the Fornarina to some one behind her.

'*Ah, buon di, Eccellenze!*' saluted the Padrone (keeping well on the safer side of politeness till he knew who was who), appearing in full view, bowing low, smiling sweetly, cap in hand.

'Good morning, good morning, excellent Signor. Behold us!—for the last time we come. Three months—two hundred and fifty lire a month.'

Shaking his head, and wagging an erect forefinger in sad negation, the Padrone retreated within the house, but beckoning all the while, till the party found itself once more in the room with *the* window.

'What a view! what a light! Oh! make a higher offer,' whispered Mr. Hullah.

But the thrifty treasurer held to the 'three months at two hundred and fifty lire a month' as long as possible.

'Alas, alas! *signori miei*, how unreasonable, how impossible is the thing you propose, how utterly *impos-si-bi-le!*'

Casting a last but despairing glance from *the* window over the splendid prospect, the travellers turned resolutely away, saying, 'Good, good, as you will, sir, but you will regret the *three hundred lire* a month as you roam through your empty rooms; and we, what shall *we* think of Roman landlords? *Addio, ad-dio-o!*'

After them swiftly came the Padrone. '*Chè—chè*—when the matter is put thus! Ah, but the English are eccentric; they must have *their* way. *Va ben!* Would their excellencies descend to the study and just settle the little formalities at once?'

Down the dark winding staircase he toddled, followed by Mr. Hullah and the Fornarina, while Mrs. Hullah sped away to the agent, and rushing in, breathlessly demanded, 'A clerk and a form of agreement, for yon Padrone yields.'

Mr. Shee was incredulous, but furnished the articles required, and gazed half an hour later at a duly signed document setting forth the conditions of the letting with amazement, and an odd expression of apprehension on his face. Midday saw the successful bargainers installed. Mr. Hullah at once appropriated the window, arranged his chair, and sat down radiantly in the midst of his books, maps, and other impedimenta, the Fornarina—henceforth known as Felice—bustling about in high satisfaction. Unpacking effected, it became needful to make sundry housekeeping arrangements, in which Mr. Hullah basely declared he could take no part whatever, 'for common Italian he didn't know —Dante being all *he* could manage!' So Mrs. Hullah, following certain directions from Felice, proceeded on a voyage of discovery, which resulted in the regular matutinal arrival of a bottle of milk stopped with a fig-leaf, a pat of butter wrapped in a vine-leaf, two eggs, some dainty appetising loaflets in snowy linen within a fairy basket; and, at the *Ave Maria*—neither sooner nor later—of a tin box with a heater at the bottom and four courses of a dinner on shelves above. Next—Felice still directing—a store of charcoal and sundry groceries was laid in, and lo! the *ménage* was started; the *ménagère* returning with a rich addition to the 'common Italian' but lately so conveniently ignored by her companion, who, however, had, when left to his own devices, found himself possessed of a sufficient stock of the *vulgo dicto* to get up quite a snug little afternoon tea, over which he was ready to preside as one to the manner born, meanwhile discoursing on many topics with Felice, who stood in admiration at his proceedings, asking at intervals pertinent questions as to when they rose in the morning, when they would require early coffee, when breakfast should be served, when other wants would have to be attended to. All these details being satisfactorily learned, Felice departed to her own regions, and never again throughout the term of her service did she require to be reminded a second time on any one point. She was never late, never untidy, never cross. Sometimes a troubled wrinkle altered the serene expression of her lovely face; sometimes a strange paleness added a beauty quite ethereal to the exquisite features; but if asked if she were unwell or in grief, she would turn away with a patient assurance that 'all was well, she was but a little sad, for she feared that she and her good man would have to spend the burning summer days in Rome'—the only thing on earth that seemed to distress poor Felice. As soon as she had decided in her own very firm mind that she should ' get on ' with her *forestieri*, she began to deck the rooms with flowers, putting aside the first offer of payment with a gesture so eloquently expressive of wounded pride that it was impossible to approach the subject again from the pecuniary point of view. In her own time she explained that, her husband being a gardener, a handful of flowers more or less was nothing to anyone. The only thing that seemed likely to call forth Felice's wrath was disregard to the dinner hour. So surely as the *Ave Maria* sounded from the Church of the Trinità, Felice's lovely head might be seen at the open door, looking anxiously about for the lagging diners, and a smileless admission was their punishment if they were late; while, on the other hand, if they came in with ten minutes to spare she was all hearty approval, for then there was ' no chance of a chill from eating while too hot.'

But to return. Tea over, Mr. Hullah's activity revived. ' Now for books and a piano,' he said, and before another hour was past several of the former and one of the latter necessities of civilisation were added to the little home. There was nothing more to interfere with the grand occupation of seeing Rome, which was resumed the next day. In the course of a week both felt fairly at home all over the city, and devoted a day to the distribution of introductory letters, with the result that the already pleasant life was made yet more pleasant by the occasional society of a little circle of acquaintances, which included a few members of the Sistine Choir, one or two leading musicians, heads of two or three Colleges, two Liberal Monsignori, and a few well-known English residents. Among them were some with good gifts of songs, which by-and-by made it possible for Mr. Hullah to enjoy at home some of Palestrina's music. One of these ' Palestrina ' evenings was especially successful, for among others there came Signor Meluzzi, Maestro di Capella of San Pietro, and all his family, consisting of wife, two daughters, and a son; Padre Carletti; Miss S—— C—— and Miss B—— T—— (but lately fallen a victim to the climate of England), whose lovely fragile person was but a fitting home for a voice of such sweetness and such power of expression that an auditor was led to say softly one day, ' Surely it was just such a voice Fra Angelico heard, and just such a face he saw, while he painted his Angels.'

Altogether the sojourn in Rome was rich in incident and beyond all expectation delightful. Many gratifying compliments were paid to Mr. Hullah, of which, perhaps, he most liked being made a member of the Society of Santa Cecilia. His only disappointments were, the difficulty of getting to hear the Sistine Choir, for the great services were things of the past, though not without hope of revival. By dint of patience, tact, and diplomacy Mr. Hullah did contrive to hear, or, more accurately speaking, *over*hear a practice of the choir. It has to be admitted that he considered the reputation of the voices overrated.

The weeks rolled by all too quickly, and the time came when, for health's sake, it was needful to seek a fresher atmosphere. Last visits were paid to favourite haunts, last adieux said to friends. The 'Fanfulla' gave the English musician 'God speed,' all wished him back again right soon, and armed with several letters of introduction from Mr. and Mrs. Montgomery Stewart, in whose hospitable house many an evening had been spent, the travellers departed on the very best of terms with the dreaded Padrone and the good Felice, her husband, the postman, the milkman, the baker, and the dinner man, all of whom had business, by some coincidence, in the immediate vicinity of the '*casa della finestra*' as the moment of departure drew near.

By Terni and Spoleto, Assisi was reached and enjoyed (!) in the company of a rabble mob of mendicants, for whose pertinacious attentions the travellers in 1877 had to thank our well-beloved guide to the beautiful, Mr. Ruskin, easily recognisable in the *Signor Rusconi* whose generosity was quoted with suggestive laudation by the *poveri* at every step.

In glorious Perugia a week was spent, especially delightful to Mr. Hullah, thanks to the constant kindness and courtesy of Signor Rossi and Count Rossi-Scotti. In the course of early morning and late evening strolls about the beautiful city, Mr. Hullah made many a plan for future loiterings among the towns and townlets, visible from the city walls and higher buildings, but for the moment it was necessary to withstand temptation to turn aside from a direct homeward route; so all were passed by except Arezzo, in which lovely little city two quite eventful days were spent. During his very first walk Mr. Hullah discovered an ideal house close to Tasso's, and was with difficulty dissuaded from hiring it on the spot. 'To recover his equanimity,' after the frustration of this practical scheme, he turned into the public library, where he immediately became an object of interested observation to an old gentleman, white and cool-looking as a snowflake. Under a most transparent pretence of searching out a volume, the old gentleman—a mere miniature edition of adult humanity—stepped after Mr. Hullah till he overheard him ask a question in Italian, which, with a joyful smile and a bow, he answered himself, and thus made an opportunity for the presentation of his card, 'Il Sindaco.' Mr. Hullah returned the compliment. More bows, caught up by a gathering circle of attendants, suddenly waking up to consciousness that, to break the dull monotony of life in those musty, silent rooms, an incident was occurring.

Two seconds more and the Syndic had constituted himself cicerone to the English 'Inspector of Music in the Training Colleges of Great Britain,' and had sent the attendants flying here and there in search of the treasures possessed by the library. A mighty cloud of dust was raised, and piles of books, doubtless of deep interest, were laid before Mr. Hullah, but, scarcely giving time for a glance at them, the Syndic hurried his new friend away to the cathedral, and with a courage born of excitement, tackled the sulking Padri Gesuiti concerning *their* treasures. Little enough he got out of them, either of treasures or politeness. It was evident that relations between Church and State were strained, and the Syndic was visibly relieved to find himself again outside the holy precincts. Once more on his own territory, the little man explained, with solemn gesticulation and in sonorous phrase, ' that in fact there *was* a misunderstanding between the higher powers of Church and State, and that the clergy of Arezzo were undergoing a most undeniable snub all round.' Their moroseness, therefore, had to be excused—even by the Syndic. Moreover, on the following day (Sunday), the Fathers were preparing—it was

thought—to launch forth from the cathedral pulpit no less
than thrice in the day against the temporal power. Hence
the priestly ill-humour, not perhaps quite unleavened by
apprehension as to the possible consequences.

While the Syndic thus prepared his friends for a better
comprehension of the coming stir he also led them deftly
towards their hotel, and there, with many salutations, wished
them ' *buon appetito*,' and ambled away for ' three hours of
rest,' devoted to dinner and *siesta* by him, to further investigations by the travellers, who, it must be confessed, were rather
tired out by the time the Syndic returned, equal to more lionising, which he insisted on carrying through according to his
own light with a conscientiousness and zeal worthy of a larger
sphere. Betimes on Sunday morning, almost with the first
clash of the church bells, arrived a messenger from the Syndic
to herald his coming; also the messenger brought a card of
invitation for a gathering of notabilities that afternoon. The
envelope was addressed to

' Lord John Hullah,'

the Syndical rendering, it appeared, of ' Illustrissimo '—the
excellence of which had so seized on his imagination that
many subsequent explanations were necessary before he could
be induced to alter it. Possibly the Syndic had but appreciated
prophetically an inspector's office at its just importance!

To refuse so flattering an invitation was, of course, out of
the question, so an acceptance was drafted in the best Tuscan
at command, and pondered, with a view to correction, while
both travellers set to work to make their worn and ruefully
rusty holiday best fit to be seen. They were in contemplation
of the result of their labours when the Syndic was announced.
With his assistance a formal reply to the invitation was
prettily set forth, largely sealed, and despatched. Then, headed
by the Syndic in lustrous black with an order on his breast,
and standing quite four feet six inches on his Molière heels,
procession was formed for the Duomo. The church was
already closely packed with a congregation alert and attentive
to the extremely seditious utterances against the king and
his government, but of active sympathy there were not any

signs, and, to judge by the fragments of conversation caught in moving slowly through the crowds, inside and outside the church, the emphatic denunciations against the temporal power and its supporters of all conditions had passed in at one ear and dropped out at the other. But if the sermons delivered on that Sunday were not productive of unpleasant consequences to the irate Fathers, it must have been by grace of that policy of clemency followed by the Italian Government, so far with excellent results.

Florence necessitated a sojourn of many days, for Mr. Hullah was anxious to see, not only picture galleries and buildings, but something also of the teaching, especially the teaching of music, in the public schools. Under the guidance of Signori Cammerota and Casamorata he visited several classes, and became quite enthusiastic over the beautiful quality of the voices and the intelligence with which a new idea was seized by the students, as in the case of the 'inflected syllables.' These were fairly mastered by a scratch class in about a quarter of an hour. On the other hand, Mr. Hullah found much merely superficial knowledge, and great inaccuracy of time and of tune.

The next move was to Bologna, that delightful city of arcades. All that there was of interest was eagerly visited, but the season for *villeggiatura* had set in at Bologna as in Florence, and no one was left from whom Mr. Hullah could have sought information on educational matters.

Milan brought them at last within reach of friends, a visit to whose country house in the depths of the Brianza had long been arranged. Here, remote from picture galleries, theatres, and crowds, they had a new and most agreeable experience of life in an Italian family, living on its own estate, farming its own land, and especially engaged in cultivating enormous quantities of silkworms. Each member of the household took a share, more or less active, in supervising the entire process, but the most indefatigable was the Dowager Contessa, who was up early and late, here, there, and everywhere; on the best of terms with every peasant, priest, and neighbour for miles round, and yet maintaining without the slightest effort an undisputed sway over all. Mr.

Hullah, of course, took never-ceasing delight in watching all that went on, and soon had an acquaintance with half the neighbourhood—an acquaintance limited, to his great regret, to smiles and bows, by reason of his inability to master at once the dialect; not but that he tried his hardest to acquire Milanese, and considered himself a promising student by the time his visit drew to its close. A sad day was the day of parting! With deepest regret, and plans for future meetings, the travellers bade adieu to their kind hosts and wended their way back to the noise and crowd of city life. Passing through Milan they travelled on to Arona, where it was found impossible to get a small two-seated carriage for the journey across the Simplon, and a large laudau had to be shared with chance companions. Fortunately these turned out most agreeable, and added much to the liveliness of the journey to Brieg. Once more on the railway no further dallying could be indulged in, and the return to England and home was effected as quickly as possible. Scarcely giving himself time to examine his 'Minims,' Mr. Hullah sat down to read and dispose of his vast accumulation of letters. Among these was an announcement, in highly flattering terms, of his election as honorary member of the Musical Institute of Florence.

CHAPTER XXX.

BIOGRAPHICAL.

1877—*continued.*

IN capital physical condition Mr. Hullah set out on his tour in August, writing so brightly and cheerfully about everything that there was no occasion to feel any commiseration for his solitary state. Indeed, even at Liverpool he forgot to condole with himself, and seemed to carry his own stock of sunshine with him :

> I never saw Liverpool look so little disagreeable (he says). You must come and see my Roman Catholic Training College for women. The sisters would welcome you cordially and perhaps convert you!
> . . . . The work done is most excellent, and the influence of the refined teachers beyond all praise. . . . What a funny idea your going to Oxford in vacation time ! I hope to arrive there on Saturday night, and my idea was to leave after my work on Tuesday, which is very short, for Malvern. But I suppose they would keep me another night at St. John's, and if you were sure to come on Wednesday I might stay and see you. . . .

Having reached Oxford before the family party, he writes:

> My host and hostess seem to be the only University people left in Oxford. Whether the Rector is in Lincoln or not, nobody knows, but I shall go presently and find out. I purposed getting to Malvern on Tuesday evening, but I *should* so like to see you, if only for an hour or two. I have a good mind to give it up, but that seems uncourteous, and the good lady there (who has no idea of time) evidently thinks I am going to stay a month as it is, and she is coming from —— to receive me. . . . I shall leave for you Trollope's 'Giulio Malatesta,' one of the best novels I have ever read; all about the war in 1848. It is, I imagine, pretty accurate.

Mr. Hullah had had so many pleasant talks while in Rome with Mr. Thomas Trollope, whose knowledge of Italian character and customs is equalled by few foreigners, that he, not usually given to novel reading, put himself through a tolerably complete course of Mr. Trollope's works, deriving much enjoyment from the skilfully painted scenes of Italian life. Having refreshed himself with the desired peep at his family, Mr. Hullah proceeded to Malvern Wells, 'conveniently near to Cheltenham,' where he had to examine the two Training Colleges. Thence he writes:

There is staying here a Signor A——, with whom I talk Italian! Ah! don't you wish *now* you had come? . . . I am delighted to hear of your dissipations. Fancy the Rector [of Lincoln College] doing cicerone, and asking children to supper! . . . What has happened to the dear old Rector? He seems to be coming out in the line of hospitality and personal attention in a manner altogether without precedent.

Probably there were many precedents. However that might be, Mr. Pattison certainly was on this occasion most kind to the Hullah children, solemnly inviting them to tea and supper. The interval between the repasts was spent in the gallery of the Rector's lodgings, where, seated on either side of him, they listened untiringly while he read aloud pieces from Wordsworth, Goldsmith, and some short pathetic bits out of a volume of Bret Harte's poems.

As Mr. Hullah progressed from town to town on his work, he never failed to send the 'daily news,' and was eager to get details of home life.

I hear much talk about my Report, which, it seems, has in some shape or other appeared in almost every paper of town or country, among others in the 'Times.' This is new.

From Winchester.—As usual, life here has been made delightful. . . . I examine at Chichester on Wednesday and at Brighton Thursday, which will be the close of Act 1 of my Inspectorial Drama. On Thursday evening I shall be home again. (At this point please to imagine three cheers!) . . . Warburton and I have had a walk, and called on your brother. He walked down with us home, was asked in to tea, and introduced to Mrs. Warburton, who has invited him to dinner . . . . and I doubt not he will turn out an excellent, moderate, high and dry Churchman.

During the flying visit to London, Mr. Hullah, by way of *entr'acte*, examined metropolitan and suburban schools, and attended committees at the Borough Road Schools, at which was discussed the question of a more thorough extension of the existing system of musical inspection. At odd moments, while at home, he elaborated with great satisfaction several letters in Italian, in reply to numerous communications from correspondents whose acquaintance he had made during his recent visit to Italy. He had also to acknowledge the honour of being elected a Vice-President of the College of Organists in London.

Scene I. of Act 2 of his Inspectorial drama opens in Dumfries rather sensationally:

I could not write yesterday, for I had to lie in bed the greater part of the day. I woke up on Sunday night with a sense of sea sickness. . . . It being about getting-up time, I had H—— summoned, who came to me in a moment, and was soon followed by Mrs. H——. . . . They sent for the doctor, who proved a bright, sensible fellow, and let me off with two very small pills. . . . This morning I got up, and I am all right—'better as new.' The worst part of the matter was that the H——s had invited people to dinner, who had to be put off, but are coming to-night.

From Glasgow:

I left the H——s this morning in time to visit a school at Dumfries, consisting exclusively of quasi-criminal children, who have been taught to sing, in my way, by a Mr. Gooden, of Dumfries. The results were quite extraordinary. . . . I am again perfectly well; my good state being greatly enhanced by the sun, which streamed into my room gloriously. I began my work here this morning, and got on favourably. Since leaving off I have had a walk, during which it did not rain ! . . . . 9*th*.—I have had a long and somewhat worrying day at the training school. The music master (a very good man) is leaving, in consequence of rows of all kinds, and I have to-day had interviews with the three most eligible candidates. . . . 11*th*. . . I saw the deaf and dumb schools here, where they have begun lately to teach lip-reading as they do at Siena. The whole thing is very interesting. . . . I have come across some pleasant people, among them a (Frankfort) German, who speaks—*i.e.* pronounces—English better than any German I have ever met. Fancy his being alive to the offensiveness, to educated English people, of an affectation of familiarity with our language on the part of a foreigner ! . . . The new 'Halls' here are to be opened next week with the 'Messiah' and a new cantata by Macfarren, who comes to-morrow. 13*th*.—I have been in a whirl of excitement during the last few days. In addition to my ordinary work, which takes me from ten till three, I have had to meet committees, examine candidate music-teachers, visit board schools, and I know not what besides. Nor was there much rest on Sunday, though I devoted my morning to writing in my own room; for, in the afternoon, I went up to the University, was presented to many of the Professors, and after the service went to Sir W. Thomson's, with whom Professor Bell, the inventor of the telephone, is staying. He got a wire laid on to the attic, and from the drawing-room carried on a conversation and sang songs which were heard with perfect ease. This has been done, it seems, at a distance of 250 miles. I am going to another lecture of Professor Bell's to-morrow night, and to-night to the 'Faculty Hall,' to see a man who is speaking with an artificial larynx.

Concerning this man Mr. Hullah subsequently had some correspondence with Dr. Foulis, who performed the operation necessary for the use of the artificial larynx. There is an interesting passage in one of Dr. Foulis' letters which it is most convenient to give here :

The point alluded to as the breathing not causing a sound is explained by the fact that the force required to vibrate the reed so as to produce sound is greater than that of ordinary respiration. When we intone, we use a stronger current of air than usual, and the same is the case with my patient. It is very interesting to notice the change of *timbre* or quality of voice to which you allude. With ivory, horn, and vulcanite reeds we get quite different sounds, and even brass reeds differ in quality. The oral cavity, therefore, is secondary to the reed, and there can be no doubt that the differences in our voices as between man and man depend, to some extent, on differences in the density, elasticity, and cellular structure of our vocal chords. The case opens up various interesting problems, and I trust we shall be able to set these at rest.

The sojourn in Glasgow city proved this year less of a martyrdom than was usually the case, and Mr. Hullah went off to Aberdeen in excellent spirits, though this mental condition may be largely accounted for by the fact of his destination being the house of Professor Geddes, for whom he entertained a quite enthusiastic admiration.

My host is a most delightful creature, brimful of literature, about which he has been talking till just now, when we suddenly found out how late it is. I fear you will hardly make your way up here, but I *quite* expect to find you in Edinburgh on Monday. P.S. *Friday.*—A lovely morning! . . . . I have finished my second school here, and I am much enjoying my [Sunday] rest, and the prospect of a walk by the sea, on this the loveliest day that can be conceived. Not in the recollection of the 'oldest inhabitant' has such weather been known in Aberdeen. . . . *I* don't see why you should not come at once to Edinburgh. The severities of the summer and autumn have entirely passed away, and the winter has set in with sweetness and serenity unsurpassable as unprecedented. . . . I go to-morrow to Edinburgh, where, during my visit last year, it snowed, with intervals of cold thaw, incessantly. All over the north there seems to be a kind of summer, and the thermometer is still rising. . . . That delightful Geddes will be back directly, so I must shut up. . . . The people here—University Professors—are most kind. I have just heard that at the time of the election [for the Reid Professorship in 1865] at Edinburgh, the people here, and also in other parts of Scotland, sent a petition to the Senators to elect me. . . . *Edinburgh.*—Ah, the weather changes. You won't come ! . . . I am glad you have been to T——, and more glad that you have come away. . . . I sympathise with you in respect to your sufferings under those Low-Church parsons. . . . You will doubtless enjoy yourself greatly at Oxford ; at least I would fain think so, for *I* am enjoying myself greatly. . . . On Monday I dine with the Royal Society (marrow-bones always !). I have just come away from a meeting at the Musical Society, to the members of which [students] I made a speech which was well received . . . more tomorrow,

Thursday night. . . . This afternoon I sent off a letter to Milroy about our Principalship [of Queen's College, Harley Street]. I told him I would vote cordially for Dr. Farrar or the Rector [of Lincoln College, Oxford] ; for the latter *most* cordially. But we shall do very well with either, and I incline a little to Farrar, simply because he lives in London. We have suffered much from absenteeism. . . . We have had a dinner-party. Sir Wyville Thomson is a capital fellow. I am going out on Saturday to see him—somewhere at Linlithgow. . . . To-morrow I go to the Episcopal Training School ; after to the University to see some ' deep sea ' creatures ; and after that to dine with the Secretary of the Education Board in Scotland.

Saturday. . . . I am just back from Sir Wyville Thomson's. Were you ever at Linlithgow ? It would be a delicious place to spend a day in, in fine weather, with one's sketch-book. . . . I am glad Oxford is proving interesting. . . . I should like to have heard Ruskin on ' Carpaccio ' [as a fact Mr. Ruskin discoursed on many subjects, and was eloquently interesting for an hour and a half or more, but of Carpaccio said not a word on this occasion], of whose capabilities I think I know somewhat. . . . You cannot think what a lot there is to do here. Yesterday, before I set off to Linlithgow, I had to give a lesson to a man [Oakeley's assistant] who is using my old books, and who had not heard of the *inflected* syllables now in use at St. Peter's, Rome ! His enchantment was ravishing to witness. I want also, before I leave, to see the *two* schools here for the deaf and dumb, about whose training, in *speech*, I am meditating an article.

Following his usual route, Durham—where he heard two ' excellent services, some of the best at which he had ever assisted,' and a ' splendid sermon from the Dean of Manchester '—and Darlington, he arrived at Lincoln, whence he gladly wrote :

This will prove, I hope, all but the last letter I shall send you for some time to come. Not that I grudge the letters, but the absence which necessitates them. And this (D.V.) will come to an end next week. . . . This is a delightful house to be in. It contains at this moment *four* young ladies; two daughters, a niece, and a friend! All very lively and well informed. . . . Yesterday I spent two hours in the cathedral library, and this morning we have been to the cathedral, which is as glorious as ever. Good-bye . . . for two more days only. Hooray! P.S.—Come and meet me.

He came back for Founders' Day at the Charterhouse, and brought the Inspectorial drama to a close with Norwich and Bishop's Stortford. He was decidedly less knocked up than usual—a pleasant fact set down to the credit of the Italian journey. Almost immediately he took in hand his Report, and soon after the new year began had completed it, and an article on the falsetto voice, long due, for Grove's 'Dictionary.'

The Report for 1877 necessarily ran closely on the lines of that of the previous year.

Mr. Hullah notes with satisfaction ' improvement in sight singing,' and the Training Colleges of Cheltenham, Borough Road, Shortlands, Southlands, Peterborough, Edinburgh, and Glasgow are instanced as furnishing exceptions to the rule of ' monophonous practice.'

But it is to the effects of the ' Memorandum on the Application of Sol-fa Syllables to Musical Notes,' appended to my Report for 1872, that I am able to refer your Lordships with the greatest pleasure (continues Mr. Hullah).

In this memorandum, after having described the two modes of application of sol-fa syllable in common use, that known as the movable *Do* and that known as the fixed *Do*, I showed the difficulties, inconveniences, and inconsistencies of the former mode in its application to any but the very simplest music, and strongly recommended the adoption of the latter, admitting, however, as I have always done, that it involved, as heretofore used, some theoretical imperfection and even practical inconvenience. For these I suggested a remedy, based on a natural law, which I thought ought to remove every reasonable objection to it. Several musical instructors at once tried this remedy, and others, even among those who had heretofore used the movable *Do*, soon followed their example. That it has proved efficient would seem to be shown in the following facts :

There are now seven Training Colleges in Scotland and forty in England and Wales.

Of the former, in three (Edinburgh and Aberdeen, Church of

Scotland, and Edinburgh Episcopal) the established notation, with the movable *Do*, is taught; in two (Glasgow Church of Scotland and Edinburgh Free Church) the established notation with the movable *Do* and a short course of tonic sol-fa. In the two others (Glasgow and Aberdeen Free Church) the tonic sol-fa notation is used exclusively, except by those students who learn the pianoforte. These amounted last year, at Glasgow, to fifty-four among the sixty-six female students, and at Aberdeen to twenty among the thirty-five.

Of the English and Welsh schools, in four (Bangor, Homerton, Hammersmith, and Westminster) the tonic sol-fa, together with the established notation, is taught. In three others (the Borough Road, Durham, and Chester) the established notation exclusively, with the movable *Do*. The remaining thirty-three colleges have adopted the use I recommended in 1872, that of the fixed *Do* with inflected syllables.

To this extensive adoption of a method which is consistent with itself, and the application of which need never involve a moment's hesitation where its single law is understood, may be to a large extent attributed the generally increased 'sympathy of eye and ear,' the greater facility in uttering written and recognising uttered sounds, and even the improvement in style of execution of what has been already studied, on which I have latterly had to report. Doubtless a careless student sometimes forgets that B♭ should be called not *Si* but *Se*, F♯ not *Fa* but *Fe*; but the hesitation in giving names to notes to which I referred in my first Report is now exceptional though not extinct, for it still more or less hangs about the comparatively few scholars still taught through the movable *Do*. Like their predecessors of 1872, they still hesitate in naming notes, in more than two or three keys, systematically ignore modulation, and finally, if left to themselves, take refuge in 'inarticulate moans.' The movable *Do* may be likened to the *stock* of the soldier, long defended by military authorities of a former school, on the plea that in action he always threw it away.

In giving some of the results of the (paper) examination in the theory of music, he says that 3,661 students in Training Colleges took the established notation questions and 289 the tonic sol-fa; 1,234 'acting teachers' took the established notation questions, sixty-six the tonic sol-fa. It must have cost the veteran 'Apostle of Music' a pang to write:

> I verily believe that the art of singing from notes is now less commonly taught in elementary schools than it was during the years immediately following the impetus given to the subject by the Committee of Council on Education in the year 1841, an impetus the effects of which just lasted long enough to show that the art was as accessible as its possession was advantageous to the children attending those schools.

His comments on teaching by ear and the instance he relates of scientific teaching and its results are interesting :

That the effects of this impetus, permanent in the country itself, lasted no longer than it did in elementary schools is attributable to several causes; more than any other to the fact *that they never have been either estimated or recorded.* At present, with here and there an exception, singing (so called) in elementary schools is altogether 'by ear.' With very few exceptions it is so carried on even in the practising schools attached to the Training Colleges.

No persons, however well disposed to it, find such difficulty in learning to read music as those who have been long in the habit of singing by ear; and no passages are so difficult to sing correctly, even to persons who could otherwise have sung them with ease, as those which have been caught up by the lazy practice of unconscious imitation.

But singing by ear is not only mischievous, considered in relation to future musical culture, it is absolutely unnecessary; a clumsy and tedious process, even for the teaching of the simplest half-a-dozen songs to the youngest child, who may as readily—I might say more readily—be taught these songs and a great deal besides, *scientifically* as otherwise. This has been shown again and again, and years ago; very recently in an instance which I will particularly describe.

At the close of my examination of the Home and Colonial Training College in 1876, I requested the principal of that institution to allow an experiment in 'scientific' musical teaching to be made in his infant school. Immediately after the Christmas holidays last year a class of children, sixty-five in number, between the ages of six and seven, was formed and placed under the care of one of the teachers, Miss Elizabeth Crocker. For their instruction, twenty minutes every fortnight, with now and then five minutes during recreation time, was allowed; surely not an extravagant allowance, either for the experiment or its exponent. What these children had been enabled to do at the end of (say) five hours, distributed over twelve weeks, was exhibited, I am told, at a meeting of subscribers in the month of April last. I examined them myself at the end of October, after my visit to the Training College. I found that the majority could name correctly and readily any sounds within the limits of the same diatonic scale, and give utterance to any such sounds when called upon to do so. They could beat time with their hands, and distribute notes of various lengths into measures of two, three, or four beats—*e.g.* of a crotchet and two quavers, of two crotchets and two quavers, of two quavers, a minim, and a crotchet, and the like. I touched on my hand the notes of a tune they had certainly never before sung, and they sang it, with one or two exceptions, accurately. Finally, they sang various simple passages, still 'at sight,' which were written on the black-board.

Now it is no exaggeration to say that these children, whose

interest in the 'work' they had been made to do was manifestly intense, at the end of their (say) eight *hours'* instruction, had attained more of that 'sympathy of eye and ear' which most goes to make a 'musician'—had become, in fact, better musicians— than two out of three of the candidates for admission to our Training Colleges, to the musical instructors in which such an amount of preparatory training *at the same early age* would save nearly a year's work. It is to be desired that the training of these children be carried farther; but I venture to say that, even should this not be done at present, they will, should the opportunity be presented to them, take up the subject at any distance of time with a facility which nothing but the very short but sound course of instruction they have already had could have enabled them to do.

With a few earnest remarks on the futility of teaching music by rote, Mr. Hullah closes his Report.

CHAPTER XXXI.

BIOGRAPHICAL.

1878.

MR. HULLAH now turned his attention to other work for his pen. He first disposed of arrears of correspondence (which had been gathering up against him for months), which included an especially long letter to Monsieur Bourgault Ducoudray, on the system of choral singing adopted in England—on which subject much communication would seem to have been already held—and many shorter letters requesting the co-operation of several of his musical *confrères* in the preparation of a hymn-book for the Sunday School Union, which he had undertaken to edit. Very readily all responded in the same friendly spirit which dictated the reply of Dr. Monk, of King's College : ' Anything you ask can have but one reply from me—*i.e.* " yes." '

With great reluctance Mr. Hullah decided to resign at Midsummer the professorship he had long held at Bedford College, the work of which was becoming difficult in conjunction with other more pressing claims. The council of the college expressed much regret on receiving his resignation, and passed a highly complimentary resolution, adding that ' they would be glad, with his permission, to nominate him a permanent member of the college.' A resolution to the same effect was passed at the general meeting of the college, which took place on July 18, and in due time he was, as proposed, elected a permanent member of it.

Though always closely at work, Mr. Hullah was by no means indifferent to, or negligent of, social pleasures. He took his full share of his favourite ' little dinners ' in agreeable houses, attended concerts and the like. Now and then he notes in his Diary how he heard such and such a piece of news at such and such a house. As, when dining one night with the L——s, Professor Beesly (?) announced to the gentlemen gathered about the hearth that the University of London had that day consented to grant degrees to women. The Diary tells how indefatigable he was, too, in his attendance at the Philharmonic, the Madrigal Society—where he sometimes took conductor's work—at the meetings of the Bach Choir, and at the charming *matinées* of Mr. Ella's Musical Union. Twice he heard the 'Sorcerer.' On these occasions it was most curious to his companion to watch the little outbursts of mirth excited, not at all by what he saw, but by what he heard in the music itself—the musical jokes, in fact, which seemed so droll to the musician's ear, and yet suggested nothing in the least comic to the non-musical auditor.

The vacation frivolities began with a visit to Paris, where Mr. Hullah was anxious to hear the choirs which daily met in competition at the Trocadéro. The English choirs, conducted by Messrs. Leslie and Sullivan, held their own right well, Mr. Hullah said; but he added that from the fuller throats and more powerful lungs of the Swedish singers came volumes of sound more impressive at a distance. There was just time to go twice to the theatre and to dine once with Madame Coignet, a clever and interesting contributor to the 'Revue Politique' and other periodicals, at whose weekly gatherings many French people of note in the world of letters or art were to be found.

It had been necessary to return to England before the full holiday weeks were expended, which afforded an opportunity to go and see some old friends of his wife. The visit to Yalding proved a great success. 'How is it that I have never been taken to that delightful, altogether unique household before?' said Mr. Hullah on the way to the station. Then, after a reflective pause, he added, 'It would be a distinct gain to know that no remaining year of one's life would pass without a few days spent with that brilliant, learned old man, as brilliant and as learned as my dear old Dean of Salisbury.'

Once more, before the Rector of Yalding passed away, full

of years and crowned with love such as falls to the lot of few, Mr. Hullah did enjoy the privilege he so well knew how to appreciate.

The happy holiday time was now over, and Mr. Hullah departed for Warrington *en route* for Liverpool, where his wife joined him, and he had the satisfaction he had so long promised himself of introducing her to the ladies of N. D. de Namur, and the still greater satisfaction of finding that she derived from the introduction even greater pleasure and interest than he in his most enthusiastic moments had predicted.

The opportunity of seeing together Mr. Reay's collection of pictures (which includes some famous Rossettis) was not neglected, and then they parted once more.

From Bangor he writes:

I got yours of Tuesday with great delight; for it was a real letter, full of news [abstracts, probably, of all the letters found at home], although 'written at a shop.' . . . Really you are very good, and not at all as bad as you might be. . . . I go to-night to the P——s at Carmarthen, and to M—— D—— at Swansea, when, if they ask me, I shall stay over Sunday. *Swansea* . . . . [after a lively description of his social surroundings] Mr. and Mrs. M—— W—— make (as somebody would say) a great deal too much of their present guest. . . . I am here till to-morrow, in very delightful quarters. There is a billiard-table in the house, in the room (very large and commodious) in which we spend the evening. I have played a lot of games, and won several, which is a great satisfaction, for Mr. W—— is a tolerable player. I send you several documents, which will interest you, and which you will attend to . . . . How are *you* getting on at Bognor. Dull? . . . . [but ruefully, he rightly guessed] . . . . I have had three hours' perfect quiet in a charming little room, and I have cleared off my letters [to the Training College, among others] pretty thoroughly . . . .

Cheltenham, Sept. 9; 9 *p.m.*—Arrived an hour since. . . . Yesterday afternoon we drove over to see Miss Bostock [so well known in connection with Bedford College], about ten miles from Swansea. She is living in the most lovely conceivable spot, in the best-planned and prettiest house and garden imaginable—all of her own design. . . . *Malvern Wells.*—I finished at Cheltenham two very long days' work yesterday. Mrs. —— and I are going over to the [Worcester] Festival this morning, when Dr. Arne's oratorio, 'Hezekiah,' is to be done. It is years—six at least—since I have heard music—*i.e.* with an orchestra—in a cathedral, and nowhere does it sound so well.

About this time the Education Department decided to send Mr. Hullah on a continental tour of musical inspection. When they learnt this decision, he and his wife were panic-stricken to find, on mutual examination, how little of the German tongue available for colloquial use had stuck by them, and they lost no time in applying themselves to a daily portion of grammar on the rival systems of Bernays and Ollendorf.

Writing from Bristol, Mr. Hullah says :

I receive inquiries about my mission every day and from everybody. What if the Treasury, after all, should refuse to make the grant ? . . . . I am glad you are going on bravely with the German. The incessant travelling, work, and society have prevented my doing much during the last few days ; but I mean to do a great deal to-morrow. The journey (to Truro) is long enough to learn *all* languages in. . . . On the 24th I hope to be with you at Bognor. We will *drive* thence to Chichester. I should like you to see Miss Trevor [the Head of the Otter Training College] and her college ; though you will find nothing equal to our beloved sisters of N. D. I was yesterday at Fishponds (six miles from Bristol) at ten, and had not done till five. On my return here I went to the Asylum for the Blind, where I found a most interesting matron, Mrs. Stanley, and heard the pupils sing and play very well indeed. I made a little address to them, but nearly broke down more than once. [He all but gave way, and made but a poor speech on a similarly trying occasion, when addressing the pupils of the Blind School in St. John's Wood.] Mrs. Stanley told me her first work among them nearly killed her.
. . . . *From Exeter.*—My work being finished, I shall go for a long walk, which will be a real treat, not to say *rest*. *From Salisbury.*— Mr. Morrice came to receive me—most kindly, as always. We then went off to the cathedral, where I stayed for about three-quarters of an hour after the service—playing on the new organ, the grandest and most perfect I have ever touched, or, I think, heard. Then I called at the Training College to arrange about to-morrow ; then at the Dean's, where I saw Mrs. Hamilton, and engaged to lunch on Saturday ; then, lastly, at the Chancellor's, where I stayed last year. . . . . I seem at last to have got again into a civilised county as to postal arrangements—after Wales and Cornwall.

The 22*nd.*—Luncheon with the Dean (and Mrs. Hamilton), who was brilliant as ever, and sent pleasant messages to you. . . . I heard a most magnificent sermon at the cathedral from the Chancellor [Swain]. . . . I have made a purchase of two old china vases (blue), which I think you will like.

In spite of the rather wearisome journey to Bognor, and to and from Chichester, the short stay by the sea, and rambles on the shore with the children, did him much good, and sent him off to Lincoln greatly refreshed, though very 'cross' that he had again to go alone. He tried to pass the time cheerfully by devoting himself to the study of the Teutonic tongue:

> As my only companion, an old lady, slept all the way (he reports) I got on very well with Peter Schlemil, which is clever; only those sensitive Germans always conjugate the verb *weinen* on every possible occasion. . . . The household here [at Lincoln] disapproves of your defalcation. There is evidently going to be a huge dinner to-night; for, like the little boy of Dickens, Master Barlow, I have peeped into the cupboard, and seen some *horringes*.

Returning home, he wrote, in the intervals of examining St. Mark's, Westminster, and other metropolitan and suburban schools, the paper for the Social Science Congress in Cheltenham, the time for which was rapidly approaching. Taking Oxford on the way, he arrived at Cheltenham on October 24, and had the pleasure of staying with one of his old Charterhouse friends. On the following day, his paper read, he hastened home to prepare for a much longer absence on his 'Northern Circuit.' He found throughout his tour, and was naturally much pleased to find, that his utterances at the Social Science Congress had been extensively read, and were being much and hopefully talked of, especially north of the Tweed. Greatly as he relished finding traces of this, the clammy atmosphere and muddy streets of Glasgow, as usual, tried his temper and depressed his spirits:

> The weather till to-day (he says) has been lovely. Yesterday the sun was visible from morning till night. To-day—doubtless on account of 'the Sabbath'—he hides himself behind a set of very dirty-looking curtains. Instead of sitting down at once to my writing yesterday, I went out, tempted by the sun and the look of things in general, and called at each of the training schools just to show myself and make acquaintance with the *new* Principal of the Church of Scotland School. I found him and also the *new* inspector for this district, an old acquaintance from Aberdeen. . . . The proof of the Social Science paper has come. . . . It reads fairly, but these things want the effect to be given to them by *delivery*. . . . I am glad you have heard from poor ——, who is, like many of us, a dual personage; *i.e.* she often does wrong, being *at the same time* thoroughly able to criticise her wrongdoing most rightly and justly.

This was invariably his kindly and considerate tone about

even those who were troublesome to him, and who would, as a rule, be most severely judged and condemned.

I have had a long consultation with Miss Galloway (Higher Education of Women) and Mrs. S——, the 'President*ess*.' I am going to give a lecture on Saturday afternoon, about the theory of music, at the Society of Arts, &c. &c. What I am to say I don't yet know, but I dare say something or other will present itself. They are evidently much in earnest, these good people, about their 'higher education;' but it is clear that what they want is the *lower*. . . . *Nov.* 6.—I have had an easier day, and finished up at the Church of Scotland Training School. . . . Answered no end of letters, and went out . . . to the cathedral—a fine, well-proportioned building, with coarse detail. . . . The place where the altar should be monopolised by an enormous pulpit ! . . . I went on my way to and fro through streets I have never before seen, of unspeakable squalidity. I don't think I shall visit that part of Glasgow again in a hurry. This evening I am going out to tea with Dr. Peace, the great organist; after, we are to visit one or two new organs said to be very fine. To-morrow I begin at the Free Church School. Tonic sol-fa by way of a treat ! This will last till Saturday, when I give my lecture at three . . . . to which, I believe, a good many people are coming. . . . *Sunday.* . . My lecture yesterday was a success. Sir Henry Thomson took the chair. There were so many people that, had not the great hall been occupied at the time, we should have moved into it. As it was, a side room had to be opened, and the corridor was crowded down to the steps. The people in the latter could have profited little by my expositions. [It is quite probable that they heard very fairly, for Mr. Hullah's voice could on occasion reach an immense distance, and his enunciation was always clear and distinct.] I had no time to prepare more than a few notes; so the whole thing was extempore. Eight or ten of the Professors from the University came and sat on the platform, among them Sir William Thomson, who took the chair. I am going this afternoon up to the University sermon, and afterwards to dine with Miss Galloway and her father, a very nice old gentleman, who went last year to Norway by himself. He can *read* Norwegian, but gets on among the people through—the Aberdeen dialect ! I have made several new acquaintances, and met again the Dr. Foulis who performed that tremendous operation on the larynx of a man whom I saw last year, and who is still living and likely to live.

From Aberdeen.—The snow this morning was so deep that Mrs. Geddes insisted on my driving. So I got down to work quite comfortably, but walked back in what proved to be a rather fierce storm of rain. However, when I got in, at about four, I found a glorious fire in my bedroom, and 'every luxury of the season' that could be desired. To-night we have had a great dinner-party which has been very pleasant and amusing. To-morrow we dine at Mr. W——'s. He has a very fine collection of modern pictures ; among them some Turners. . . . How I shall regret to say adieu to-morrow to such a host and such a hostess! There is comfort in the thought that I shall turn southward. . . .

From Edinburgh. . . . Here I am safely on the way 'bock again.' The dinner at the Whites was most brilliant. . . . To-night I dine at Mr. L——'s to meet Dr. Blackie. . . . I have done with the Free Church [Schools] having taken leave of the students this afternoon in a very long and reproachful speech, and I am consequently very tired and looking forward with much satisfaction to to-morrow's rest. Miss Flora Stevenson came to see me at the Free School to-day. . . . I think you will have to set up as a musical critic! I consider I have *heard* your two foreigners and Miss T——. . . . I have called on Miss Flora Stevenson and found her full of my paper [read at the Social Science], and the circulation thereof in Edinburgh, especially among the members of the School Board, of whom, as you know, Miss S. is one. Whether she can do any good remains to be seen. Professor Blackie has been to luncheon, and was as . . . amusing as usual. . . . The thought of turning homewards is very pleasant, though I have had a most agreeable fortnight.

From Edinburgh he plodded on, until arrived in York he named a day for returning home, adding: 'When I come back I mean to be very idle for some time.' Accordingly, being come back, the 'idle time' extended to *fully six hours*—the whole of the first evening at home, in fact! The next day he attended a committee at Spencer House about the Royal Academy of Music, and the following day the idle Inspector went to Norwich, after which indeed his travels for the year were practically over.

The labours of the examination ended with the Royal Military Asylum, and on the last day of the year this incorrigible idler placed in Metzler's hands a motett for female voices (the third of a set of four), entitled, 'We wait for Thy loving kindness, O Lord,' and forthwith addressed himself to examination papers, cleared off at the rate of one hundred a day, and to the Report for ' my Lords ' during those forenoon hours kept inviolate for work.

In the opening paragraph of his Report, Mr. Hullah observes with much satisfaction that there is a 'growing conviction among college authorities that music is an *educational* subject,' and that the talk about music '" as a relief to grave and more important studies "' is a thing of the past. Looking back to the early causes of the unprepared state in which candidates too frequently present themselves for admission to the Training College, he offers the following interesting remarks :

> Moreover, a truth has latterly been dawning upon me, for the confirmation of which more experience is perhaps as yet needed, but which I so far believe to be a truth, and even one of universal application. The young men and women in the training schools, probably all others, who have indifferent voices—I find none who have 'no voice '—are simply those *who have never sung as children.* Whenever I have questioned a student, whatever the quality of his voice, in regard to this statement, the answer has always been confirmatory of this statement. The student with an indifferent voice, too often an indifferent ear also, is found never to have sung as a child. The student with a good voice and a good ear has invariably had some instruction or practice at school, sung in a choir, or been taught by one or other of his parents. 'Father began to teach us all to sing, as soon as, almost before, we could speak,' said an unusually accomplished female student to me last year. If only fathers or mothers with the slightest musical knowledge or skill would, for a few minutes every day, apply either to the cultivation of the musical ears of their children, what a musical people we should be in a few years' time!
>
> A bad quality of voice is not only a personal misfortune, as obvious in speech as in song, but it is often. I find, confounded by unlearned hearers with false intonation. Forty years ago, when I began the work to which my life has since been devoted, false intonation was certainly the rule. I have known a new class of adults sink a *fourth* in the course of a simple exercise of sixteen bars— *i.e.* begin on C (*Do*) and end on G (*Sol*), having taken every sound a little falsely in reference to the sound before it. By no contrivance, I believe, could such a result as this be attained now. The national ear, even among those who do not study music, has improved, and as a fact those who sing ' out of tune ' are now a very small minority, at least among those who come before me. Nor are voices of disagreeable quality anything like so numerous as they were.

Without being able to answer with precision a common inquiry as to what part of Great Britain yields the best voices, Mr. Hullah gives the result of his own observation, derived from the fact that the students of the York (male) and Warrington (female) Training Colleges are principally natives of the West Riding and Lancashire, those of the Bangor (male) and Swansea (female) of Wales, and those of Truro (female) of Cornwall. 'These, without exception,' he says, ' present bodies of voices which for quality and force I do not commonly find equalled elsewhere.' The concluding paragraph on this subject contains some useful hints to those about to build school or other rooms for similar uses :

Some of the apparent superiority in voice of the York students, not of this or that, but of every year, is possibly due to the proportions and arrangement of the room in which I hear them. This I find to be 50 feet long, 25 feet wide, and 25 feet high, proportions from which good results might have been expected. With the exception of a small organ and a stove, it is without fixtures of any kind. The students *stand* to sing, from movable desks; as many as five or six sometimes reading from one book, quite possible with a little mutual concession among the readers. This arrangement is, for singing *practice*, incomparably superior to that of fixed desks and seats. It admits of any grouping of voices at a moment's notice, and enables the teacher to move about among his pupils and ascertain what *individuals* are doing. The standing position is, I need not say, far more favourable than the sitting to the production of the voice.

The choice of songs prepared for the torture of the Inspector's ear still angers Mr. Hullah—though his wrath is somewhat appeased by the 'clear and natural manner in which the words are uttered '—a point to which he draws the attention of amateurs and ' even artists.'

The prolixity of answers to papers (complained of equally by Mr. Barrett and Mr. Bliss) also remains a source of dissatisfaction, though, as he says, 'language' being 'to many students a new instrument, a little ostentation in the use of it may be pardoned to them, always supposing it to be rightly used for the revelation of knowledge, not the concealment of ignorance.'

Mr. Hullah's statistics in regard to the notation used by the students in the preparation of the examination papers are, briefly, that out of a total of 5,572, ' 5,131 were done in musical notation and 441 in tonic sol-fa.'

With a strong appeal to ' my Lords to encourage, recognise, and reward scientific musical teaching in elementary schools, Mr. Hullah ends his Report for 1878.

At all sorts of odds and ends of time he took up his German books and worked away after the pattern of his fellow-student of former days, Sir Arthur Helps. Many were the disturbing unconjugated verbs and undeclined nouns that broke on the stillness of the foggy winter nights during the months of

January, February, and March—all in preparation for the impending journey, for which at last marching orders arrived. By this time a considerable quantity of German had been reconquered by Mr. Hullah and his 'assistant —a strictly honorary appointment, be it understood.

CHAPTER XXXII.

BIOGRAPHICAL.

1878.

THE final act of his official drama ended, Mr. Hullah was glad to take a week's 'idling' among his books; but even in his idling there was system and order. Each morning he began with a dip into some volume of Newman's 'Parochial Sermons' before he turned to one of his other favourite authors, piled comfortably about his seat. Voltaire or Balzac, Dante or Milton, the old English dramatists, or perhaps 'Don Quixote,' whiled away the hours delightfully till luncheon time, when he would issue from his study bright and beaming. As for the hateful German verbs, they were consigned to the topmost shelf for that one week, at the end of which Mr. Hullah declared himself ' all right,' though several friends found cause for affectionate uneasiness in his worn and tired looks—an aspect quite exceptional to him. Suggestions were even ventured that the projected journey be given up, but to these he turned a stone-deaf ear. The very thought of postponement spurred him to extra exertion for an even earlier start.

It happened that a very unusually large amount of writing was in arrears, so to gain a little more leisure he anticipated by some months the resignation of his harmony classes at Queen's College, with the less hesitation that his place was filled by Mr. Edward May.

In April he read a second paper on ' Musical Education ' at a meeting of the Social Science Association at Cheltenham, returning home to make preparations for the start to Paris as the first stage on the continental journey. Now the 'getting ready' had proved a period of serious domestic *Sturm und Drang*; for the Inspector, on luxurious travel bent, wished to take so many appliances in the way of despatch-boxes and books, that the whole of the by no means liberal 'grant' would have been swallowed up in paying for overweight of luggage! —a misapplication of public money to which the 'assistant' (whose office included those of courier, interpreter, keeper of the seal, purse-bearer, quartermaster and commissary-general, physician, and envoy extraordinary) felt bound to resist. Moderation born of experience won the day for once, and the start was made in light marching order—not, alas! maintained for long, for even before leaving Paris, on the eve, be it remembered, of a long and troublesome journey, Mr. Hullah was caught—caught in the very act!—of packing away two enormously bulky volumes, newly acquired, among his dress clothes! Needless to say the conflict of wills was renewed; nor was peace restored save by a curtailment to *nil* of the Inspector's pocket-money—a harmless measure, for many weeks elapsed before he had further leisure for again indulging his bibliomaniac tendencies, the object of his journey completely absorbing his serious attention. The distances to be traversed, and the shortness of the time at his disposal, made the special work extremely laborious, the fatigue and worry being incalculably increased by the necessity for night journeys, and by the unceasing noise, the glare, and the general discomfort of the German part of the tour. The inspection visits sometimes began at 7 A.M., and usually went on at short intervals till 3 or 4 P.M.—immediately after which hour the inspector went off post-haste in one direction and the assistant at equal speed in another, in order to catch head-masters or mistresses at home for the purpose of making arrangements for the next day's visits to the classes.

Odd difficulties now and then occurred in getting at the superior officers of a school after teaching hours, for as soon as the schools were cleared and the class-rooms tidied up, it seemed to be customary for the house master and staff to depart on private affairs, leaving the gate or door in charge of some superannuated and usually deaf substitute, who, not being able or willing to mount the many stairs which, as a rule, divided the Principal's rooms from the street, would simply admit the visitor, indicate the way up by a backward action of the thumb, and disappear, ignoring any further attempt to utilise his services. There was nothing for it, therefore, but to wander about passages and knock at doors persistently till some one said ' *Herein*,' and to obey, though occasionally the result was embarrassing to both sides. Sometimes the head-master would be caught performing the elementary stages of a *toilette de promenade*, or, calmly seated at work ankle-deep in school papers, in ' off duty ' costume of unconventional shape and airy texture, when, poor man, he would be reduced to the verge of apoplexy in his frantic efforts to resume an outer garment ; or, after prolonged researches through an apparently untenanted house, a babel of tongues would suddenly reveal the presence of fellow-creatures somewhere on the other side of one of the numerous doors, and a repetition of tentative taps would at length result in a shrill permission to enter, which, being acted upon, would admit the inspecting assistant (she it was who usually took the preliminary visits to female colleges), to her horror and dismay, into a room containing a score or so of ladies, all chattering, and knitting as if for their lives, around a central figure—clearly the headmistress and hostess of the *Kaffee-Kränzchen*—who would look up at the unhappy intruder and peremptorily bid her advance and state her mission. With one consent, tongues and needles would cease to operate, in order apparently to give undivided power of application to eyes and ears, while the wretched assistant would meekly march up the room and begin, in a paroxysm of nervousness, beneath the unwinking gaze of all those critical eyes (counting the very threads perhaps in the texture of her gown), to string together verbs all unconjugated and nouns all undeclined, which were listened to either in grim silence or interrupted every now and then by a pitiless ' *Wie ? Was ?* ' on condescending assurance that the English language was *perfectly* familiar to the hostess.

Ah ! how sweet a revenge it was then to use the mother-tongue as a weapon of torture and humiliation against the boastful mistress, her Teutonic vanity, pedantic intolerance, and selfish effort to profit by every opportunity of improving her knowledge of school-acquired English, and to watch the growing bewilderment on her face, as sentence after sentence, spoken in the politest of tones, but intentionally complicated and not too clearly pronounced, fell without meaning on her ear, and reduced her to:

'Ach! gnädige Frau Inspectorin, bitte! bitte! You shall not speak so *rasch* wen I shall onderrstand.'

'Ah, so? I spoke as to a countrywoman. You surely said, gnädige Frau, you understood English *perfectly*?'

'Surely, surely—only want of practice! But it might be the Frau Inspectorin would prefer to explain in German.'

Courage having been during the little contest somewhat regained, German was again resorted to, and a rapid agreement was soon arrived at as to when the classes could be inspected; and with a crab-like movement towards the door, dispensing bows right and left to the hungry-eyed ladies (each of whom dropped her ball of wool in rising, and immediately scuttled after it), the wretched *Frau Inspectorin* made her exit, to reappear next day with the head inspector, who never but once failed in the shortest interview to become a *liebenswürdiger Mann* in the eyes of head-mistress and lady examinees.

That one failure was in Vienna, when, though specially recommended through the *Ministerium von Cultus und Unterricht*, all his best and sweetest blandishments (made from the outer side of a *grille* in the convent reception-room) were ineffectual in reversing the decision of the sister superior that her pupils should *not* be inspected, and that she should *not* be made to waive her right ecclesiastical to admit or exclude anyone at her pleasure. His non-success much disconcerted Mr. Hullah, for he was anxious to compare the work done at Vienna with that carried on at Liverpool by the ladies of Notre-Dame de Namur.

Before such preparatory visits were well over the dinner-hour drew near. After dinner the day's work was discussed and posted up. Whenever it happened—as it fortunately did, not infrequently—that some *fête* day broke the continuity of school work, the opportunity was seized of visiting persons whom it was useful and agreeable to know, or in lounging about public galleries. In this way the monotonous routine of inspection was enlivened by contact with persons and things of more or less interest. But the wear and tear of nerves while in Germany and Austria was most serious, and induced the breakdown which occurred the next year. Everyone shouted, or chattered, or banged. To drive in the streets of Berlin, and Hanover more especially, was like a thundering progress over miniature boulders. Spine and brain suffered, or seemed to suffer, displacement. Sleeplessness resulted, and Mr. Hullah (likewise his assistant) was in a fair way of breaking up altogether by the time the German frontier was crossed into Holland. Everyone to whom Mr. Hullah had an introductory note had been kindly and readily responsive. He found his name and his labours known and appreciated. Almost everywhere he had met with cordial courtesy. Nevertheless, words fail to give any idea of the relief experienced by poor jaded Mr. Hullah when he passed into a land of calmness and quiet, where, as a rule, people do not walk heavily on the heel, nor habitually shout as if the hearer must be deaf or a mile off, nor do everything with a crash, from the shutting of a *porte-cochère* to the closing of a 32mo volume. Then what a change in the hotels—at least at the Hague! Instead of undecorated walls, bare floors, albeit of parquetry, undraped beds, uncurtained, or, at best, lace-curtained windows, what comfort—nay, what luxury, to be shown (and with gentleness) into a cool, shaded room, amply curtained, adequately carpeted! And then how charming to dine again in the midst of people who, though all talking, talked in deep-toned voices, instead of in those direfully strident tones by which the German guests at *tables d'hôte* may be singled out at once, whether in their own or foreign countries! And then the pleasantness instead of the horror of bed-time! With a sigh of weariness and an exclamation of deep thankfulness that he was out of 'noisy Germany for ever—and ever—Amen!' Mr. Hullah sank into a sleep which lasted from ten o'clock on Tuesday night till midday on Wednesday. In all probability that long restorative sleep—the first sound sleep for many weeks—saved him from an immediate illness. The fortnight spent in Holland partially set him up. He walked or sat out

in the quiet, staid streets as much as possible, and never tired
of discovering 'bits' which might have served De Hooghe—
his favourite among Dutch painters—for endless charming
pictures. Then the acquisition of specimens of quaint glass or
blue china, sought under all sorts of picturesque circumstances,
put him once more into a holiday frame of mind, and enabled
him to do his day's task with facility and pleasure. And he
much enjoyed, too, his evenings passed in easy flowing talk
with one or other of the official gentlemen with whom he had
been brought into contact. The passage through Belgium,
though busy and exciting, lasted but a short time. Home
was reached when London was deserted, and there was
abundance of enforced leisure to prepare deliberately for his
autumn work among the Training Colleges.

The Report which Mr. Hullah drew up for 'my Lords is
a fitting close to this fateful chapter of his life. It contains
much that is interesting beyond the professional criticisms
which would, as a matter of course, be looked for in such a
document. The final paragraph, with a passage taken from
his observations on the notation used in Geneva, give, moreover,
a simple and concise statement of his attitude in regard to the
Tonic Sol-fa movement, or indeed any other movement having
for its object the introduction of a system of *notation* differing
from the recognised musical symbolism which has, exclusively
thus far in the history of modern music, found favour with
composers of standing and weight.

Then, again, his sense of justice was offended by any form
of experimental teaching imposed exclusively on the children
of the classes who necessarily must use the elementary schools.
The educational value of experimental notation was well gauged
by him when the teaching of music by the Tonic Sol-fa symbolism was under discussion in his presence:

Surely (some one said) it is analogous to teaching drawing by
the exclusive use of that nursery appliance, an outline placed beneath
a sheet of ground glass, on which the infant artist traces what he
sees below.

That mode of teaching drawing (said Mr. Hullah) will be quite
as useful practically to the pictorial artist as will music, taught
exclusively on a fancy notation, be to the musical artist.

Mr. Hullah begins his Report by enumerating the countries

through which his mission took him—'Switzerland, Würtemberg, Bavaria, Austria, Saxony, Prussia, Holland, and Belgium.' He recalls that 'Reports addressed to the Education Commission of 1861 and 1864 by, among others, the late Rector of Lincoln College, Oxford, and Mr. Matthew Arnold' have appeared, 'but,' he says, '*music in elementary schools* has been but slightly treated by any, or altogether left untouched by all of these writers.' Dr. Burney would seem to have omitted any inquiry into the state of educational music during his travels in the last century.

Mr. Hullah remarks that he entered on his journey with

... large expectancy as to German [musical] achievement; recognising in the Germans the people who in modern times have given to the world the most and the best musical works, I ... expected to find the readers and performers of these more numerous in their country than in any other, and the teachers, in whatever class of school, more skilful, and the methods of teaching better.

How little these expectations were fulfilled will doubtless surprise many who still hold—to follow Mr. Hullah's example, and quote Mr. Edward Holmes—'that the authority of one born in Mozart's country, and speaking like him, would scarce be questioned.'

In Basle, the schools being in vacation, Mr. Hullah was forced to gauge the state of elementary musical knowledge by what he could get to hear in institutions similar to that managed by Herr Schäublin—an orphanage on a very considerable scale. Herr Schäublin illustrated his system of instruction on a piece of music new to his scholars:

The practice of this he prefaced (says Mr. Hullah) by a catechetical lecture on various points in it—key, time, modulation, and the like. [The pupils] then *read* the notes, first without musical intonation, and then with calling them A, B, C, &c. They then read the notes, beating the time, and finally sang them. Herr Schäublin never sang *with* his pupils. When they read falsely he stopped them, that they might, if possible, correct themselves. If they failed in doing this, he selected one pupil, whom doubtless he knew to be in advance of the others, and never ceased till he or she had made the necessary correction, which was soon adopted by the rest of the class.

With his expectations raised to a 'very high pitch,' Mr. Hullah passed on to Berne. Here his opportunities were less restricted, though the classes were in some cases numerically smaller than usual, in consequence of the temporary absence of some of the older scholars on agricultural avocations—a practical and suggestive reason, which, with many other points equally interesting, Mr. Hullah was not able to mention for want of space.

At Geneva, and at Geneva alone, Mr. Hullah came upon a system of notation other than that 'in universal use,' the 'arithmetical symbols of Mons. Chevé' being substituted.

The teachers said with one voice, that children learned it more rapidly and easily than they could musical notation. I ventured to inquire whether they had ever tried to teach children the latter, and they admitted equally with one voice that they had not.

In Zurich, Mr. Hullah found the teaching, whether elementary or more advanced, excellent, the voices of incoming candidates (he had sat through the individual examination of about thirty) being 'neither better nor worse than those of English youths in like predicament.' He notes 'the frequent change of posture' during the lessons, and he cannot refrain from saying a word about the neatness and cleanliness of the scholars' appearance, in spite of the too frequent evidences of extreme poverty, both in the quality of the clothing and in the stunted growth of the children.

I left Switzerland (he concludes) with high admiration of nearly all I had seen and heard, results as they were, indirect or direct, of the efforts the governments of the different cantons are making for the education of the people. The schools they have recently built are magnificent; the class-rooms numerous, light (the light always *to the left* of the seated pupils), and well ventilated, the access to these (stairs and corridors) capacious and well lighted. The teachers are numerous, and, so far as my observation, not always confined to my own subject, enabled me to judge, they carry on their useful and honourable work with as much cheerfulness as advantage to their pupils. Music is obligatory in all Swiss schools, and, as a rule, every Swiss teacher is the music master of his own class. To quote Schülinspector König, of Basle, '*Il n'y a pas de maîtres de musique à part.*' This *rule*, however, is liable to many exceptions.

In Stuttgart, two Protestant schools—one primary, one secondary—were first visited. Mr. Hullah thus gives his experiences:

They sang mostly, I think, ' by ear,' certainly always without
books. . . . Two or three teachers assisted their scholars by using
a violin, not unskilfully. In the secondary school, which I subsequently visited, I found the work somewhat less unreal, though
still very unsatisfactory. What was done was done chiefly ' by
ear.' The theory was of the meagrest possible description, and
the talking generally as little ' educational ' as it was possible to
make it. The teachers, each occupied exclusively with his own
class, seemed to have no common plan, and indeed no knowledge
of what was being done or attempted in other classes. One of
them expressed his amazement at my expectation that boys of
eleven or twelve should be able to ' read ' music, however simple,
at all, and another remarked that he thought that about ten per
cent. of those in the classes would never be taught to sing. This,
having regard to the teaching, I had no difficulty in believing. . . .

The performance at a blind asylum Mr. Hullah found very
inferior to those at St. John's Wood and Bristol.

In Munich he learnt ' that in the schools of Bavaria, as of
some other parts of Germany, singing *from notes* is not begun
till *after the age of ten years* '—' four, possibly five years too
late,' in his opinion.

Speaking of ' combination schools,' he says :

I visited many such schools in the course of my journey, and I
think that they were among the best that I heard. . . . The difference of sex seems to act as a stimulus to their interest in music.

The performances at a male training school at Freising
(to which he was escorted by almost a namesake—Dr. von
Hüller), where the students ' enter at the age of 13 and leave
at 18,' ' three [of these five years] being devoted to a preparatory course and two to a pedagogic,' are highly commended, and, with the exception of a few lines descriptive of
the schools of Leipzig, close for the moment his remarks on
Germany.

On his arrival in Vienna, Mr. Hullah's expectations were
reduced to a very low ebb in the course of an interview with
a gentleman high in office, who assured him that very little
teaching of music would be found in the elementary schools of
Austria, which proved to be most true. In all the elementary schools singing ' by ear ' was the rule. In most of the
normal schools visited by Mr. Hullah the power of *reading at sight* was the smallest conceivable. A century ago

Dr. Burney recorded that in Bohemia he found 'little children of both sexes, from 6 to 10 or 11 years old, who were reading, writing, playing on violins, hautbois, bassoons, and other instruments. The organist (and schoolmaster) had in a small room of his house four clavichords, with little boys practising on them all; his son of nine years old was a very good performer.'

. . . . Full of the impression produced by the reading of these and many other passages by other writers (says Mr. Hullah) I reached Prague in the belief that it would prove a veritable elysium of music, to discover that not only were 'the violin, the hautbois, the bassoon, and other instruments' no longer to be found in the Bohemian school, but that even singing was little practised there, and singing from notes scarcely at all! Further inquiry thoroughly confirmed this statement.

But if he found little knowledge and much inaccurate time, he found an almost limitless capacity for music among the students. Of this he cites an instance from the *Bohemian Female Training Schools*, where they were gathered together to the number of ninety expressly for his benefit. He has to say of this capitally representative collection of the swarthy singing race:

I found what may be best described as the cumulative results of many generations of practised vocalism. No such sound from choir or band had ever before fallen on my ear; no vocal organs so sweet, so strong, so extensive in compass, so beautifully modulated, so perfectly in time.

But then it turned out that it was all 'ground' into them, and that of independent power to *read music* they possessed none! so that, after two or three failures, he had to give up testing them. 'The sympathy of eye and ear, which above all things goes to make a musician, was wholly wanting in these gifted students,' was the only conviction possible to Mr. Hullah. 'There is no teaching by note in the elementary schools of Dresden—*à fortiori*, in the provincial schools of Saxony,' sounds so conclusive a remark, that of Saxony there would seem to be nothing more left to say; but, though teaching 'by ear' was in 1879 the rule in the Saxon Volkschulen, there was no lack of real teaching in the higher institutions, such as the Normal Schools, the Kapellknaben, and similar institutions, and in the famous Normal School at Nossen.

The military precision of the Prussian schools was at once noticeable, accompanied by a harshness of manner and voice between teachers and pupils which, encountered early in the morning, left a singularly uncomfortable feeling for the rest of the day. Except in the Jewish schools, the teachers, male and female, wore an overdriven look.

Mr. Hullah found teaching from notes very common and satisfactorily practised in the Prussian schools, but, as a rule, reading at sight was indifferent; yet of the thoroughness of the teaching, so far as it went, Mr. Hullah is constrained almost in every case to speak highly.

In Hanover, the musical question in reference to 'the people' had evidently not been taken into grave consideration, and matters were in a sadly backward state, there being in 'the elementary free schools of Hanover' . . . 'no singing from notes,' and, in the judgment of an important official, 'a large number of the children in Hanoverian schools' having 'no ear'—a statement which must have aroused in Mr. Hullah a spirit of contradiction. He does not, however, record what protest he felt called upon to enter, but concludes his remarks on Germany by a few words of very general application:

Why (he says) are the humbler classes in so many countries debarred the acquisition and exercise of this beautiful accomplishment, for which they have at least as much aptitude as their 'betters,' and a year's cost of the enjoyment of which would easily be paid for by a fortnight's abstinence from beer and bad company?

Early in his peregrinations through the schools at the Hague, Mr. Hullah came across the satisfactory spectacle of combined classes of both sexes, 'generally taught separately, but brought together once a week for practice.

They not only sang what they knew (he continues), various songs in three parts, but one or two easy passages which I wrote on the board, readily and correctly. . . . In teaching the first and second classes by ear, I noted here, as afterwards in other Dutch schools, that the teacher *beat time*, and that consequently his pupils *kept* it.

In this particular school the *reading at sight* test failed, but was generally successful in the Dutch schools with older pupils.

Apart from the mere routine of teaching, Mr. Hullah calls attention to the excellence, both in its conception and practical results, of a system of volunteer inspectorship which exists in Holland and in Belgium, and he speaks likewise of the self-possessed and quiet manner and tone of the Dutch pupil-teachers in managing their classes, drawing a comparison, in no unkindly spirit, between them and our English pupil teachers, not altogether flattering to the latter.

After giving special details of the teaching in several of the free, model, and commercial schools in Brussels, Mr. Hullah says comprehensively:

I may say that in every [school] I visited, the children, almost without exception, answered every theoretical question I put to them, and read at sight every passage I wrote for them, correctly, easily, and in many instances even with some style.

The elementary schools of the Continent present

three striking points of difference from those of Great Britain. (1) The scholars remain longer in, and are more regular in their attendance on them, than with us. (2) The amount of teaching force brought to bear upon is greater than on ours. (3) More power of attention and more eagerness to learn are generally exhibited by continental than by English children.

Accounting for this, he continues:

A school time of from three to six years' duration, broken in upon by every conceivable accident, contrasted with one of from six to nine, scarcely ever interrupted, and classes of indefinite size contrasted with classes rarely exceeding thirty pupils—these are evils which an increased estimate of the value of education on the part both of parents and school managers may in process of time remove. Inferior power of attention, and less eagerness to learn on the part of the children, may also be increased through the same means. That there should be any greater inherent aptitude for this or that subject in Swiss, German, Dutch, or Belgian children than in English I have seen nothing to induce me to believe. To speak only of my own art, musical practice continued through many successive generations, as among the Bohemian people, may induce a more ready receptivity of musical impressions than among our own; but (he further insists that) the so-called 'natural' musical power of the English people is equal to that of the German or any other people. If the greater musical fecundity of the German nation be adduced as evidence to the contrary, it must be borne in mind that this fecundity is of recent growth, and may in its turn prove to be but temporary. In the fifteenth and first years of the sixteenth century the Belgians, or Gallo-Belgians, were the music masters of all Europe, and music was more largely and thoroughly cultivated in their country than elsewhere. To them subsequently the Italians owe their long uncontested supremacy in the art. This in turn has undoubtedly in more recent times been transferred to the Germans. But, then, it should be remembered that Germany, in the modern acceptation of the expression, comprises a vast extent of country, and the so-called German people a vast variety of races. To the edification of modern German musical reputation not merely have Austria, Prussia, Bavaria, and Saxony contributed, but Bohemia, Poland, Hungary, Scandinavia, and even the Netherlands.

A more extended system of musical inspection, voluntary as well as salaried, is much pressed on the notice of ' my Lords,' with further suggestion that the inspectorial signification of the word ' singing ' should be restricted to the power of singing from *musical notation* :

I entreat your Lordships (urges Mr. Hullah) to bear in mind that the question here raised is not one of methods but of notation. Let who will teach, and who will learn, on whatever method he pleases, but let not the sanction of your Lordships be further given or implied to a notation or alphabet absolutely unknown out of Great Britain, the closest acquaintance with which fails to enable its possessors to read music as it is written by musicians.

CHAPTER XXXIII.

BIOGRAPHICAL.

1879.

THOUGH by no means recovered from the fatigue of his recent journey, Mr. Hullah started on his tour of inspection in exceptionally hot, sultry weather in August, beginning with Salisbury, where he was again the guest of the Rev. J. D. Morrice. He saw, among other friends, the Dean ' as bright as ever, but weaker than last year, but who showed great interest in the recent travels.' The writing of this, the first, as of all other letters written during his absence, betrays weakness. His cheerfulness often failed so soon as he was alone, and he could not conceal how great was the need that the strain of work should be relaxed. Railway whistling and other noises incidental to travelling began to harass him and haunt him for hours after the immediate cause for irritation was over. He complained if but a day passed without news of home doings, so that it was necessary to keep him acquainted chattily with all that was going on, and to make the most of any passing incident. Herein lay the difficulty : for incidents are the exception, by no means the rule, of life at Bognor, to which placid and sleepy place the quondam assistant had been compelled to retire by the necessities of a most dilapidated travel-worn condition. He was not difficult to please, fortunately, so that 'nonsense letters,' helped out by pictorial illustration, and both whipped up by imagination, kept going quite a lively stream of gossip as to the sayings, doings, and thoughts of the family circle. Mr. Hullah continually acknowledges these epistles :

Your letters come in at all sorts of odd times—sometimes two together, but come when or how they will they are very consoling. ... I was much amused by your account of the sermon, the youthful criticisms thereon [from the 'Minims'] and your sketch of the preacher. What a creature! ... Having got through my Training College at Bangor, I was making up my mind what next to do, when Mrs. W—— (of Malvern Wells) made her appearance, having run over to see whether I had got her letter, which I had not yet answered. Really she is a good-natured soul! I went back to Llandudno with her and came on here [Liverpool]. ... I am free from the Training College for an hour, and I hasten to acknowledge the arrival of the last of the 'sleepy soliloquies' and 'sea-side sighings,' also of your 'revised edition' of my memoranda. [He was so good as to keep 'idle people at the seaside out of mischief' by sending a constant supply of work to be 'rough blocked.'] I send on to you a packet of letters. Deal with those I have marked for me. The work here [he writes from Liverpool] is pretty constant. The Sisters welcomed me cordially, and inquired after you. You ought to have come back to have your *conversion completed*. ... They are engaged in a great work. Besides their normal they have a practising school and five others of different grades and ages in their house, which they are enlarging again. They teach also some other schools in Liverpool. ... After nearly six hours' incessant work I have written a number of letters in answer to my foreign correspondents. One of these is from Monsieur Landa, of Brussels, asking a number of questions about the 'inflected syllables,' which he purposes introducing into his particular school—the *Ecole Modèle*. ... Another letter comes from M. F. Gedeking, of the Hague. I send it. [In this letter Mr. Gedeking explains that, having borrowed a copy of 'Time and Tune in the Elementary School' from Inspector Van Aken, he desires permission to 'publish an edition in Dutch, not a mere translation ... for use in our schools. [It] would do much good to the singing instruction in particular,' he continues, 'and to the public interest in general.' And yet another very gratifying letter he has to tell of.] I received a day or two ago a letter from Visetti, who has been at Milan, and finds that his translation of my 'History of Modern Music' is actually printing. He sends a request from Ricordi, that I will add to this Italian edition something more about Verdi. This is quite reasonable, and can easily be done.

Very naturally he was much pleased and cheered, and, on the whole, was in much better spirits by the time he got to Cheltenham, where, having examined the students of the Male Training College, he went off to Malvern Wells for a whiff of his native air and a warm reception.

Ah, these beautiful Worcestershire hills! (he exclaims). The rest and quiet after the work and the incessant racket of railways, and of occasional hotel life, are very refreshing.

A few days later brought him home. He was visibly worn, and an assistant for the coming work in Scotland was pressed on him, but not yet would he listen to any suggestion of help. After examining many of the suburban colleges, and those of Norwich and Lincoln, he departed for the north in rather forced spirits. But by-and-by he felt better, and reported himself as stronger, and 'very well looked after by friends everywhere.' Even Glasgow was less wearing to him than might have been feared. While there he saw much of Miss Galloway, more intent than ever on the Higher Education of women, and desirous of securing Mr. Hullah's assistance for the following May; had a pleasant chat with Mr. J. C. Robinson, travelling in the north at the moment, 'who knows lots about pictures, and is acquainted with all painters whatever,' attended concerts, went to parties, did not fail to hear Dr. Pease play on the organ, and was assiduous in his examination of those schools which he found so 'huge' that, when the time came for going to Aberdeen, he could not but rejoice and be glad, even though it was not possible for Professor Geddes to receive him as a resident guest on that particular day. In Edinburgh he went, of course, to Professor Douglas Maclagan, and was more than ever the object of the kindest care to the whole household. It must be admitted that life in the Modern Athens was pretty equally divided between work and play. He might well say:

> The work and the dissipation make it hard to write. . . . On Wednesday we dined at the L——. Yesterday the Doctor and I dined at the Medical Society's Club, which was very lively. I am invited to a *wedding* and banquet afterwards at the Lord Justice General's, and on Wednesday to Dr. Rutherford's. To-morrow afternoon I am to be taken over the new hospital by the house surgeon, and the museum on Wednesday by the curator. Sir Herbert Oakeley has a meeting on Monday at the University, to which I have promised to go. . . . I met Sir Daniel Macnee last evening—a capital *raconteur*—from whom I have learnt more stories.

The next move homewards was to Durham, whence he writes:

> I have been in such a whirl during the last few days that I do not know when I last wrote; certainly it could not have been yes-

terday. At Durham I did not tell the Arnes (or anybody else) that I was coming, but took my things to the hotel and engaged a room. Having done this, I set off to their house and found Mrs. Arne at home. She began to rage at me for not coming to them straight. The upshot of it all was that I had to go back to the hotel and fetch my things here; and here I am, by a very nice fire, writing this note before getting ready for dinner, having had a short walk and been to the cathedral. How very fine it is, especially lit up, as it is now, for evening service! . . .

At last came:

I do long to be home again, and I am coming.

On December 9 he came home worn and thin, but owning to nothing beyond a little fatigue from 'over pressure;' and, with one thing and another, the strain was kept up till the very last day of the closing year left him beginning his Report of the Training Colleges which he had so lately examined. The chief points of interest noted by Mr. Hullah in his official Report for 1879 are, the large increase in the number of students studying music instrumentally, and in those singing by *note* in the practising schools attached to several of the colleges. He notices also a marked diminution in the number of musically unprepared students.

Mr. Hullah's Report, as a whole, tends to show improvement in every branch of musical study, as do also the Reports of Mr. Bliss and Mr. Barrett.

CHAPTER XXXIV.

BIOGRAPHICAL.

1880.

UTTERLY weary of his desk, and of all other sedentary work, Mr. Hullah was seized on New Year's Day with an alarmingly energetic desire ' to set things generally in order.' Against his method of arranging books, music, and papers there was nothing worse to be said than that it was inconvenient for the rest of the family to feel faint with dust, and to find neither vacant chair nor couch, nor clear six feet of floor, to faint upon. But when, having preliminarily studied the method on which ' *l'ami Fritz* ' managed *his* cellar, he sought to apply it to his own receptacle for wine—a range of iron bins built up in a cupboard within the flat—the result generally was chaos, and the accidents so calamitous, that at the end of a week his deposition from the post of cellarman was proposed and unanimously carried by an influential meeting of Home Rulers. With suspicious humility, as of one who had had more than enough of his own failures, he retired to the vantage-ground of his study, to plunge forthwith into the correction or preparation of examination papers, of which he notes 593 were cleared off in six days. The remaining thousands were, without his permission, sent off to his ' assistants.' Though the leisure thus gained for him was instantly turned to other account, the substituted work was of a less wearing nature. It consisted largely of correspondence with America, whence came inquiries about ' schemes for teaching ' and ' instructions how to overcome special difficulties in the conduct of musical education ;' and about this time there was an exchange of letters between Mr. Hullah and Mr. Francis

Galton on a subject which the latter was then investigating—the 'visualising' power of artists generally and musicians in particular. There had been some previous interchange of pamphlets, disposed of in a sentence or two. Then Mr. Galton continues:

. . . . May I ask whether you can . . . . briefly give me any information by which I could form some statistical conclusions as to the distribution of the faculty of mentally reproducing music with vividness? . . . . By vivid representation of music I mean a mental reproduction of it that is lifelike, or comparable in power and definition to the sound of music actually heard. It so happens that in the course of my inquiries about visualising I have only incidentally heard of *one* very marked case of this. The person in question has described his power with great detail and careful self-analysis, and has sent me what is certainly a most interesting and instructive paper. I should be very curious to learn whether the power is always, or even commonly, possessed by great composers and musicians. Paradoxical as it may seem, I should be quite prepared, from the absence of the visualising faculty in the case of many of our highest living painters, to expect that it was not. The mind works in many different ways, and there are more symbolic methods of dealing both with objects of sight and of sound than by direct visual or audible representation. I gather . . . . that you entertain a somewhat similar view; I mean when you speak of one sense doing the work of another as well as its own, and, so to speak, of *hearing* with the *eyes*. Am I right in my supposition?

To this letter Mr. Hullah sent the following reply:

. . . . No doubt 'the mind works in many different ways;' but I am disposed to think that, among the *greatest* poets (dramatic especially), architects, painters, sculptors, and musicians, whole works are, more than sketched, *seen*, by the mind's eye, before they are presented, even to the artist himself, in any visible form. This seems to me to be less wonderful in literary and plastic art than in musical. Language is, in *some* degree, a universal gift; and ideas cannot be said to be *formed* till they are put into it. We have no proof that a man who could not build, paint, or model a cathedral, a picture, or a statue could design it; whereas a melody (for instance) could be, and often has been, invented, and *sung*, hummed, or whistled, by one who could not write it with even approximate correctness. Many melodies have been presented to me, on paper, of which I could make nothing until the composers had sung or even played them, when I found, as I knew must be the case, that they had not written *what they intended*. The realisation of *visible* music—the converse of writing, or trying to write, what is already in the mind—is not at all a rare power; indeed one who has it not cannot be called a *musician*—the primary condition of whose existence is that he *knows the sound of what he sees*. I have myself repeatedly *conducted* from a full score I had never seen till I entered the orchestra. This, I need not say, involves not only the appreciation, at a glance, of the *character* of each movement, but the power of detecting notes falsely written or read; indicating to performers when they are to begin again after a silence of any duration, &c. &c. This power is not at all uncommon, and is the property of one or more persons in every town of musical Europe—or America. Musicians know, and sometimes intimately, a vast quantity of music they have never heard—never will have a chance of hearing. Some, of very exceptional powers, can *read* one piece of music while another is being performed within their hearing. The late Sterndale Bennett gave his composition lessons in a room adjoining the orchestra at the Royal Academy during the hours of rehearsal. Other men have *composed* under like circumstances—probably the easier process of the two, as demanding closer absorption in one act. . . . .

Recently Mr. Galton has suggested that it would be of interest to another question with which his name has become associated—the heredity of genius—were the source of Mr. Hullah's musical ability traced.

It is unfortunately not practicable to work out a genealogical table of his talent, for the Hullah family would not seem to have been very numerous in past generations, and there is little else to go upon in regard to the generation immediately preceding his own than what Mr. Hullah has himself told in his fragmentary autobiography.

It will be remembered that Mr. Hullah mentions incidentally that his father had a pronounced taste for instrumental, and his mother a remarkable gift for vocal, music. It is known that his brother was also highly endowed in this latter respect, but the cultivation of his gift was scarcely carried far enough to afford evidence as to the comparative quality of his musical abilities.

The only other blood-relative known to persons still living —his father's sister, Mrs. Smart—possessed no more than a taste for music in the abstract.

It may be inferred, therefore, that so far Mr. Hullah was himself the highest development of the musical aptitudes of his paternal and maternal ancestors.

But if it be interesting to inquire into the origin of his musical talent, it is irresistible to remark in passing how much more interesting it would be to follow to its source in some remote ancestor his more pronounced, albeit little used, gift for architecture. Bearing his foreign origin in recollection, it seems not wholly impossible that with opportunity and leisure at command such an inquiry might lead to a discovery that some one or other of his race built, in the golden age of Gothic architecture, one of those glorious cathedrals, like Chartres, or Rheims, or Noyon—the contemplation of which never failed to move him to the depths of his soul.

From his speculations concerning visualising power and kindred subjects Mr. Hullah had to turn to the more immediately practical and utilitarian schemes of the Coffee Music-Halls Company, promoted by Mr. and Mrs. Ernest Hart, Miss Cons, and other enthusiastic advocates for bringing light and pleasure to cheer the toilers for bread on their way in life.

It seemed but natural Mr. Hullah's co-operation should be desired, since, as the secretary very truly said, 'no one could speak better on the subject,' 'being the pioneer in popular *good* musical entertainment for the people.' Having once responded to the call, he, in his usual conscientious way of doing things, felt himself under an obligation to investigate personally the state of matters in existing music-halls, and in the pursuit of knowledge wasted much valuable strength going from one to the other—to arrive at the only conclusion that would seem possible to a person of ordinary refinement, namely, that for the most part the performances in these music-halls are less harmful than had been reported, but inconceivably dull, and more often than not vulgar.

He had an opportunity of expressing his views on the subject at some length at a meeting held in the Jerusalem Chamber in February. This pursuit of knowledge in the interests of philanthropy, added to many examinations—notably one at Dulwich College—and attendance at numerous committees, several of these being in connection with the new Training College of Music, kept him frequently exposed to irritating noises and changes of temperature—too long absent, in fact, from the comforts of home, where, though he worked incessantly, he worked, at any rate, in that state of peace and quiet which was becoming daily more essential to his well-being.

There came a lull, however, at last, and he was able to

spend some hours daily in his own study, where his occupations were pleasantly diversified one day by a discovery among the children's Christmas gifts of a volume of verse with illustrations by Miss Kate Greenaway. These he quickly provided with musical settings, which were effectively rendered by the 'Dodos.' Alas! the poor Dodos had had no manner of teaching from him for many a long day, and were enchanted to receive some attention again. Under their father's guidance they carolled with infinite glee of the manners and customs of ' the twelve Miss Pellicoes,' and of the joys of ' sitting on a rail ' and ' conversing with the birds ' on ' a hot September morning.' Naturally enough everyone wanted to see and know the charming artist, so Mr. Hullah set out one morning betimes to call on Miss Greenaway, who lived far away somewhere towards the North Pole. Late in the evening he returned, and recounted to the children how he had climbed up to the topmost floor of a house to find Miss Greenaway in her own pretty nest of rooms, where she dreamed her elegant fancies, and wrought them out and lighted them up from that inward storehouse of seemingly inextinguishable sunshine—her bright imagination.

She had given permission to Mr. Hullah to use her verses, and promised to come and see him. So, as a children's party was imminent, she was asked to come to that. She came, and in the course of the evening listened with evident pleasure to the singing of her verses by the youthful choristers, led by their father, as merry, and not much less bright-eyed, than the youngest of them.

A few days after this children's party—the last, as it proved, he was ever to assist at—he was dining with Canon T——, after a day of unceasing exertion, when the first stroke of paralysis deprived him partially of the use of the left leg and arm. He described subsequently how he felt the numbness coming on during dinner, but suppressed all sign of uneasiness. After dinner he succeeded in getting upstairs, when the sense of a coming catastrophe became unbearable, and he beckoned his wife to him and asked to be taken home.

With remarkable self-possession and tact their young hostess made departure easy, and he was spared the dangerous excitement of hearing sympathy from friends among the company. Under the calm support and reassuring treatment of Dr. Allen Sturge, Mr. Hullah rallied surprisingly, and was able in a few weeks to go down on a visit to a friend at Malvern Wells, till his wife could follow and make a temporary home for him in the place he was so fond of. He sent daily reports of himself, making quite the best of his condition:

> It is weary work (he writes). I gain strength but slowly. I cannot walk more than a few yards at a time. Writing is a little difficult. Happily I can read without headache or difficulty of any kind. My hostess is kindness itself and anticipates my every wish. . . . Write constantly till you come, and come soon. . . . Your arrangements with Mr. Barrett [who henceforth took charge of nearly all Mr. Hullah's unfulfilled professional engagements, and undertook to be ready at a moment's notice to visit any or all of the Training Colleges] are altogether most satisfactory. . . . Mrs. W—— talks to me and to everybody as she writes to you, about my staying on. Of course it won't do. But I do not contradict her *yet*. There is a whole week before us for discussion, and every day I am getting stronger, less and less of an invalid, wanting all kinds of things which *she* says are not to be had in the lodging; but I have been to the lodgings, and they are in perfect order and look really nice. . . . The sun is shining and is certainly welcome, but he is a deceiver, inciting poor broken-down folks to encounter bitter cold east winds ' neither good for man nor beast.' How welcome will be the Blunts, won't they? Do confirm their resolution to come if need be. How I should like to have some talks and even walks — for my legs are getting stronger—with him. . . . People say I am getting on very fast, but *I* should say very slowly. If the wind did not pierce to the very marrow of one's bones it would certainly promote a quicker return to one's normal condition, if that return ever come. I look up at these beautiful hills and wonder if I shall ever climb them again as I used to do. Meanwhile everybody is most kind. I really had no idea there were so many people here who cared or seemed to care about me. Mrs. W—— is kinder than ever; no relative could be more devoted. But you will see all this when you come. We are happily in the last days of an absence from one another. Be sure you come by the first train. I am looking forward impatiently to Thursday. . . . Tell the chicks to bring their Dodo books with them.

The stay at Malvern Wells was prolonged into May, but the east wind prevailed the whole time. He was much worried by expensive litigation cruelly forced upon him by a firm of music publishers. Still there were consolations of a social sort, numerous and pleasant. Not only were the residents at the 'Wells' universally sympathetic and kind, but occasionally other friends came and stayed a day or two and cheered him up, and once two American gentlemen came all the way from London to talk over musical matters in connection with education with him.

Each day brought letters full of affectionate commiseration for him, and offers to lend a house here, a cottage there, and invitations rich in promises of tender care. He was deeply touched, but the genuine alarm felt about his state by intimate friends was not always successfully disguised, and he was quick to penetrate how many thought that for him life's work was practically over. 'The pitcher which goes often to the well is at last broken,' wrote one, and that phrase seemed to echo for ever in Mr. Hullah s ears. As the summer drew near an attempt was made to induce him to send in his resignation to the Education Department, but the bare proposition so irritated him that it was deemed best to let him have his way. 'Better to wear out than to rust out,' he said. After many weeks Mrs. Hullah was obliged to return to town, and Mr. Hullah went to Staunton-on-Wye. While there he was anxious for a day or two about his wife's health.

To think of your being so ill and I not to know it! I thought you were only over busy and could not write. . . . If M—— were not with you I should come at once, useless though I am. M——, dear little soul, is always ready to come to the front, and has doubtless by this time installed herself as head nurse and housekeeper in chief. . . . I read the children's letters always more than once with infinite delight.

Dr. Sturge advised that Mr. Hullah should be kept out of London as much as possible. He therefore returned to Malvern Wells, always under the impression that the air suited him. At the end of May he was so far recovered as to be able to say:

This morning I think I feel better than I have done since I came. . . . Ballantynes have nearly finished the new book of exercises and figures [to Hullah's method]—a prodigious load off my mind. Anybody could now see the manual through the press, having this to refer to.

And then, being in a chatty frame of mind, he continues:

Your *notelet* of yesterday was very welcome, for a *one* line day is just a hundred times better than a *no* line day. There is absolutely no proportion between them. . . . The dear old May [his brother professor at Queen's College] descended serenely on us yesterday; and after his arrival we took him a drive round the Wynd's Point and up the Hills, so that he had a long sniff of the mountain air. . . . Did I tell you that Boyle—an old, very old Charterhouse pupil of mine, who has just been made Dean of Salisbury—is here recruiting? He has succeeded *our* brilliant Dean. . . . I leave this for Swansea on June 15.

This announcement was alarming, for it meant that he purposed doing the work of inspection himself. The resolve was not approved by anyone, but yet it was thought best not to excite further nervous suspicions about himself by insisting on absolute abstention from work. On condition that he accepted a good deal of help from Mr. Barrett, Dr. Sturge gave his consent, and a letter explaining the nature of Mr. Hullah's recent illness preceded him to each friend as he moved about; with what effect will be gathered from the following passages from Mr. Hullah's own letters. Having reached Swansea, he writes:

Up to the last moment my hostess [at Malvern Wells] was inconceivably kind. . . . You are right indeed in supposing that I find 'every living soul helpful and kind, and anxious to spare me all possible exertion.' Here I am offered more comforts and conveniences in a day than I could avail myself of in six weeks! . . . *From Carmarthen.* . . . The Principal at Swansea came with me from the College to the station, and from the station to Landore, where there is a junction, and insisted on seeing after my ticket and belongings till I was fairly seated in the carriage to Carmarthen *junction*, where again I was met by my host Mr. P——, who had borrowed the vicar's pony and carriage, that I might be spared more changes. As to Mrs. P——, she offers me cups of tea, glasses of wine, and all other luxuries every time we meet, and insists on my breakfasting in bed. This morning I examined twenty students, and shall easily get through the remainder to-morrow. I am to stay over Sunday, and on Monday I go to Bristol.

Set on his way with kindly forethought, he was again a guest at Clifton, whence he writes:

June 21.—My journey to-day has included a steamboat *trajet* with a going up and down of steps, so I am a little more tired than usual, and must come to an end soon. Yesterday I could not write to you. There were such heaps of letters [sent through the Education Department] waiting answers—two or three in reference to the College of Music. It will be curious if my suggestions (in my Report) about the teachers should prove of real use to the College, which seems possible. [The passage Mr. Hullah had in his mind will be found at the end of the Report for the year 1880, page 275.]

Helped on by a constant repetition of acts of kindness, he went on his way to Truro, thence to Cheltenham, before returning to London in July. Possessed by a strong desire to go abroad, opposition was too evidently hurtful to him, so he again had his own way. Accompanied by his wife and a young Oxford friend, who had just taken a Double First, and needed an easy holiday, he started *viâ* Dover for St. Omer. By short stages they went from St. Omer to Ypres, Bruges, Blankenberg, Ghent, and Courtrai to Tournay, Mr. Hullah enjoying the architecture for a short while each day, but not able to do much of anything. At Tournay it had been arranged he should remain with Mr. Tylden, while his wife returned to Calais to meet the children and bring them back with her, but just at the last moment a sudden change occurred in his bodily state which decided him not to stay behind. Once in Calais, it was evident that it would be sheer madness for him to encounter any more inland journeys. The heat was great, and every hour on the railway injurious to him. Very reluctantly he consented to remain where he was, till some particularly calm day should ensure him a safe passage back to England. Once more at home, he was not allowed to remain within reach of London noise and excitement.

For special reasons Bognor was chosen as a suitable place for spending the weeks that had yet to pass before the inspection of Training Colleges could be resumed. When that time came, he seemed really in a tolerably satisfactory state, so marked was the benefit he derived from the quiet and sea air. Accompanied and aided by Mr. Barrett, he got through the greater part of his work in the north of England and in Scotland very well, returning home at the end of October to resume his old routine of life, subject to certain rules in respect to early going to rest and late rising, the first of which he found very distasteful, since it practically debarred him from any share in social enjoyments. Of all things, however, late hours were forbidden, and medical opinion being in favour of a winter out of London, as quite the wisest of precautionary measures, a decision to that effect was taken.

Mr. Hullah begged, if he must go, that some place out of England—some place in Italy—be selected.

Unfortunately, anything so pleasant was utterly impracticable, and nothing better could be managed than a second migration to Bognor, which he had rather liked in the summer, but soon learned, alas! to detest, in spite of the truck-load of books he took down wherewith to solace himself. But the much-abused Bognor may be said to have prolonged his working life by a year at the very least. Dull it was beyond all power of description, but the weather was beautiful for England, the sunsets exquisite evening after evening, and the walking easy even for one in Mr. Hullah's condition. The silence calmed his nerves, the air braced them. Little by little he grew stronger, and during the forenoons he contrived to get through a good deal of work. Among other things he made notes, and sketched out a slight plan, for his autobiography. He composed but little, though frequently, when left alone, he would go to the piano and jot down a few notes.

Occasionally, when the weather was very mild, he would take a sketch-book and draw a little, with a touch not much less firm than usual. Or, wrapped in a thick shawl, he would sit awhile on the rocks at Felpham and read aloud or recite from memory passages from his favourite writers, English or foreign.

His correspondence was large, and now and then some one would write and tell him pleasant things about his books. In Italy he learnt that many 'good things' were said and written of his 'History of Modern Music;' or that in different parts of Germany his Report of 1879 had received much attention, in spite of the general tone of disapprobation of the musical teaching in the German schools. It pleased him much to receive letters, even in the unloved German character, from several of the principals of schools in Bavaria, Saxony, Bohemia, and Prussia, giving him the fullest credit for fairness and thoroughness.

From his correspondent at the Hague, the translator of Hullah's 'Method of Teaching Singing,' came a long letter, describing the visits of a French Inspector, Monsieur Danhauser, and of Mr. McNaught, of the Tonic Sol-fa faction. The quotations are given in Mr. Gedeking's own English and orthography:

> One of my best teachers had begun teaching the manual signs according to 'Time and Tune.' The pupils effectuated them with much pleasure, and Monsieur Danhauser was contented with it.

Concerning Mr. McNaught, the object of whose visit was a puzzle to Minherr Gedeking, he says:

> After a moment's discourse he was one and all admiration for the Tonic Sol-fa method, the excellence of which he tried to prove with a sort of table, on which were written different numbers. . . . As much as possible [the difficulties of a foreign language taken into consideration] I refuted the arguments of his apology for tonic sol-fa; and while disputing, we heard singing in the different classes. . . . Mr. Naught had some exercises sung at sight from a paper he brought with him (entitled 'Advanced Staff Notation Exercises'). Two difficulties soon surmounted by interfering (?) a tone of the chord in which we were singing urged his observation that pupils taught after the Tonic Sol-fa method would never make such faults (it was in modulations). I answered that, after my opinion, the difficulties were by the tonic sol-fa only avoided, not surmounted; and that we valued much such a degree of development in our pupils that they feared not such difficulties, but attacked and surmounted them. Some days afterwards I heard Mr. De Cock (you know, of Rotterdam) say that Mr. Naught had also made a visit to the Rotterdam Normal School, and had there *not insisted on the use of tonic sol-fa.*
>
> . . . .
>
> All I have heard about your book here is very much praise. . . . My first teacher in music . . . who is one of the teachers at the Amsterdam Music School, has introduced there most of the exercises. . . . I hope . . . that we may preserve your system an honourable place in our musical instruction in schools.

An important item of the work in hand was, of course, the Report to 'my Lords.' Mr. Hullah's Report takes rather the form of suggestion for the future conduct and extension of the system of musical education in the Training Colleges:

> REPORT, *for the Year* 1880, *by* JOHN HULLAH, ESQ., LL.D., *Inspector of Music, on the* EXAMINATION *in* MUSIC *of the* STUDENTS *of* TRAINING COLLEGES *in* GREAT BRITAIN.
>
> MY LORDS,—I find myself under the necessity of bringing under your Lordships' consideration an impression difficult to resist, that [the improvement] has been carried as far as it is at present likely to be carried, and, seeing that nothing long maintains a stationary

position, progress will ere long be replaced by regress, unless measures are taken to check the causes which ere long will assuredly bring it about.

The study of music, unlike that of any other subject in the curriculum of the school teacher, has hitherto been carried on in the Training Colleges without any special or recognised object or purpose. But that this accomplishment has any direct bearing on their positions as schoolmasters and schoolmistresses must, under present circumstances, be regarded by the [students] as a matter of considerable uncertainty. [They know] that *singing from notes*, taught at such an expense of time, pains, and money in every Training College, is rarely even attempted in the elementary schools for the conduct of which they are undergoing preparation; and that success in teaching it where attained will meet with neither estimate nor reward. The knowledge of this fact—for fact it is, though as yet comparatively inoperative on the better class of students—has begun to act on the idle and careless class, and must ere long drive all students to throw their energies on subjects that are——*more remunerative*.

The little or no direct results in elementary schools of the teaching of music in training schools has led to a very widespread belief that this teaching is, in a large number of instances, all but useless; and with a view to supplement its shortcomings, a number of persons, doubtless well meaning, but obviously ill informed on the circumstances of the case, have been induced to form themselves into a society for the training of music teachers in elementary schools. How little they can have known of the work which has been going on in the Training Colleges for so many years past may be gathered from the following table, in which is shown the number of students who have left those colleges in England, Wales, and Scotland after two years' training since 1872, the year in which they were first placed under systematic musical inspection:

Year	Male Students	Female Students	Totals
1872	677	716	1,693
1873	793	856	1,649
1874	839	989	1,828
1875	805	1,007	1,812
1876	847	1,092	1,939
1877	843	1,098	1,941
1878	833	1,115	1,948
1879	858	1,153	2,011
1880	816	1,099	1,915
Total	7,311	9,125	16,436

We have here a list amounting to 16,436 students, every one of whom (save a few last year) I have personally and individually examined.

The time seems to be come for completing the examination of elementary schools by subjecting to it such musical work as is done in them. The means for doing this are quite accessible, and to be brought to bear with a little preparation and at a moderate cost.

I propose that there be placed at the disposal of each of her Majesty's Inspectors one or more assistants especially skilled in music, who shall annually examine, in conformity with the following scheme, each of the schools under his inspection, and that these musical assistants be paid for their services either annually, *per* day, *per* hour, or *per* school, as may hereafter be determined.

That the majority of the inhabitants of Great Britain living in towns, the experiment of musical examination be first made in town schools, and that subsequently it be extended to such schools, whether in town or country, as make formal application to the Education Department for it.

These musical assistants might be drawn from the following classes, representatives of which are located in every part of Great Britain:

(1) The musical instructors in the Training Colleges;
(2) The adult members of cathedral choirs;
(3) Organising music masters;
(4) Various professors who have given special attention to class teaching.

The subjoined scheme (subject, of course, to revisal) will show what teaching in the various 'standards' of elementary schools my Lords might safely recognise as 'satisfactory' and worthy of recompense.

I must preface the details of this scheme by remarking that the primary condition of its being worked at all must be the appropriation of a defined and sufficient place in the time-table of every school for musical instruction and practice. This work, where it is at present done at all, is done at all sorts of otherwise unoccupied times, and is invariably the first made to give way to any other thought to be of greater importance.

The shortest time to be devoted to it in every school or division thereof with any chance of success should be, I conceive, three half-hours in every week.

STANDARD I.—Very simple and short passages in the 'natural scale' to be *sol-faed* from dictation, or from the pointer applied to the ladder representing the sounds of that scale.

Measures or bars, consisting of minims and crotchets only, to be recited (without musical intonation) from dictation, or *sol-faed* in monotone.

STANDARD II.—Simple passages, involving occasional modulation into the scales of the dominant and sub-dominant of the natural scale, to be *sol-faed* from dictation, or from the pointer applied to the ladder.

Measures or bars (as for Standard I.) comprising semibreves and quavers in addition to minims and crotchets.

Ear tests.—Passages similar to the above to be sol-faed or played on an instrument by the examiner. The notes composing them to be named by the scholars individually and collectively.

STANDARD III.—Simple unrhythmical passages to be written in musical notes on a board by the examiner, and to be sol-faed by the scholars not more than three times each.

STANDARD IV.—Barred phrases written in musical notes to be first read (without musical intonation) and afterwards sol-faed, each process not more than three times.

STANDARD V.—Barred phrases written in musical notes involving common modulations to be sol-faed, first without reference to the lengths of the notes composing them, and afterwards in time.

STANDARD VI.—A song, round, or other piece, in at least two parts, previously practised, to be sol-faed and then sung, under the direction of the school teacher.

In this exercise correct time and tune will be regarded as indispensable, and the performance recorded as fair, pretty fair, or good accordingly. Other and higher qualities (*timbre* or quality of sound, pronunciation, &c.) to be recorded as very good, excellent, and the like.

The musical examiner will not direct or interfere with this last exercise, save by silencing or removing any one or two scholars whom he believes to be 'leading' the others. He will do this in the examination of all the other standards whenever he thinks it to be necessary.

I therefore recommend that after 1882 singing *by ear* be no longer regarded as *singing*, and that no award for singing be made after that date save for singing *by note*.

Towards the close of a 'Report on Musical Education Abroad,' in 1879, I said: 'The musical instruction given in our normal schools might, in special instances, be carried further than it is, and students who show special talent for the subject might, at the end of their two years' training for the elementary school, be sent to the projected Royal College of Music at South Kensington, with a view to their formation into a body of music masters in towns or districts where a sufficient number of schools to occupy the time of each one of them could be found together.' 'Teachers of this class,' I added, 'need not anywhere supersede the schoolmaster in his musical work, but they might aid him, both in the higher and lower. Schoolmasters who did not need such aid, and who felt sure that without it they could meet the requirements of a competent inspector, could and would do without it.'

To this proposition I will now venture to add another: that the candidates for the office of musical examiner in elementary schools be required to attend a course of special instruction at the Royal College, at the close of which their general musical knowledge, and especially their skill and tact as examiners, should be tested and certified by the professors of that institution. By this means your Lordships and the country at large would have as good an assurance as it is possible to provide that the work of musical inspection was likely to be done efficiently.

It is not necessary that I enter into further working details of this scheme, which, in some shape or other, must, I feel sure, come under the consideration and receive the sanction of your Lordships at some time or other.

Four years have passed since the capable and experienced educational musician penned these words, but neither 'my Lords' nor the authorities of the Royal College of Music have seen their way to follow out his suggestions, though at the time that he made them they were received as admittedly excellent on all grounds, and practical into the bargain.

CHAPTER XXXV.

BIOGRAPHICAL.

1881.

WITH the exception of a few days in London, in January, during which Mr. Hullah refreshed himself by visits to the Education Department and Society of Arts, conferences with Mr. Barrett, and dinner and musical parties in the evenings, the stay at Bognor was unbroken by the smallest incident of importance, till the famous snowstorm of January 18 caused endless speculation as to how long the stock of coals and provisions would hold out in the town. Rumour said the period of suffering, possibly of starvation, was close at hand, whereupon life, which had long been considered a bore, immediately became well worth living. But the excitement was soon over, and with the end of January came deliverance from thraldom, and Mr. Hullah returned jubilantly to London to stay a few days with Mr. and Mrs. Henry Deacon, while the flat was being put into habitable order. This interlude was turned into quite a continuous *fête* for him, during which he enjoyed himself immensely, for it was a long while since he had had such delightful talks about musical matters or seen so many musical acquaintances. He immediately resumed his work at Queen's College, and was able throughout the rest of the term to be fairly regular in his attendance. He was also able to busy himself somewhat with the doings of the Victoria Coffee Music-Halls Company, to attend examinations at the Training School for Music, and to prepare, in conjunction with his fellow-examiners, a Report, which met with the approbation of H.R.H. the Prince of Wales, on the results of the teaching since the school had been called into existence.

In May he insisted on keeping his engagement to conduct the examinations for the Society of Arts in Glasgow, which again brought him into frequent communication with his friend Miss Galloway.

Before returning home he stayed a few days with Professor Douglas Maclagan in Edinburgh, where his old friends were grieved to notice that he was much changed.

But so soon as the rigours of winter were overpast, his natural buoyancy of spirit and excellent constitution kept him up, and he went through his usual work uncomplainingly, though sometimes there was a feverish impatience of manner that was as yet unaccountable. By an exceptional arrangement he began his inspection of Training Colleges early in June. As he travelled from place to place he was, as ever, kindly welcomed, and even more than ever treated with all imaginable consideration for his visibly diminishing strength; but he did not like to have it thought that anything beyond fatigue ailed him. A few days' rest, he always said, would set him up, but rest for days few or many seemed just the unattainable luxury. Rather it seemed as if further claims were to be made on his time and powers, for he was elected a member of the council and executive committee of the proposed College of Music, and he fully appreciated the compliment, and was more than willing to give the best of himself.

Then, again, there seemed literally no end to the stream of people always wanting to see him about projects of general utility, or affairs of their own. Once admitted, the visitors often forgot that they had but asked for ten minutes, not for an hour of exhausting talk, and Mr. Hullah was always ready to be interested in all intelligent schemes, and never able to be other than kind, considerate, and polite to strangers. Sometimes it happened that he was really pleased with his visitor, and found matter for real interest, as was the case the very evening before his departure for the country, where friends were to take him and ' spoil him a little,' when he had to receive an inspector of schools from Brooklyn, U.S., who had written beforehand:

I have come from America specially to see and converse with you, for not more than half-an-hour, on the subject of public school music.

Never was half-hour turned to better purpose for the acquisition of desired knowledge. Every question was clear, concise, penetrating, and racy; so put that the answer almost of necessity had to be as clear, as concise. Fortunate it was that Mr. Hullah was a man entirely after the interlocutor's own heart. Mr. Caswell went away rejoicing, and seemingly content; but he returned to the charge—by letter!

In August came the question as to whether Mr. Hullah should or should not examine in person the Training Colleges. Dr. Allen Sturge had already taken that question into consideration during his visit to England in the spring of the year, and had come to the conclusion that, if accompanied by Mr. Barrett, Mr. Hullah might do much of his own work. By the happiest of coincidences the Rev. W. Warburton (of Winchester) found that his work would take him on the same round at the same time with Mr. Hullah, and wrote to suggest companionship during the journeys. Anxiety at home was thus alleviated, and he was sent off to join Mr. Warburton. Together the inspectors visited Truro and some other of the distant Colleges in the south of England, and failed not to enjoy the evenings when work was over. Later in the year Mr. Hullah had again the advantage of Canon Warburton's company as far as Darlington. Mr. Barrett then joined him, and the work in Scotland was next carried through, and he paid his usual visit to Professor Maclagan.

Durham, York, and Peterboro' were taken on the way home. Throughout his journey he had steadily kept to the old habit of despatching daily *due righe di biglietto*, touching far more than usual on purely personal affairs; but the cheerful tone of his letters (and in the main they are wonderfully cheerful) was frequently too apparently forced, and the handwriting often gave strong evidence of physical exhaustion.

From home Mr. Hullah, always accompanied by Mr. Barrett, got through, in the course of several long days, the suburban schools, his little stock of strength barely lasting the necessary weeks. The excitement of work removed, he sank for a few days into a state of complete exhaustion—utterly unable to stand up longer against the general weakness, which extended, in a very slight degree, even to his power of reading with pleasure. But care, long hours spent in bed, with books around him, and absolute immunity from interruption, light and nourishing food, good wine, plenty of air with easy exercise, did much—he aiding by the strongest conceivable desire to be ' up and doing '—in bringing him once more to the condition of enjoying occasional society at home and abroad. His recuperative power was truly surprising. Very soon he was doing much as usual, and wrote his Report for 1881, from which a few remarks on what may be described as musical discipline are taken :

> The knowledge and skill of candidates for admission to Training Colleges are greater than they were some years since, but they are still deplorably small. The knowledge has in many cases been got up a day or two before his or her application for admission to a College, and the skill in general is absolutely nought.
> There is, it is to be feared, a greater variety in the *times* allotted to music in the different Colleges than there is in their time-*tables*.
> The teachers, however they may be measured, certificated, and the like, vary in knowledge, skill in its application, tact, and, more than all, belief in the certain effects of their own work. No child, unless it were suggested to him, ever yet doubted his own capacity for the utterance and imitation of musical sounds. No good teacher should ever doubt his own power to cultivate this capacity.
> Though I have always regarded method of instruction as an interesting subject of inquiry, I have never regarded it as one with which I was called upon to interfere. My business I have, from the very commencement of my inspections, always considered to be not with methods but with their results. Only on one matter connected with them have I insisted, that the students should follow implicitly the directions of their teacher, and adopt the processes and use the terms about which *he* had made up his mind. As early as in my Report for 1874 I said, ' I have been surprised to find that teachers here in some cases allowed students to continue practising on methods not approved by themselves or sanctioned by the College authorities. It would be hard to say whether such a course was likely to be more injurious to the music of a Training College, as throwing difficulty in the way of the teacher, or to its *morale*, as fostering conceit in his pupils. Whatever be the method of instruction adopted in a Training College, the students should be required during their term of studentship to adopt it, first for the sake of discipline, which the student surely must conform to before he can enforce, and, secondly, because the method which the teacher *thinks* the best *is* the best for him, if only because he believes in it and is most familiar with it.

CHAPTER XXXVI.

BIOGRAPHICAL.

1882.

THOUGH still going about like other people, Mr. Hullah constantly showed signs of diminished strength, and probably felt weaker than he looked, for he quietly began to ' set his house in order,' frequently spending hours in sorting letters and memoranda—destroying much, and neatly arranging all he decided to keep. When tired of this occupation, he would turn to the friends on his book-shelves, and hold communion with them with unabated enjoyment and appreciation; or now and then would be heard from the piano grave chords, melting into snatches of melody which, thus slightly sketched, sometimes in his memory only, were set aside for elaboration at some other time—that other, happier time that came no more! The immediate inducement to make definite efforts at composition was a request from Ricordi, of Milan, that he should write three songs for their firm, the words to be selected from the works of Giosuè Carducci, and of Lorenzo Stecchetti—a poet of great promise, whose life had recently been cut short in its prime.

Both writers were new to Mr. Hullah, and he began their acquaintance by listlessly cutting the leaves of a volume of Stecchetti's posthumous verse, passing over poem after poem, outpourings of unhealthy passion, the sentiments and imagery of which could have had no charm for him—for he loved not the fleshly school of poetry, albeit often expressed in language rich and melodious—to choose six or eight pieces, delicate in feeling and highly finished, from which he had taken portions to set to music. There is a mournful interest in following the musings of the invalid's mind in the marked passages of this and other volumes he took down from his shelves during the hours he spent in his study this winter. Now, his mind would seem to have reverted sadly to memories of long-past days—passionately to have recalled the hopes, fears, ambitions, and dreams of his youth and early manhood—feverishly to have lived again in imagination the active, brilliant life of his middle age, yearning the while for renewed vigour to bring to completion the riper schemes of his later experience; and now to have looked onward and pictured in the poet's words how it might be with some he loved and was leaving.

To fragments of melody, vague, sweet, indescribably heart-searching, he from time to time linked words of saddest meaning. Had he spoken the thoughts of those hours of silent retrospect or foreboding he had surely said with Southey:

> My hopes are with the dead: anon
> My place with them shall be,
> And I with them shall travel on
> Through all futurity;
> Yet leaving here a name, I trust,
> That will not perish in the dust.

But however severe the mental agony of those solitary hours, he strove, generally with success, to come back to the family circle with outward calm, if not cheerfulness, and often took occasion to observe that of all the winters of his life he thought this winter of 1882 was the calmest and, in that sense, the happiest. But, though his quiet hours of a forenoon were respected, he was never allowed to be alone at other times, and many distractions came unsought to prevent him from brooding too long. Scarcely a post failed to bring him something to divert him, and convince him that the outer world had by no means done with him. Sometimes proposals came from America that he should visit the United States. The long letters full of allusions to his past life brightened him up, though at the same time they made him wish more fervently than ever that he could drink a long draught of the elixir of youth.

He was particularly gratified with all that was said of him

and to him at the meeting held at St. James's Palace on February 28, for the Royal College of Music—when the Duke of Edinburgh, Mr. Gladstone, Sir Stafford Northcote (now Lord Iddesleigh), and others, spoke of his past services with so much kindly feeling that he came home tremulous with emotion. Éven pleasurable excitement was beginning to wear his nerves and produce intense fatigue. 'Ah,' he said to his wife, 'I wish you could have been there' (ladies had not been asked). 'I should like you to have heard all that was said. It was very flattering, but I wish they would pay me in the higher form of flattery—imitation—and carry out all my ideas in regard to musical teaching.'

For his convenience it had been arranged that some of the Colleges were to be examined immediately after Easter, for, as the Italian proverb has it, 'he who goes slowly goes safely.' So jogging slowly from place to place, kindly looked after everywhere, and not seldom set on his way by some anxious friend with a little leisure on his hands, Mr. Hullah got well through his work, and announced that on May 24 he should pitch his 'tent in Edinburgh for ten days.' It need hardly be said his tent pegs went into his usual ground in Heriot Row, where he and the Professor and family were jubilant over many a good story, followed by a 'crack' over the post-prandial whisky toddy. Not that social pleasures were confined to Heriot Row—by no means! There was a dinner and *levée* at Holyrood; a dinner given by the company of archers; another, on June 3, by the 'Æsculapians,' a purely social club, instituted in 1773, and strictly limited to twenty members, all of whom are Fellows of the Royal College of Physicians or the Royal College of Surgeons of Edinburgh, who are supposed to introduce as guests none other than members of their own profession. 'This rule has rarely been departed from,' says his host, Dr. Maclagan. It was therefore an exceptional privilege that Mr. Hullah enjoyed when he sat at the banqueting table of the members of the healing art, and after dinner sang to them 'The Three Fishers,' and 'When he who adores thee,' with other Irish melodies, 'with exquisite taste,' as described in the minutes of the meeting. But doctors, learned and great, as are the Æsculapians, did not remind Mr. Hullah he was half an invalid and ought to retire early, and he, all unmindful of home injunction, stayed as late as anyone, notwithstanding that he had examined in the forenoon about thirty students, and had a like prospect for each succeeding day. When he bade adieu to Edinburgh he was so cheerful that none suspected he would be seen there no more. He went on with his work, saw his old friends at every place, and at last named a day for his return. About the middle of June he arrived grievously exhausted in body but alert in mind, and anxious to irritability to take his share in all that was going on, and that was not a little.

For his seventieth birthday a party of old friends—alas! how many gaps death had made in the muster roll!—with just a few of later date, had been made up for him. He enjoyed himself fairly well, but when all his guests were gone he fell into sad depression without being able to explain why. Then, as London began to empty he grew restless, and wanted to go abroad as usual, insisting that what had always set him up was a continental journey, a ramble in the French cathedral towns. But the 'faculty' would give no consent, and he betook himself for a few weeks to the Malvern Hills, where a pleasant time was contrived for him. According to old custom he wrote home every day, but not such circumstantial letters as of old, nor by any means so cheerful. Indeed the vein of sadness that runs through them all is very pathetic.

As it had proved impossible to persuade him to resign his inspectorship, and as his medical advisers, Dr. Barlow and Dr. Sturge, had positively set their faces against his doing any more such work, it was necessary to devise some means of securing to him enforced, however unwelcome, leisure. To this end a preliminary six months' leave of absence was asked and readily accorded. Almost immediately on this followed a letter from Mr. Gladstone, announcing in highly complimentary language that it was Her Majesty's pleasure that Mr. Hullah's name be placed on the Civil Service pension list. He accepted, without realising that acceptance barred the way to a resumption of his inspectorial duties ' when he should get better.' ' Now we will go abroad and I shall get all right,' he said to his wife. When it dawned upon him that he would never again go back to his active life, his distress and discouragement were painful to witness. 'Far better have let me wear out than rust out,' he would say, with the nearest approach to resentment of which he was capable towards those he loved.

Premature though he believed his rest to be, it came too late to save him, in the sense that those to whom he was dear would have had him saved.

All that could be done by kindly hearts to cheer his life was done. He might have spent the year round with country friends if he had liked. His interest in his own particular subject—the spread of music among the people—was constantly kept alive by applications for advice and assistance from teachers and other musicians at home and abroad. Some came from the colonies, some from America. Several hours a day might have been spent in replying at length to the minute questions of his correspondents, not to speak of the time that was required merely to acknowledge letters from old friends—some of them long lost sight of—who, seeing news of his ill health in the newspapers, wrote in affectionate sympathy. Then also some of the work he had done for years was still under his hand—the Charterhouse on Sundays, the Queen's College classes, the numerous committees on which he served. But nothing comforted or consoled him. To write the annual Report, knowing it would be his last, was too much for him. He could not do it, and no Report appeared.

He grew more and more restless, more and more irritably anxious to try what a sojourn abroad would do for him. Even his books, heretofore the joy of his spare hours, though often taken down, were but listlessly glanced at, and replaced with a sigh. He was urged to go on with the notes for his autobiography, but he found the work sadden and weary him. To give him peace and something to look forward to, a promise was made that *coûte que coûte* he should go to the Riviera as soon after Christmas as possible. Meanwhile he was sent off to Oxford. A letter he wrote thence to one of his adopted 'cousins gives a tolerable idea of his now normal state of mind:

It is always a great pleasure to hear from Heriot Row (he says), especially when the hearing comes in the form of such a pleasant letter as yours—full as it is of good news. The treat of answering it I left for a day or two, and here is the result. For the first time since I left your pleasant land, I have been out of London for a few days, and my wife and I have been separated. She stays in London for a day or two and I make an excursion to my old Oxford friends—possibly even to Malvern Wells, whither I am already half way. I have lately been leading a very idle life. You know I broke off my inspection work in the early autumn and have done none of it since. As a matter of fact I suppose, and I am told, that I am much better. I don't altogether believe it. We have been for some time past in a queer transition state—trying to manage for our trip to the Riviera, where the weather has been, I hear, such as to occasion rejoicing at being at home. So far we have had no winter, and we are beginning to think the clerk of the weather has neglected us in these latitudes. According to you he has not forgotten Edinburgh! I rejoice to hear that you are going on again with your 'Challenger' work, which I trust will prove as interesting to you as ever. Your accounts of your father and mother are most cheering. I suppose I shall see them again before long . . . and carry on the cheery conversations we never finish. . . .

Ever your trusty and well-beloved cousin,

J. H.

CHAPTER XXXVII.

BIOGRAPHICAL.

1883-4.

BEFORE returning home in January 1883, Mr. Hullah had spent a few days at Malvern Wells; but, though the winter was mild, that place, so largely favoured by nature, cannot but be cold, playground of the east wind as it is, and he had begun to suffer much from cold at all times. He could not, therefore, be said to have derived any benefit bodily from his little outing, but he was more cheerful, and began to make preparations for his journey to the south. Meanwhile he returned more calmly to his desk, and went on with the sorting and arranging of papers, weeded out his musical library, made abstracts from his Diaries, took a few classes at Queen's College, and dined out not infrequently with something of the zest of former years. The evening before he and his wife left England was spent with Mr. and Mrs. Charles Eastlake, when he felt so well that it was a little difficult to draw him away early, in view of the start next morning. Stopping one night in Paris, and one night in Marseilles, Nice was reached in tolerable comfort. Dr. Sturge and the late Mrs. Bovell-Sturge, M.D., had hospitably offered their one visitors' room to Mr. Hullah, and the opportunity of giving him the great advantage of being under their roof was thankfully accepted for him, his wife installing herself in a hotel close by, so that he could at any moment walk across for a chat or a stroll. After a while she was compelled to leave Nice, the climate not suiting her, and he had the pleasure of getting traveller's letters, but to which he was unable to make the prompt and chatty replies that used to flow so readily from his pen in former days.

Apart from the misery of his weak state, his life was pleasant and happy enough. Several acquaintances of former days came across him at the Sturges' house, and helped to pass away half-hours innumerable, when his doctor hosts were out on their professional rounds. The beauty of Nice and its suburbs enchanted him, and short drives he would enjoy thoroughly. So time slipped away till June, when, his wife having returned, trunks were repacked, and, under medical advice, Mr. Hullah was taken to Pesio, in the Savoy mountains. When *en route* Savona was reached, a strong desire came upon him either to retrace his steps and visit Avignon, which he had never succeeded in seeing, or to go on to Florence, and gaze once again on the pictures in the Pitti and Uffizi galleries. But it was so sadly evident that his strength was barely equal even to the little walking required in small inns, that it was impossible to countenance any further trial which would have ended in certain disappointment. On to Pesio, therefore, they pursued their way. As the mountains were approached, and miles of splendid trees came in view, he became quite reconciled, and looked out in ecstasy, and inhaled the freshening air with delight.

The whole distance from Savona to Cavaller Maggiore—where a lengthened halt has to be made for the train from Turin, which eventually carries the traveller on to Cuneo—presents ever-changing and always beautiful scenery. But the keener the enjoyment the greater the fatigue; consequently the poor invalid was weary and exhausted, and much in need of a resting-place, when he was helped out of the train at the dismally dirty and distracted heap of ill-constructed buildings which does, or did, duty for a station at Cavaller Maggiore. A glance into the waiting-room proper was enough. The room literally swarmed with winged things, all madly a-buzz in the stifling heat. A further search for some place in which the travellers could sit down in the shade, and in comparative silence, seemed at first likely to be fruitless, but by-and-by the kindly, courteous Italian nature, on this, as on many other occasions, came to the rescue. In a sort of lean-to attached to the station by poles and fragments of rope, with here and there a broken board helping to support an awning overhead, lay, lounged, or sat about a dozen peasants. Here, in a corner, were huddled in sleep two young men, with a sheaf of grass poised on their stooping heads to ensure them against sunstroke, and a picturesque *chevaux de frise* of scythes and other agricultural implements stacked around them; while on a grimy bench lay at full length a satyr-like creature, little better than a skeleton clothed in tatters and shaggy hair, chaffing at his ease (and with brilliant success, judging by the stentorian roars of laughter that followed his sallies) the group massed in various attitudes around a table, on which stood in disorder a few glasses and *fiaschetti* of red wine, with which the sunbeams made rare effects of colour, as they glinted through the waving vine leaves which had wandered downwards over the edge of the awning. Among these merry folk the advent of the strangers created naturally first curiosity, then interest in their evident discomfiture as they turned away from the picturesque but noisy scene. Then came a lull, followed by a gathering together of limbs, readjustment of seats, and by sounds in chorus which were taken by the discomforted to mean ' *s'accomodi, s'accomodi* ' (be seated), and gratefully acted upon with alacrity, accompanied by much pantomime of thanksgiving.

Off his bench rolled the satyr, scrubbing hard with his fragmentary sleeve to make it less grimy. Away to the furthest edge of shade retired the group at the table. Only the sleepers beneath their grass-sheaf slept on unmoved. Little by little, while shawls, cushions, and bags were being arranged to support a weary back and tired head, the voices fell into whispers, and eyes alone were in uncontrollable activity at the strange culinary operations which succeeded Mr. Hullah's deposition on the satyr's bench. A muffled burst of surprise greeted the flaming up of the *réchaud* Lang, while the most absorbed attention was given to the concoction of soup from Liebig's extract of meat, seed sago, and pinches of powdered herbs, which went, like witches' philters, one after the other into the miniature caldron. Then the strengthening drop of cognac being added, poor Mr. Hullah had to sip his beef-tea beneath the furtive but intense gaze of four-and-twenty black eyes, which all seemed to say, ' *Povero,*

povero! but how strange are the ways of these foreigners! Presently, the necessity for a *siesta* being well understood, peace and solitude were secured by simply spreading a pocket handkerchief over his face; whereupon, there being nothing else of interest to watch, these dear good *contadini* softly departed, each insisting by gesture on a separate adieu.

Lulled to sound slumber, Mr. Hullah took his nap regally, while his more wakeful companion wandered out and about, and presently fell into conversation with two non-commissioned officers on their way to Valdieri for military service. Both these men had excellent manners, but one was clearly Prince Charming in disguise, so soft his glance, so sweet his voice, so pure the Tuscan in which he said clever things about statues, pictures, and beautiful objects in general, seen during his travels, and so fascinating the air with which he insisted on carrying to the train—when, after long delay, that train appeared—as much of Mr. Hullah as he could support on one arm, the other being laden with the bags and other things out of which a couch had been improvised, before, with a parting salute, the grace of which words cannot describe, he departed.

Arrived at Cuneo just when the evening chill was swooping down from the mountains, it was consolatory to catch sight of a well got-up *portier* (with 'CERTOSA' in shining letters on his cap) whose broad face beamed with joy, the measure of which seemed excessive, till it came out that the travellers just arrived were the first of the season. As harbingers of good luck they were coddled and covered and tucked up in places of their own choosing in the Pesio *diligence*, and so soon as the luggage was collected, crack went the whip, away rushed the steeds at a capital pace over the smooth plain which lies between Cuneo and the nearest mountain range, on the higher peaks of which the snow was still lying in considerable quantities. For an hour an even trot was kept up; then gradually the pace slackened as the road grew steep and in places rugged. As on and on, upward and upward they went, the trunks of the serried ranks of chesnut trees seemed to be of larger and yet larger girth, the masses of foliage more and more impenetrable to such fading light as was left, except where at long intervals the icy winter wind had proved too strong for the trees, and kept a free right of way for itself.

A short pause was made at a sort of farmhouse, inn, post office, and general store all in one, at which, with infinite difficulty, the *portier* procured a flinty piece of cheese and a fragment of bread (with which a ship's biscuit would have compared favourably)—wherewith to appease a sudden pang of hunger developed in Mr. Hullah by the mountain air. Nibbling his bread and cheese, he sat enjoying in silent ecstasy the sound of the river below and the rustling of the leaves above, while he listened to the *portier* describing how in the remote days, when the Certosa was a monastery, the ladies of travelling parties lodged *there* in that now lonely homestead, while the gentlemen went up and enjoyed the hospitalities of the nobly-born brethren.

'It was a grand place even up to the time of Napoleon,' said the *portier*, with a sentimental sigh, 'and then that *grand vaurien* despoiled it, carried away all the treasures, dispersed the remaining brethren, and devastated the world, and——'

Suddenly he broke off and jumped down. Almost at the same moment a strange, unpleasant odour came down on the evening breeze, and presently a sound of pattering feet drew nearer and nearer, followed by the passing to the right and to the left of streams—never-ending streams they appeared—of sheep, goats, and larger horned beasts, with wildly glittering eyes and steaming nostrils—for none of which things the horses cared a pin, though often pulled up short to let some blundering inferior quadruped go safely by. For a while the movement of so many animals was curious to watch, but the smell was decidedly oppressive, and most welcome was the *portier's* announcement that the carriage was just about to enter the gates of the Certosa. With accompaniment of wild whoops, fearful thwackings, and ear-splitting cracks of his leathern whip, the driver turned the *diligence* sharply across the descending stream of animals, and presently crossed by a narrow strip of a bridge the foaming torrent of the Pesio, jolted and stumbled under an archway, trotted gaily up a short avenue, and pulled up in style beneath an enormous arch at the foot of a steep flight of stairs, just sufficiently lighted to reveal the eagerly descending figures of the landlord, landlady, and staff. A few minutes afterwards the travellers found themselves in rooms with vaulted ceilings and stone floors, that were too cold to be pleasant at that time of night, and before supper; but after supper everything looked much more cheerful, and especially the beds. Much delighted with his journey, Mr. Hullah speedily betook himself to his own nest, and after some refreshing sleep he was quite eager to get up in the morning to look out of the window on the river rushing by, over stones and fallen trees, and round sharp curves, and through natural arches, with a dull roar to which he had listened far into the night, promising himself walks and sketches without end. Dressing quickly, he took a short turn round the open cloistered passages of the building, which once was a Carthusian monastery, looked out into the peaceful quadrangle, the fourth side of which seemed like the beginning of an interminable forest, and gazed up at the distant snow peaks overhead, and came back to report that ' Paradise was reached,' and must be enjoyed *à deux*.

He looked for the moment absolutely transformed! Accordingly, breakfast being disposed of, and Signor Mengharini, the landlord, at liberty to act as cicerone, a saunter was taken, in the course of which they learnt the position of the original groups of cells running along the open cloistered passages, wherein of old some great and notable warriors or men of the world had lived out in solitude the remnant of their days.

Then descending slowly, half-way to the river level, was reached the site of the original chapel, on one remaining wall of which may be made out a faded, broken fresco, attributed to Luini, and assumed to have been done by him in grateful acknowledgment of hospitality. Close by are some of the ancient baths, usable still by the strong and venturesome; and not far off in the bend of the river are the quiet pools where once fish culture was largely carried on, and where still at times troutlets of tender age loiter and fall a prey to the wily angler.

In passing from point to point it was difficult to avoid turning aside to follow some flowery path evidently leading to enchanting sylvan shades; but the landlord, wisely inexorable, partly in regard for Mr. Hullah's weakness, and partly because he had a marked respect for the rights of vipers on their own territories, went on his way, finally leading his guests to the higher level of the present chapel, and placing Mr. Hullah on a sun-warmed bench, whence he was able to survey the river below and the mountains flecked with snow rising up on the other side range over range, while, by slightly turning his head, he could look up towards an umbrageous plateau, enthusiastically recommended by Signor Mengharini for contemplative strolls. Said the Signor Padrone, ' Cavour and Massimo d'Azeglio—not to speak of Victor Emmanuel—had found that plateau the most delightful spot of all. Who could tell, indeed, how many of the grand schemes of the statesman had been planned, or how many of the beautiful thoughts of the writer had been conceived, beneath the magic influence of the Monk's Walk? Who——.' recommenced the landlord, with a fresh stock of breath, when the tide of his eloquence was checked by a summons from *la padrona*, using her lungs bravely from some distant angle of the building. Hastily apologising, and making them free of his domain, away went Signor Mengharini, and the Hullahs found themselves *tête-à-tête*, to wander whither they would. After a sufficient rest the ascent to the magic walk was effected—a region of delight indeed!

Trees of many sorts, grouped by Nature's artist hand, afforded habitation to birds innumerable, whose unceasing song made rival music to the sweet tinkle of some very distant bell, or twang of stringed instrument, or waves of rippling laughter and snatches of vague melody, wind-borne from children at play in the valley fields beneath.

Day after day, during hours long, the pleasantness of that spot was enjoyed with ever renewed delight.

Within the building life was quietness itself. Now and then came up a passing traveller, English, Russian, or American, spent a night and departed. Mostly *avant-coureurs* these of larger parties for the warmer, finer months of July and August. Mr. Hullah began to feel like the oldest inhabitant, and the servants to treat him as one who had a right to be told of expected guests. Thus it came to pass that it was announced to him one day with intense satisfaction that the landowners of the whole district, a Signor and Signora Garanti, of Turin, were imminent, and that likewise a company of Alpini (a body of mountain volunteers) were coming by that way, and would bivouac about the old monastery. The excitement, therefore, was immense when one morning a bugle (extremely out of tune it was) was heard coming nearer and nearer, followed helter-skelter by about a hundred little men, all walking with that curious gait, half swing, half spring, peculiar to the Italian infantry soldier, and dressed quite *sans gêne* in a grey uniform with red facings, each man carrying his rifle in a happy-go-lucky fashion, most shocking to a trained military spirit. Here and there, on wall, or stone, or fallen tree trunk, the wee warriors attitudinised unconsciously in a way most provocative to sketching proclivities—only, alas! no facile pencil like Mrs. Butler's was at hand to touch off graphically, in a line or two, the characteristics of the picturesque groups that composed and recomposed themselves all day long. Hours had passed delightfully in watching them, when a waiter, known to the Hullahs as *Il Veneziano*, because of his resemblance to so many of Veronese's supple, graceful figures, came scudding down the long passages to announce that dinner was served. The usual leisurely entry into the refectory followed, when, lo! all round the lengthened tables sat bronzed men in uniform, representing three or four branches of the regular army—these being the officers come up to inspect the Alpini.

At the head of the festive board, made gay with flowers, extra plate, and wine flasks, sat Signor and Signora Garanti as hosts. Very gracefully they had refrained from excluding from their circle the oldest inhabitants. 'What a chance of hearing Italian!' gleefully whispered Mr. Hullah, as, returning with effusion the special and general salutations, he took his seat.

The next minute every creature in the room was talking, not the hoped-for Tuscan, alas! but Piedmontese, which no one can be expected to understand! It was a dreadful blow! and no doubt both looked distressed—Mr. Hullah certainly did. At any

rate, at a fitting moment the hostess leant forward towards
him, and urbanely enquired if Italian was comprehended.
Being assured that ordinarily it was, especially if spoken at all
clearly, she smiled, said something to her husband, who also
smiled, and as a result it came to pass that the nearest guests,
with the kindly courtesy of the nation, slid into Tuscan, and
continued the subject of conversation, thus enabling the poor
foreigners to take a share, though only a silent share, in topics
of interest. The military party broke up that night, but
during the succeeding days both Mr. and Mrs. Garanti were
kind and courteous, and would probably have become friends,
but for the catastrophe which overtook Mr. Hullah. During the
fortnight or more that had passed he had made steady progress.
Each morning he wrote a little, and read much; strolled
about for an hour, and sat out while the sun shone;
sketched now and then; talked polyglotically to everyone,
from the 'Padre,' engaged as chaplain for the summer, to
the laundress who trudged up twice a day from the valley
below; ate the well-cooked dinners, and drank the capital
wine with real enjoyment. There arose a little flame of hope
that a definite change for the better was coming—that indeed
a miracle was about to be performed, when, on his birthday, a
second stroke of paralysis, affecting the lower limbs, prostrated
him. His courage, in his anxiety not to increase his wife's
alarm, was beyond belief wonderful, more especially in a man
so constitutionally timid. Far from trustworthy medical advice,
and with no more than travellers' appliances—though these
were, happily, many and excellent—it seemed at first unlikely
that his exhausted state could be successfully combated. The
first day and night were passed in unremitting efforts, happily
successful, to restore circulation to his deadened limbs. By the
morning he was sufficiently recovered to give good ground for
belief that death was at least not imminent. It was decided
that a move should be made as soon as possible, and all arrangements were carried through by the landlord of the hotel
and his staff with all imaginable zeal and good-will, though
sorely against their judgment. The railway was reached at
Cuneo, and here again the fullest courtesy met the travellers
from the railway officials. From the station-master to the

humblest porter every man was willing and anxious to help,
without apparent thought of the *buon mano* for which the
Italian is calumniously supposed to be ready to sell his soul.
At Turin the same attention met them, and Mr. Hullah found
himself gently carried from the train to the hotel, and set
down in a large room, quickly provided with everything that
an invalid could desire—everything, that is, that depended
on the *personnel*; for outside the din was maddening for him,
making sleep impossible, so that he was eager to escape.
Getting an invalid carriage, in which he could travel to Paris,
was not to be arranged, however, in a moment, so a second
night had to be passed in Turin. But now that he felt life
was to be spared him yet a while longer, he begged that no
medical advice might be sought till Paris should be reached,
where it was hoped Dr. Sturge might be intercepted on his
passage through to London.

Telegrams and letters had, however, missed him, and no
Dr. Sturge appeared. But, except for the moral support
afforded by the presence of a medical man who is also an es-
teemed friend, it mattered little. Mr. Hullah had recovered
so far as recovery was possible, and nothing was left to contend against but dire weakness and consequent depression.
By slow stages home was reached, and amidst his own comforts he seemed to revive. Once more he took down his
favourite volumes, once more he resumed the morning habit
of laying out paper and pens, note-books and memoranda.
Once more he saw friends whose society was always a pleasure to him, but nothing pleased him for long. Restlessness
induced by disease was gaining ground on him daily. A constant desire for change set in, and yet scarcely was the change
effected than the fancied benefit faded away, and he feverishly
longed to be home again. In this sad state he passed through
the summer and autumn months. As winter drew near he
was seized with a passion of longing to breathe again his
native air, and to look once more on the Worcestershire hills.
The wish was so natural, that but for the anxiety felt about
his going anywhere alone (he had long ceased to walk out
unwatched), and the impossibility of accompanying him, he
would not have needed to plead at all. The friend at Malvern

Wells, with whom Mr. Hullah had often stayed before, decided the question, responding with kind intention to his wish, and inviting him as her guest, giving every assurance that he should be guarded from all preventible harm. A week passed, during which bulletins of his state came mainly from the hand of his hostess, he adding a word or two. But towards the end of the week he began a long letter to which he would seem to have added the final sentences on Sunday. After telling all the local news, and the incidents of the 'interior' in which he found himself, even to a sharp touch of criticism on a manuscript novel which had been read aloud to him, he says :

> I go to bed early and get up late, both, I suppose, good things, the effects of which are still to be ascertained. We have been quiet this morning, and are going to church presently. We expect Mr. Peel to luncheon. . . . Love to Millie and little Ann Procter, and all who care about it.

On Monday a telegram arrived—too late to admit of his wife's departure by the evening express. On Tuesday, by the first train, she went down to Malvern Wells, to find him insensible, with two medical men in attendance. It appeared that about four o'clock in the afternoon of November 12 he had wished to go out 'only as far as the gate,' that he had gone alone and ventured a few yards beyond the gate, that he had fallen—no saving arm within reach to break the fall—and had struck the back of his head just at the base of the skull.

Five terrible weeks—terrible in spite of universal sympathy for, and kindness shown to, him, by none more than by the young doctor, Mr. Holbeche—passed before he was taken home, in one of Redding's carriages specially constructed for such uses, and surrounded once more by familiar objects, the sight of which afforded him daily pleasure. Many a time the monotony of a bedridden existence was for a few minutes relieved by the sound of the piano softly played, and of his children's voices singing in the drawing-room. Now and then it was possible to pass away a short time for him by reading aloud from Milton, Wordsworth, the Psalms, Dante, or Petrarch, passages which he knew—knew so well that he would often finish a line, seldom, ill as he was, making a mistake. On the other hand, he was frequently so very ill that, with one exception, he did not recognise people about him.

In gloom died out the troubled year. January passed. February was drawing to a close. Such changes as had been observable to Dr. Barlow and the nurses for some weeks had been judged favourable on the whole. Suddenly, on the night of the 20th, there came a change so marked as to be recognised as the immediate foreshadowing of death. He became at once aware that deliverance was at hand for him, and bade his wife adieu with labouring breath and words barely audible; but what the tongue failed to clearly tell, the eyes, wide-opened and luminous for a few fleeting moments, eloquently conveyed. In the faltering, whispered words that fell from his lips, his faith and hope seemed expressed in the words of the last simple verses which had concluded a short forenoon reading:

> We'll meet and aye be fain
> In the Land o' the Leal.

His eyes closed; he spoke no more. There was a brief period of suffering, followed by sleep, placid and painless, during which the troubled expression passed from his features, and life ebbed slowly away, until with the last gleam of daylight on the 21st his spirit glided gently through the gates of Death to that land where it were best in all humility to trust that his own ideal of happiness—labour blessed and illumined by love—has been granted to him—

> .... the journey is done and the summit attained,
> And the barriers fall.

On February 26, 1884, he was laid in Kensal Green Cemetery, in the sunny spot where twenty-one years before he had placed in the tomb the companion of his earlier years.

PRINTED BY
SPOTTISWOODE AND CO., NEW-STREET SQUARE
LONDON

For EU product safety concerns, contact us at Calle de José Abascal, 56–1°,
28003 Madrid, Spain or eugpsr@cambridge.org.

www.ingramcontent.com/pod-product-compliance
Lightning Source LLC
LaVergne TN
LVHW040733250326
834688LV00031B/269